FUTURE MULTILATERALISM

MULTILATERALISM AND THE UN SYSTEM

Programme Coordinator for the United Nations University
Robert W. Cox, Professor Emeritus of Political Science, York University,
Ontario

Published within the International Political Economy Series,
General Editor: Timothy M. Shaw, Professor of Political Science and
International Development Studies, and Director of the Centre for Foreign
Policy Studies, Dalhousie University, Nova Scotia

Titles in this subseries include:

Robert W. Cox (*editor*)
THE NEW REALISM: Perspectives on Multilateralism and World Order

Stephen Gill (*editor*)
GLOBALIZATION, DEMOCRATIZATION AND MULTILATERALISM

Michael G. Schechter (*editor*)
FUTURE MULTILATERALISM: The Political and Social Framework
INNOVATION IN MULTILATERALISM

International Political Economy Series
Series Standing Order ISBN 0–333–71110–6
(*outside North America only*)

You can receive future titles in this series as they are published by placing a standing order.
Please contact your bookseller or, in case of difficulty, write to us at the address below with
your name and address, the title of the series and the ISBN quoted above.

Customer Services Department, Macmillan Distribution Ltd
Houndmills, Basingstoke, Hampshire RG21 6XS, England

Future Multilateralism

The Political and Social Framework

Edited by

Michael G. Schechter
Professor of International Relations
James Madison College
Michigan State University
East Lansing
Michigan

United Nations
University Press

TOKYO • NEW YORK • PARIS

First published in Great Britain 1999 by
MACMILLAN PRESS LTD
Houndmills, Basingstoke, Hampshire RG21 6XS and London
Companies and representatives throughout the world

A catalogue record for this book is available from the British Library.

ISBN 0–333–69813–4 hardcover
ISBN 0–333–73465–3 paperback

First published in the United States of America 1999 by
ST. MARTIN'S PRESS, INC.,
Scholarly and Reference Division,
175 Fifth Avenue, New York, N.Y. 10010

ISBN 0–312–21549–5

Library of Congress Cataloging-in-Publication Data
Future multilateralism : the political and social framework / edited
by Michael G. Schechter.
    p.   cm. — (International political economy series)
Includes bibliographical references and index.
ISBN 0–312–21549–5 (cloth)
1. International cooperation.   2. International relations.
3. Security, International.   4. Environmental policy.   5. Human
rights.   I. Schechter, Michael G.   II. Series.
JZ1318.F88   1998
327.1'7—dc21   98–16508
                                                          CIP

© The United Nations University 1999
The United Nations University
53–70, Jingumae 5-chome
Shibuya-ku, Tokyo 150–8925, Japan

This book is printed on paper suitable for recycling and made from fully managed and
sustained forest sources.

10   9   8   7   6   5   4   3   2   1
08   07   06   05   04   03   02   01   00   99

Printed and bound in Great Britain by
Antony Rowe Ltd, Chippenham, Wiltshire

Contents

Preface

The essays in this volume are part of the MUNS (Multilateralism and the United Nations System) programme which evolved during the first half of the decade of the 1990s under the intellectual stewardship of Robert W. Cox of York University in Toronto. The programme, whose scholarship has articulated a commitment to greater social equity, greater diffusion of power among countries and social groups, protection of the biosphere, moderation and non-violence in dealing with conflict, and mutual recognition of the values of different civilizations, was generously supported by the United Nations University. Takeo Uchida, then senior academic officer at the UNU, served as the programme's key administrative and intellectual leader there.

This particular volume, the final one to be written in the MUNS programme, grew out of a symposium organized by UNU and the Facultad Latinoamericana de Ciencias Socialese – Programa Costa Rica (FLACSO, Costa Rica). Our host, Rafael Menjivar, and his very capable assistant, Abelardo Morales, worked very hard to ensure that it was an intellectually stimulating two days for all who participated.

In addition to the papers in this volume, which were presented in draft form in San José, we also provided each participant with a background paper or 'Guide for paper writers', authored by Robert W. Cox. Unfortunately, two of the papers that we had commissioned for the symposium could not be written, as the press of events in the authors' respective countries prevented them from writing them. These were to be by Xavier Gorostiga (Rector of the University of Central America) on multilateralism and democracy in Central America and by Pino Arlacchi (Vice President of the Italian Senate) on transnational criminal organizations and networks.

Each of the papers at the symposium was carefully read and critiqued by one or two scholars selected for those papers. The volume is considerably improved as a consequence of these efforts. For this activity we turned to coordinators of prior MUNS symposia as well as a number of Costa Rican scholars. In this capacity, we are indebted to Manual Aaraya (of FLACSO, Costa Rica), Robert

W. Cox (York University, Toronto), Stephen Gill (York University, Toronto), Keith Krause (Graduate Institute of International Studies, Geneva), Daniel Masís (Universidad de Costa Rica), Abelardo Morales (FLACSO, Costa Rica), Yoshikazu Sakamoto (Peace Research Institute and International Christian University, Tokyo), J. Pat Sewell (Brock University, Canada), Luis Guillermo Solís (Ministerio de Relaciones Exteriores de Costa Rica), Joaquín Tacsan (Center of Peace, Fundación Arias para la Paz y el Desarrollo Humano, Costa Rica), and Takeo Uchida (Chuo University, Tokyo).

Finally, appreciation is expressed to Tim Shaw, general editor of the International Political Economy series of Macmillan, whose creative idea of a MUNS subseries we eagerly embraced and whose patience we sincerely appreciate as we revised and re-revised the efforts of this truly interdisciplinary, multinational undertaking.

Subsequent to the symposium, tragedy struck two of our participants. Both Claude Ake and Joaquín Tacsan were killed in a plane crash in Nigeria on 6 November 1996. The entire international community has suffered tremendously from their deaths; their superb contributions to our symposium and this volume are illustrative of their central role in the study and practice of multilateralism.

Acknowledgements

The work of many people went into the preparation of this book and the San José, Costa Rica, symposium on which it is based. Pre-eminent among them is Robert W. Cox, the intellectual steward of the MUNS programme. He assisted in shaping the key questions for the symposium and identifying some of the principal participants, authors and commentators. Takeo Uchida, formerly of the United Nations University, assisted both with logistics in Tokyo and intellectually in San José. Moreover, the symposium never would have been possible without the help of Abelardo Morales, of FLASCO, Costa Rica.

I also wish to express my appreciation to the faculty, staff and administration of James Madison College of Michigan State University for providing me time and support in bringing this book to completion. Particular mention needs to be made of Donna Hofmeister, who processed countless versions of these chapters and sent innumerable faxes around the globe, first trying to ensure that everyone arrived in San José on time and subsequently chasing down citations. Timothy M. Shaw, the editor of Macmillan's International Political Economy Series, has proven to be a model of patience, support and persistence, essential qualities for a successful series editor.

Finally, this work would not have been possible without the love and support of my wife of over three decades, Ilene R. Schechter.

Michael G. Schechter

List of Tables

List of Acronyms and Abbreviations

ACSA	Acquisition and Cross Servicing Agreement
AFTA	Asian Free Trade Area
APEC	Asia Pacific Economic Cooperation
ARF	ASEAN Regional Forum
ASEAN	Association of Southeast Asian Nations
ASEM	Asian European Leaders' Meeting
CDC	Campaign for Democracy
CENTO	Central Treaty Organization
CEPAL	Economic Commission for Latin America and the Caribbean
CFC	Chloro-FluoroCarbon
CLO	Civil Liberty Organization
CSCA	Conference on Security and Cooperation in Asia
CSCE	Conference on Security and Cooperation in Europe
DDT	DichloroDiphenylTrichloroethane
DFO	Department of Fisheries and Oceans (Canada)
EAEG	East Asia Economic Group
ECO	Economic Cooperation Organization
ECOSOC	Economic and Social Council
ECOWAS	Economic Community of West African States
EEC	European Economic Community
EU	European Union
FAO	Food and Agriculture Organization
FDI	Foreign direct investment
FY	Fiscal year
G-7	Group of Seven
G-77	Group of 77
GA	General Assembly
GAB	General Agreements to Borrow
GATT	General Agreement on Tariffs and Trade
GDP	Gross domestic product
GEF	Global Environment Facility
GNP	Gross national product

GSP	Generalized system of preferences
IBRD	International Bank for Reconstruction and Development (World Bank)
IGO	Intergovernmental Organization
ILO	International Labor Organization
IMF	International Monetary Fund
INGOs	International non-governmental organizations
IO	International Organization
IR	International Relations
IRC	International Rescue Committee
KMT	Kuomintang
LDP	Liberal Democratic Party
MOSOP	Movement for the Survival of the Ogami People
NAFTA	North American Free Trade Agreement (or Area)
NATO	North Atlantic Treaty Organization
NDI	National Democratic Initiative
NGOs	Non-governmental organizations
NIC	Newly industrializing country
NOD	Non-offensive defense
OAS	Organization of American States
OAU	Organization of African Unity
ODA	Official development assistance
OECD	Organization for Economic Cooperation and Development
SAARC	South Asian Association for Regional Cooperation
SADCC	Southern African Development Coordination Conference
SDR	Special Drawing Rights
SEATO	Southeast Asia Treaty Organization
TRIMs	Trade-related investment measures
TRIPs	Trade-related intellectual property rights
UNCTAD	UN Conference on Trade and Development
UNDP/PNOD	United Nations Development Program
UNESCO	United Nations Educational, Scientific and Cultural Organization
UNHCR	United Nations High Commission for Refugees
UNICEF	United Nations (International) Children's Emergency Fund

UNIDO	United Nations Industrial Development Organization
USDA	US Department of Agriculture
WTO	World Trade Organization
ZOPZAN	Zone of Peace, Freedom and Neutrality

Notes on the Contributors

Claude Ake was, at the time of his death in November 1996, a Visiting Professor of Political Science at Yale University. He also served as Director of the Center for Advanced Social Science in Port Harcourt, Nigeria. He did his undergraduate work at King's College, Lagos, the University of Ibadan and the University of London. He did his graduate work at Columbia University, where he taught from 1966–9. He subsequently taught at Carleton University and served as Dean of the Faculty of Social Sciences at the University of Port Harcourt. Widely recognized as one of Africa's leading political scientists, his publications included: *A Theory of Political Integration* (Dorsey, 1967), *Revolutionary Pressures in Africa* (Zed, 1979), *Social Science as Imperialism: The Theory of Political Development* (Ibadon University, 1979 and 1982), *Contemporary Nigeria: A Political Economy* (Longman, 1984), *The Political Economy of Crisis and Underdevelopment in Africa* (JAD, 1989), *The Feasibility of Democracy in Africa* (CREDU, 1992), *The New World Order: A View from the South* (Zed, 1992), *Democratization of Disempowerment in Africa* (Malthouse, 1994), and *Democracy and Development in Africa* (Brookings, 1996).

Walden Bello is currently the Co-director of Focus on the Global South at Chulalongkorn University in Bangkok, Thailand. He also serves as Professor of Sociology and Public Administration at the University of the Philippines. He is the author of *Dragons in Distress: Asia's Miracle Economies in Crisis* (Penguin, 1991), *People and Power in the Pacific: The Struggle for the Post-Cold War Order* (Pluto, 1992), and *Dark Victory: The United States, Structural Adjustment, and Global Poverty* (Pluto, 1994).

Richard A. Falk is the Albert G. Milbank Professor of International Law and Practice at Princeton University, where he has taught since 1961. He holds degrees in Economics from the University of Pennsylvania and in Law from Yale; his doctorate in Law is from Harvard. He is the author of more than two score books, most recently *On Humane Governance: Toward a New Global Politics* (Penn State, 1995) and *A New Europe in the Changing Global System* (United

Nations University Press, 1997). For the past decade, he has served as rapporteur of the Global Civilization Initiative of the World Order Models Project (WOMP).

Peter Harries-Jones is a Professor of Anthropology at York University in Toronto. His early work was at the Rhodes-Livingstone Institute in Zambia, followed by teaching at the Universities of Swansea and Khartoum. His current interests include the study of the environmental movement, both as a global and social phenomenon, as well as the ecological epistemology of Gregory Bateson. Two of his most recent publications are *Making Knowledge Count: Advocacy and Social Science* (McGill, 1991), and *A Recursive Vision: Ecological Understanding and Gregory Bateson* (University of Toronto, 1996).

Tariq Osman Hyder is currently Pakistan's Ambassador to Ashgabat in Turkmenistan, Central Asia. He previously served in Pakistan's embassies in Washington, Moscow and Hanoi. Immediately prior to his current position he was Director-General for Economic Coordination and Environment in the Pakistani Ministry of Foreign Affairs. In that capacity, he was the Coordinator for the Group of 77 in a number of key negotiations. His accomplishments included helping to shape the Rio Declaration, the Climate Change Convention and the Global Environment Facility. He has spoken and written widely explaining the developing countries' position on environmental issues.

Javier M. Iguiñiz-Echeverria is a Professor of Economics at the Pontifical Catholic University of Peru. He also serves as a researcher at the Institute Bartolomé de las Casas (Rimac) in Lima. He earned his Ph.D. in Economics at the New School for Social Research and was recently awarded a Guggenheim Fellowship. He has been a Visiting Fellow at the World Economics Laboratory in the Department of Economics at the Massachusetts Institute of Technology, at St Antony's College, Oxford, and in the Departments of Economics at the University of Notre Dame and the University of Ottawa. His most recent books include: *Politicas de industrialización del Perú 1980–1990* (DESCO-Consorcio de Investigación Económica, 1991), *Los ajustes, Perú 1975–1993* (F. Ebert, 1993), *Buscando salidas, Ensayos sobre la probreza* (IBC-CEP, 1994), *Pluralismo empresarial, representatividad y empleo* (DESCO, 1994), and *Deuda externa en América Latina, Exigencias éticas desde le Doctrina Social de la igelsia* (IBC-CEP, 1995).

W. Andy Knight, who earned his Ph.D. in Political Science at York University, teaches International Relations at Bishop's University. He is on the editorial board of *Global Governance* and had headed the International Organization section of the International Studies Association. He is co-editor of *State, Society, and the UN System: Changing Perspectives on Multilateralism* (United Nations University Press, 1995).

Abraham Rotstein is a Professor of Economics and Political Science at the University of Toronto. He is a former student and colleague of the late Professor Karl Polanyi. He has written extensively on Canada's economy and other public policy issues. Among his publications are, as editor: *Beyond Industrial Growth* (University of Toronto Press, 1976) and *Rebuilding from Within: Remedies for Canada's Ailing Economy* (James Lorimer, 1984).

Kumar Rupesinghe is currently the Secretary-General of International Alert, an international non-governmental organization dedicated to the prevention and mitigation of violent internal conflict. He is also currently advisor to the Program on Governance and Conflict Resolution of the United Nations University and a member of the International Negotiation Network in Atlanta, Georgia. A Sri Lankan and former member of the Bandaranake government, he was forced to leave his home country in 1979, following the outbreak of violence there. He joined the International Peace Research Institute (PRIO) in Oslo, first as a research fellow, later being appointed as Director of PRIO's program on Ethnic Conflict and Conflict Resolution. He has published widely in the field of conflict resolution and travels often, addressing potential activists in different sectors. His books include: *Conflict Resolution in Uganda* (James Curry Ltd., 1989), *Ethnic Conflicts and Human Rights: A Comparative Perspective* (United Nations University Press, 1989), *Conflict Transformation* (Macmillan, 1995), and *Civil Wars, Civil Peace: An Introduction to Conflict Resolution* (Pluto, 1998).

Michael G. Schechter teaches International Relations in James Madison College of Michigan State University. He earned his Ph.D. in Political Science at Columbia University and has served as an officer in the International Studies Association, Academic Council for the United Nations System (ACUNS) and the American Society of International Law. His research focuses on international law and organization and processes of global governance. A former editor of the *Political Handbook of the World* (St Martin's), his most recent book is the *Historical Dictionary of International Organization* (Scarecrow, 1998).

Marie-Claude Smouts, who earned her doctorate in Political Science from the Sorbonne, is Director of Research at the Centre d'Etudes et de Recherches Internationales and Professor of International Relations at Institut d'Etudes Politique de Paris. She is a specialist in French foreign policy and UN affairs, having written her Ph.D. dissertation on the UN Secretary-General. Among her books are: *La France face au Sud: le miroir brisé* (Editions Karthala, 1989), *Le retournement du monde* (Press de la Fondation Nationale des Sciences Politiques, 1992) and *La France à l'ONU: premières rôles et second rang* (Press de la Fondation Nationale des Sciences Politiques, 1979). She has served as the Vice-President of the French Political Science Association.

Peter Timmerman is a Research Associate of the Institute for Environmental Studies (IES) at the University of Toronto and a Research Director of the International Federation of Institutes for Advanced Study. He is also the Director of a non-profit NGO network, the Canadian Coalition for Ecology, Ethics, and Religion (CCEER). He was one of the founders of the Green Party of Canada. His research interests include environmental ethics, climate change, and high-level nuclear fuel waste. Recent publications include *Collateral Damage* (IES, 1992), a study of the Gulf War, and a two-volume *Report to FEARO on High Level Nuclear Fuel Waste Disposal in Canada* (CCEER, 1996).

Raimo Väyrynen gained his Ph.D. at the University of Tampere (Finland). Since 1978, he has served as Professor of International Relations at the University of Helsinki and served in 1990–3 as Dean of its Faculty of Social Sciences. Since 1993, he has been Professor of Government and International Studies and the John M. Regan Jr. Director of the Joan B. Kroc Institute of International Peace Studies at the University of Notre Dame. A specialist in conflict resolution, he is the editor of *New Directions in Conflict Theory* (Sage, 1991) and the author of *Military Industrialization and Economic Development: Theory and Historical Case Studies* (Dartmouth, 1992) and *Urho Kekkonen: President of the Republic* (1994).

1 Introduction

Michael G. Schechter

The theme for this volume in the MUNS (Multilateralism and the United Nations System) programme is 'Future Multilateralism: the Political and Social Framework'. Under the intellectual leadership of Robert W. Cox, whose thoughts permeate all of the chapters of this MUNS volume as well, the goal of this book is to build on those in the series which precede it, but most particularly on its immediate predecessor: *Innovation in Multilateralism*.[1] That volume focuses on the political processes and bases for support for multilateralism in terms of the shifting power relations in world politics, institutional developments (or non-developments) in the UN and non-UN multilateralism, and the impact of evolving social movements on the institutions and policy outcomes of multilateralism.

The aim of this volume is to discuss the kinds of multilateralism that would be required to pursue some of the alternative projects of society, namely those which accord with some of the key normative commitments of the MUNS programme: non-violent means for dealing with conflict; social equity; protection of the biosphere; diffusion of power among social groups and societies. The strategies identified herein are both 'top-down' (i.e. relying on conventional international institutions) and 'bottom-up' (i.e. involving a new multilateralism grounded in civil society). This is because all of the authors see the state system as continuing for a long time into the future. None anticipates the sorts of massive power shifts in the near-term, which would be necessary in order for those with a vested interest in the current 'top-down' multilateralism to be replaced by those without such interests. That is because it reflects past global power distributions and is accountable almost exclusively to the inter-state system. But this is not to deny that the world structure is changing in ways which have already had important, and are likely to have even more significant, impacts on the form of prevailing multilateralisms and the achievement of various societal goals. Indeed the *leitmotif* of the MUNS programme is the need to take a critical approach to multilateralism because of the dynamism of the global system. The authors all recognize and take into account in their analyses that: (1) the existing state system is being transformed into a multi-level pattern of political actors, including macro and microeconomic entities; (2) dominant neo-liberal economic 'globalization' is polarizing rich and poor, included and excluded, both among countries – especially those in Africa – and within societies; (3) threats to people's lives include forces, like the biosphere, which are not contained by territorially based political entities; and (4) current concepts of world order, including Pax Americana and the United States' vaguely articulated preferred new world order, are open to challenge.

Grounded in political realism, however, the authors of the various chapters in this volume not only take into account the evolving international system, but are cognizant of the multiplicity of obstacles to the achievement of such projects and normative commitments. Indeed, few see their achievement as likely, none as imminent. Moreover, some of the authors see history in dialectical terms, few as linear and none believes that the end of history is imminent.

This volume is divided into four parts. In the first, 'Security Issues', the various dimensions of security – material, ideological and organizational – are discussed, as the problems of security management and conflict resolution must address all three. Accepting the proposition that threats to security cannot be totally eliminated in a dynamic world in which peoples remain dissatisfied with the situation, the authors in this section take as the goal of multilateralism foreseeing and moderating threats to security and providing the means for conciliation in conflict situations. Kumar Rupesinghe, who begins this section, takes a traditional approach to security, in the sense that he focuses on military security. Even with that perspective, however, he provides evidence of the dramatic changes in the nature of conflict in the post-Cold War era. The conflicts are now largely intrastate rather than interstate. The victims are largely civilians rather than soldiers, only partly as a consequence of the increased lethality of today's weapons: 'Over 90 per cent of war casualties today are civilians, which compares with 10 per cent during World War I and 50 per cent during the Second World War.' As a consequence, he notes that even former UN Secretary-General Boutros Boutros-Ghali recognized the limits to his widely hailed *Agenda for Peace*. Even if it had been implemented rather than largely ignored, it has limited applicability to resolving the problems of internal conflict. That, of course, is only natural. The *Agenda* is the product of a state-centric United Nations. Multilateralism reflective of the interstate system can hardly be expected to make proposals, which strike at its very essence: state sovereignty. It is in this context that Rupesinghe proposes a multiplicity of innovative strategies for foreseeing and moderating threats to security and especially for conciliating conflict situations. He calls this a 'multi-track approach'. Some of these involve reform of existing intergovernmental (universal and regional) organizations. But his focus is on changes in non-governmental organizations, and especially the need for unprecedented, coordinated activities amongst all types of international organizations, including grassroots civic groups. The latter, in particular, are reflective of his vision of the 'new multilateralism'. As Rupesinghe argues: 'Peace in internal conflict can only come through a process which involves the very people who were at war with each other'. He recognizes, of course, that this is a long-term strategy, one which involves further changes in the international system and within civil society. Even in terms of his more immediate and specific calls for a multi-track approach, he recognizes that alternative multilateralisms have '... differences in opinion, resources, flexibility, knowledge, commitment, competence, location and availabilities.' Still, he argues: '... when difficulties arise in the peace process – as they necessarily do – it is precisely the alliance and synergy between these different "partners" which can play a critical role in sustaining the momentum for peace.'

Raimo Väyrynen's essay begins very differently, but finds quite similar challenges in terms of policy implementation. Väyrynen begins with a systematic and comprehensive review of the multiple calls for redefining security, beyond its traditional state-centric and military-security focus. He seems persuaded that the traditional conception of security is insufficient for dealing with both the challenges of the post-Cold War era and the expanded call for the 'collective protection of group rights', often involving calls for measures such as multilateral economic sanctions and humanitarian intervention. He first typologizes various *intentional* threats to individual, group, state/nation and global security. Then he categorizes a variety of conceptions of security – which he calls common, cooperative and collective – in terms of their understanding of threat, principle, response and outcome. While this is an especially useful set of exercises for scholars, Väyrynen recognizes its limitations in terms

of coping with the dilemmas outlined by Rupesinghe and meeting
MUNS' normative commitments. He phrases this in terms of what
he calls a 'real dilemma': 'the old concepts of multilateral security
have difficulties to grasp the new meanings of security'; they suffer
from being state-centric and thus provide little help in providing
rationales for defining which group rights or which collective threats
(such as environmental ones) merit multilateral responses, much
less in what forms, when and by whom. 'But on the other hand
new concepts [of security] either do not exist or are so general
that they hardly have any meaning at all . . .'

The second section of the volume, Economy and Ecology, begins with a chapter by the Peruvian economist and social activist
Javier Iguiñiz-Echeverria. Iguiñiz is interested in the means by
which social equity can be increased, both between countries and
within countries, especially those, like his own, in the so-called Third
World. His essay provides us with a rare critical examination of
the notion of competitiveness, combined with insights into the consequences of the minimally regulated market in terms of generating un- and underemployment and the gap between the rich and
poor. Ultimately, however, Iguiñiz's analysis is a hopeful one. This
is chiefly because he believes that leading economists, including
those at and those who influence those at multilateral institutions,
most notably the World Bank and IMF, are beginning to ask the
right questions and to bring to bear their analytical skills in addressing those questions. Whereas he believes that what he calls
heterodox development theorists, most notably Schumpeter, long
ago focused on related issues; he is excited at the prospect that
mainstream economists in the twenty-first century may focus on
the 'justification of the social and geographical concentration of
technological and organizative transformation.' This he contrasts
with what he portrays as their focus in this century on 'showing
how the system was kept together, and in harmony'. Already, he
notes, the World Bank has evidenced that it is aware of the important
issues.

Harries-Jones, Rotstein and Timmerman address another topic
infrequently discussed by more conventional economists. Indeed,
their chapter makes clear why that is so. Writing four years after
the United Nations Conference on the Environment and Development (UNCED), the authors are pessimistic. In part this is because '. . . the deterioration in the ecological conditions of life
continues, masked by local improvements in some developed

countries, while intensifying elsewhere'. But the larger basis for their pessimism – and their more controversial contention – is that

> the unexpected legacy of Rio was that mainstream interests cap-
> tured the debate about the future of the earth, and framed it for
> their purposes. Among the most poignant examples of this was
> the ratification by the representatives of Southern countries of
> the Northern development model, which appears in the Rio Dec-
> laration as the highest principle of all, even before the environ-
> ment ... Another legacy, which is currently being played out in
> the international negotiations around climate change and bio-
> diversity, is a form of neo-ecological colonialism whereby tech-
> nology transfer and joint implementation agreements between
> developed and developing countries are being instituted along
> the old power lines ...

Further, they '... suggest that the momentum of the current world economic dynamic is so powerful that it has been able to deflect or co-opt the opposition of the environmental movement ...'. They posit that one plausible explanation '... for the weakness of the environmental critique is that it did not go deep enough ...' Ac-cordingly, one of the purposes of their chapter is to articulate such a *deep* critique. The essence of their critique is presented concisely:

> ... Nature cannot be treated as a mere factor of production.
> Quite the reverse. The ecology generates the economy. Since the
> economy has been cut loose and has run roughshod over the
> ecology ... we need to begin to re-embed the economic system
> within the ecology; and we argue that a start to this process of
> re-embedding begins with retrenching or intelligent downsizing
> of the global economy, rather than downsizing of the ecology.

The authors are perfectly aware that such a 'retrenching goes against the imperatives of the economic system', but the logic of their argument and the case study they present – of Canadian East Coast 'overfishing' – leaves them few alternatives. As the title of their chapter suggests, they believe it is impossible to depend on the timely signalling of the biosphere by the economic system. It simply does not work; the laws of supply and demand do not work adequately when it comes to ecology. Whether this means that it is apt to think of the biosphere as an actor in the world system as

Robert W. Cox has suggested is unclear, but what *is* clear is that this critical investigation of the notion of 'sustainable development' is long overdue.

Chapter 6, 'Environmental Rights, Multilateralism, Morality and the Ecology', is authored by one of the key Southern negotiators who worked out the compromises so sternly critiqued by the authors of the previous chapter. Not surprisingly, Tariq Osman Hyder's portrayal of events at UNCED is much more positive. He clearly makes the case that sustainable development is a viable strategy for coping with the threats to the biosphere. He believes that the South did well in Rio. On the other hand, he is not sanguine about events since the end of the Conference. He is most frustrated that the developed countries do not seem to be living up to the commitments they made at Rio, and the South – divided in the post-Cold War era – seems incapable or at least unwilling to call them on it. At the same time, Ambassador Hyder sees some hope in recent developments in the human rights arena. Clearly, NGOs – albeit *not* the deep Green organizations central to Harries-Jones' *et al.*'s analysis – were active at Rio and their role in global environmental governance has been evident since then, especially in relation to the Commission on Sustainable Development, but also in regard to the Climate Change Convention. But whether such organizations can effectively use the human rights frame – by arguing for planetary rights – is an open question. The prospects, in the short run, do not seem that promising in what is clearly still a predominantly interstate system. The best that Hyder seems to hope for is that NGOs might be able to exert some pressure on national governments in the so-called developed world to live up to their international legal obligations. Doing so, would, in Harries-Jones *et al.*'s, analysis beg the question, at best.

The third section of the book focuses on human rights and participation. Globalization figures large in both Richard Falk's and Claude Ake's chapters. After tracing the 'surprising' emergence of human rights in the post-World War II era – especially surprising in light of what was said at the time of the passage of what Falk sees as the seminal document in the entire period, the Universal Declaration of Human Rights – Falk turns his attention to the 'complicating factor' of globalization. As he boldly and concisely notes:

> There is an emergent tension between the promotion of economic and social rights at the level of the state and disciplinary

impact of global market forces. It poses difficult questions as to whether governments locked into wider competitive frameworks retain the effective discretion to ensure that their own citizens can satisfy basic human needs of an economic and social character.

Falk then goes on to trace the relationship between globalization and multilateralism, as it relates to human rights. He notes that the 'old multilateralism', particularly the United Nations, appears to have provided some considerable space for the development of human rights groups. Attention is drawn to the UN's work on indigenous peoples – a topic addressed in two earlier MUNS studies[2] – and the encouragement of a 'new multilateralism of transnational social forces', most notably in relationship to global conferences in the fields of the environment and women's rights. But here Falk enters a cautionary warning; he anticipates a 'statist backlash', as the policy elite takes greater notice of the normative predilections of these social forces: often anti-statist, pro-human rights and environment. This novel concern is above and beyond what Falk and others have noted about the tensions between calls for universal human rights and a multicultural world in which inter-civilizational differences have more often been highlighted than inter-civilizational dialogue, much less the development – in any time soon – of a supranational intersubjectivity.[3] While Falk's chapter, contrary to much of his earlier writing, focuses on the shadow side of globalization and its implications for human rights and multilateralism, he holds out some hope that regional and subregional frameworks and citizens' initiatives might take up where the 'old multilateralism' leaves off. Here he has in mind such efforts as the International Criminal Court, an institution which is surely suboptimal at best, given that it was established by the Perm-5 dominated Security Council rather than under the provisions of the Genocide Convention itself.

The Nigerian scholar-activist Claude Ake's concerns with globalization are even more pointed. Ake sees economic globalization as shrinking democratic space, especially in the so-called Third World. Even phenomena that some see as potentially aiding in the spread of democracy – like modern communications technology (for example the electronic ballot and new means for the electorate and the elected to communicate) – are, in Ake's view at the least irrelevant to those in the so-called Third World, and potentially dysfunctional. If the goal is participatory, not representative democracy, or if one is in the stage of mobilizing democratic forces rather than tallying peoples' opinions, then electronic means of connectivity are undesirable. Fortunately for many 'Third World' countries, Ake notes, they are also inaccessible. Ake readily admits that the 'old multilateralism' – including the Bretton Woods institutions – have, in some instances, provided support for democracy. He notes, for example, that '. . . some African dictators such as Ibrahim Babangida of Nigeria and Jerry Rawlings of Ghana were able to trade democratization for structural adjustment'. But the consequences, Ake perceptively notes, include tying these countries more effectively into the global economy and thus 'in poor as well as rich countries democratization of the economy, that is, the market rather than the state is what matters'. What Ake fears most, perhaps, is that attention will continue to be focused on incipient democratic movements rather than on the increasing threat of globalization to democratic space. He concludes by suggesting that perhaps now is the time to lament the demise of democracy instead of celebrating its triumph. Whereas he believes that the 'demise of democracy can be mitigated through regional arrangements of transnational governance or associational multilateralism', it cannot be mitigated very much.

Walden Bello provides us with a case study of what Falk and Ake have described in more general and theoretical terms. Bello's focus is East Asia. After assessing the degree to which the image of prosperity in that region '. . . masks a process of growth that is marked by high ecological costs, a widening gap between agriculture and industry, and increasing inequality in income distribution', Bello maps out a plausible strategy for the future. It is one where human rights, that are both universal *and* distinctively Asian, are adhered to, one in which the military security issues of the region are addressed, but not – as so often in the past – by exogenous actors, and one where the economy is made to serve the interests of the vast majority of the population and not simply a small subset of it. Bello's chapter, however, is not utopian. He recognizes the challenges to his goals, including the widely shared perception at least until very recently, that the 'tigers' are models that should be emulated, rather than be reformed. While he has faith in the potential of NGOs to make progress in achieving some of the items on his agenda, he is enough of a realist to anticipate a backlash from the very states he is calling on to reform, if not actually the subversion of his goals. As Falk and Ake before him, Bello sees some, but little, political space. But the size of the space is less significant for him than is the need to take advantage of its existence while it is there. For none of these three authors – any more than those in other sections of the book – expects the interstate system to relinquish its privileged position, much less to disappear in a generation's time. The 'calls to arms' are not revolutionary calls, but their urgency is clear.

We chose to call the final section of the book 'Representation and Accountability'. We asked W. Andy Knight to focus on the existing ways in which civil society is represented at the multilateral level from big UN conferences on global issues to institutional developments in regional, especially European, organizations (i.e. the simultaneity of the 'old' and the 'new' multilateralisms). We asked Marie-Claude Smouts to write a complementary, somewhat more speculative essay, in which she would speak to the functional and territorial bases as they might apply to a future, 'new' multilateralism.

Knight argues that

> particularly over the past fifty years, the agitation and activities of certain non-state actors have, in effect, already etched out 'space' (which in the past has normally been reserved for state actors) for civil society within the global governance context.

He further contends that

> . . . out of the dialectical interaction of 'top-down' and 'bottom-up' forces, the outlines of a 'new' multilateralism is emerging which has the potential of allowing civil societal actors (i.e. that broader community outside of political authority) an expanded and increasingly important role in the workings of global governance.

But Knight also cautions us that the creation of space in global governance for civil society

> is not unproblematic. There is no guarantee that multilateral governance will become more democratic or egalitarian as a result of the increasing activity of civil societal, or 'bottom-up', forces. Not all elements in civil society are benign or progressive. Some of them represent the [too infrequently studied] underbelly of society and others represent reactionary and exclusionary movements.

He also adds an important point that 'not all of them want to be placed under a governance structure of any type' and some – such as the environmental groups written about by Harries-Jones, *et al.* – 'become co-opted by hegemonic institutions and ideologies'. In the space available for his chapter, Knight is, unfortunately, unable to develop the factors which give rise to one set of forces as contrasted to the other, but his discussion of the 'top-down/bottom-up intersection' which characterizes multilateralism on the eve of the twenty-first century is a valuable and original contribution.

Smouts rises to the speculative challenge by calling for a democratizing of multilateralism. In particular, she reviews the accounts of those who see the emergence of a *global* civil society. She argues that many of them seem to believe that global civil society is evolving because there is evidence of a significant growth of grassroots movements. They expect this to be translated somehow – in some unspecified manner – to the global level. She is a little dubious about this. Moreover, she reminds us that social movements are not always seeking goals in accord with MUNS' normative predilections, and she warns us of the inevitability of conflicts between social movements and of the possibility of their betrayal from within. At the same time, she offers us some rays of hope, pointing toward the recent empowerment of NGOs.

NGOs, especially in Africa where civil society is weak, often find themselves turning to the state to fend off advice coming from international organizations that lack knowledge of the social context. Paradoxically, the weakness of civil society and of those states – especially in Africa – sometimes lead those very same international organizations to turn to NGOs if they want to have their policies implemented. Thus, the potential for empowered NGOs is noted. Even more speculatively, Smouts foresees the possibility of such an empowered civil society taking seriously the notion of *jus cogens*, that is the identification of peremptory norms, from which no derogation is possible.

Among the unique contributions of this volume is its testimony to the value of taking a policy-relevant critical approach to the study of multilateralism, as contrasted to a problem-solving approach.[4] By going beyond the current state of things and focusing on more than the daily problems which *must* be addressed by those policy makers most knowledgeable about them, the authors in this volume examine the likely consequences for multilateralism of increased globalization and its attendant internationalization of the state; a weakening of state sovereignty, but continuation of the interstate system; the growth of civil society, including what some call global civil society; the dangers of a world in which most leaders, governmental and not, accept market solutions to the threat of the biosphere and believe in the notion of sustainable development, and the continuation of conflicts attendant with the playing out of contested and often overlapping identities.

NOTES

1. Michael G. Schechter (ed.), *Innovation in Multilateralism* (London: Macmillan, for the United Nations University Press, 1998).
2. Bice Maigushca, 'The transnational indigenous movement in a changing world order', in *Global Transformation: Challenges to the State System*, edited by Yoshkazu Sakamoto (Tokyo: The United Nations University Press, 1994), and S. James Anaya, 'Indigenous peoples and developments in international law: toward change through multilateralism and the modern human rights frame', in Michael G. Schechter (ed.) *Innovation in Multilateralism*.
3. This notion is developed in: Robert W. Cox, 'Towards a post-hegemonic conceptualization of world order: reflections on the relevancy of Ibn Khalbun', in *Governance without Government: Order and Change in World Politics*, edited by James N. Rosenau and Ernst-Otto Czempiel (Cambridge: Cambridge University Press, 1992).
4. The distinction between these two approaches is classically deliniated in: Robert W. Cox, 'Social forces, states, and world orders: beyond international relations theory,' reproduced in *Approaches to World Order*, by Robert W. Cox with Timothy J. Sinclair (Cambridge: Cambridge University Press, 1996), 87–91. See also: Michael G. Schechter, '*Our Global Neighborhood*: Pushing Problem-Solving Theory to its Limits and the Limits of Problem-Solving Theory,' in *Approaches to Global Governance Theory*, edited by Martin Hewson and Timothy J. Sinclair (Albany: SUNY Press, 1998).

Part I

Security Issues

2 From Civil War to Civil Peace: Multi-Track Solutions to Armed Conflict

Kumar Rupesinghe

The genocide in Rwanda, ethnic cleansing in Bosnia, violence and famine in Somalia, and a resurgence of vicious fighting in Liberia are just a selection of events which mark the first half of the 1990s, and will be remembered as indications of the international community's and the United Nations' incapacity to manage crises. They were all intra-state conflicts of the most brutal kind, which flickered on television screens world wide, arousing guilt, anger, incomprehension, sadness and generosity. Humanitarian aid flowed in, but it was not enough. The causes of these conflicts are deep-rooted and long term, leaving many observers thinking there is nothing more that can be done. Robert Kaplan expressed this attitude in his highly controversial essay, *The Coming Anarchy*,[1] about internal conflicts and environmental and political upheaval. He not only predicted an apocalyptic end to Africa which is 'set to go over the edge' but also environmental and political breakdown spreading to other theatres: the 'West African coast, the Middle East, the Indian subcontinent, China and Central America'.

This is, however, a somewhat alarmist attitude, which bears little relation to reality, nor focuses on the complexity of issues which are emerging. The post-Cold War era has brought the end of superpower proxy wars, has been effective in ending apartheid in South Africa and has heralded a new freedom in Eastern Europe, but it has also unleashed new disputes, manifested in ethnic and religious rivalries, or contests over governance and power, onto the world stage. Such disputes, which are predominantly taking place within state borders, are threatening to the world at large, mainly because there is no international structure through which they can be addressed or managed. The initial task fell upon the UN, but the organization had neither the means, nor the ability to resolve the crises single-handedly. In reality, the end of the Cold War caught the international community off-guard; on the one hand attempting to reassess the benefits of the changes, while on the other hand unable to foresee or predict the effects.

In *An Agenda for Peace* published in 1992 Dr Boutros-Ghali declared his vision of a world organization capable of maintaining international peace and security, through more efficient means of peace making. Acknowledging the organization's paralysis during the Cold War era, 'the United Nations was rendered powerless to deal with many of [the] crises because of the vetoes – 279 of them – cast in the Security Council', he also stated that since May 1990, the UN had emerged as the 'central instrument for the prevention and resolution of conflicts and for the preservation of peace'. To meet these demands, Dr Boutros-Ghali presented a framework based on preventive measures, seeking to 'identify at the earliest possible stage situations that could produce conflict, and try through diplomacy to remove the sources of danger before violence results.'

'Preventive diplomacy' defined as 'action to prevent disputes from arising between parties, to prevent existing disputes from escalating into conflicts and to limit the spread of the latter when they occur', became a new catch phrase. Yet, despite intentions to prevent violence and war through diplomacy, little emphasis was actually given to the non-military potential of both governmental and non-governmental organizations. In retrospect it was evident that although preventive diplomacy, in theory, represented a more cost-efficient approach to conflict management than troop deployment, in reality the UN could not invest sufficient resources to develop a comprehensive framework for conflict prevention.

Furthermore, the cooperative spirit of the Gulf War did not *immediately* extend to Bosnia or Rwanda, and it became ever more apparent that strategic and economic interests still held greater sway than humanitarian issues. It was also evident that member states were reluctant to commit troops under a UN command. By 1995, in *A Supplement to an Agenda for Peace*, Boutros-Ghali admitted the UN's inability to meet the demands for the use of force in internal conflicts. In addition to the increasing burden of responsibility that was falling on the UN's shoulders, the pervasive financial crisis was also a limiting factor. Yet beyond the practical obstacles, there also lay a number of more conceptual issues, relating to the

Table 1.1   Armed Conflicts and Locations

	1989	1990	1991	1992	1993	1994
Minor conflicts	14	16	18	23	15	17
Intermediate	14	14	13	12	17	18
War	19	19	20	20	14	7
All conflicts	47	49	51	55	46	42
All locations	37	39	38	41	33	32

nature and complexity of internal conflicts that had become more clear to the UN, during the interim years, between 1992 and 1995.

A fundamental problem facing the UN today is that the organization has never had an explicit mandate to intervene in civil conflicts. The UN is a state-based organization where the sovereignty of the governments of member states is recognized as paramount. It has no mandate to intervene in conflicts and matters which fall under the domestic jurisdiction of member states. Consequently, the prevention and resolution of civil wars and internal disputes is largely uncharted territory.

A REVIEW OF INTERNAL CONFLICTS

Internal conflicts have replaced interstate conflicts as the 'classic' war. Of the 82 armed conflicts between 1989 and 1992, only three were between states. In December 1995, 30 major armed conflicts[2] were recorded world wide. This is not to suggest that interstate wars are a thing of the past. As recent disputes between Turkey and Greece and China and Taiwan show, there is still sensitivity over territorial issues. However, of the 11 peacekeeping operations established since 1982, all but two relate to internal conflict. Internal conflicts have caused the greatest forced movement of people since 1945. Table 1.1 shows the classification of the Department of Peace and Conflict Research (DPCR) of Uppsala University (Sweden) into minor and intermediate conflicts and war. It classifies intermediate conflicts and war as 'major armed conflict'. The figures show that the high point in this period was 1991–2 but since then there has been an appreciable and welcome decrease.[3]

An even clearer picture of the world situation can be obtained by studying the number of conflicts by region, in Europe, the Middle

Table 1.2   The Number of Conflicts by Region 1989–94

	1989	1990	1991	1992	1993	1994
EUROPE						
Minor	0	2	4	5	4	2
Intermediate	1	1	1	2	2	2
War	1	0	1	2	4	1
No. of Conflicts	2	3	6	9	10	5
No. of Locations	2	2	5	7	6	3
MIDDLE EAST						
Minor	0	1	1	2	1	1
Intermediate	3	4	3	4	5	2
War	1	1	3	1	1	2
No. of Conflicts	4	6	7	7	7	5
No. of Locations	4	6	5	5	5	5
ASIA						
Minor	7	5	5	7	6	6
Intermediate	6	7	5	6	5	7
War	6	6	6	7	4	2
No. of Conflicts	19	18	16	20	15	15
No. of Locations	11	11	8	11	8	8
AFRICA						
Minor	4	7	7	8	4	7
Intermediate	2	1	1	0	4	4
War	8	9	9	7	3	2
No. of Conflicts	14	17	17	15	11	13
No. of Locations	12	15	15	14	11	12
AMERICAS	1989	1990	1991	1992	1993	1994
Minor	3	1	1	1	0	1
Intermediate	2	1	3	0	1	3
War	3	3	1	3	2	0
No. of Conflicts	8	5	5	4	3	4
No. of Locations	8	5	5	4	3	4

East, Asia, Africa and the Americas. Table 1.2 covers the years 1989–94 and provides evidence that conflicts are decreasing in nearly every region of the world. Europe remains the exception to this pattern but as Peter Wallensteen and Margareta Sollenberg make clear, it is not surprising that the most dramatic changes in the number of armed conflicts should have occurred in Europe, since the end of the Cold War has acted as a catalyst in some cases.

Even so, the number of conflicts in Europe dropped markedly in 1993–4 (from ten to five) and compared to the situation in 1989, there has only been an increase of one major armed conflict.[4] In the Middle East the figures point to a rough stability, four major armed conflicts in 1989 and four in 1994. In Asia, major armed conflicts have fallen from 12 to nine during the five-year period and the number of wars sees a significant decrease from six in 1989 to only two in 1994. In Africa, the number of major armed conflicts was ten in 1989, and six in 1994. Likewise the number of wars has fallen from eight in 1989 to only two in 1994. The Americas have seen the biggest developments during this time. In this region, no *wars*, as defined by over 1000 deaths per year, have taken place in 1994 compared with three in 1989. The total number of conflicts has fallen steadily from eight to four as has the number of locations. Research is currently being undertaken to develop a more systematic analysis of conflict situations within each region, and to identify potentially violent disputes which may arise.[5]

THE COMPLEXITY OF INTERNAL CONFLICTS

Internal conflicts are defined primarily as conflicts which arise within state borders. Although there may be outside factors which influence these conflicts, they are primarily conflicts over governance, identity and resource allocation within a particular state. They commence when a government is unable or unwilling to handle satisfactorily the grievances of a group, within the boundaries of normal politics.[6] The parameters which govern internal conflicts are radically different from interstate wars. These conflicts may also be over problems of identity and a sense of security. Often the state is a party to the conflict and will command power, resources and military might over the contending force. Usually, the relationship between conflicting parties is 'asymmetrical',[7] meaning that one party is strong while the other is weak. Strength is not just a measure of military power, but also refers to legitimacy within a domestic and international system. A government has legitimacy, sovereignty, armies, resources, the media, and allies. It has an international support structure. The insurgents – often faced with marginalization, brutality, and suppression – are fighting for that legitimacy and the redistribution of power and resources.

Certain features characterize internal conflicts. Unlike interstate conflicts which are monitored and mediated from the early stages, the escalation of internal conflict rarely elicits attempts at mediation by outside parties in the formation stages. Consequently, these disputes can escalate into war, and continue for years, as in Chad, Sri Lanka or Cambodia. The massive diffusion of small arms in the world has increased the scope and lethality of such wars. Increasing militarization of society leads to a breakdown in communication between different segments and groups and renders civilians passive to the violence that surrounds them. What is common in these conflicts is the fragmentation of society and a breakdown of all socio-political and legal infrastructures that are necessary to the sustenance of a secure civil society.

The tasks of the UNHCR and other humanitarian agencies have grown out of all previous proportions, as civilians have become more and more involved, in most cases involuntarily. Over 90 per cent of war casualties today are civilians, which compares with 10 per cent during World War I and 50 per cent during World War II. Of course, this is partly related to the increased sophistication and lethal power of weapons and landmines which continue to be used indiscriminately. More significantly, however, it is in the very nature of internal conflicts, that are so often fought along religious or ethnic divides, that implicate everyone: man, woman and child. The golden rule of war in the late-twentieth century seems to be that there *are* no rules of war. The most vulnerable persons and groups are continually at risk and the enactment and acceptance of human rights and humanitarian international law has not prevented continuing examples of genocide and massive human rights violations.

In countries like Somalia, Liberia and Sierra Leone, the conflict landscape contains not only regular troops and rebels, but also diamond and drug dealers, mercenaries, child soldiers and private warlords who prey on the vulnerable. The growing influence of warlordism and militia movements means that the monopoly of violence once enjoyed by the state is disappearing. Increasingly, private militias are arming themselves in retaliation against what they perceive as the growth of states which are no longer concerned about, or capable of representing, their interests and defending their needs. In Somalia, General Farah Aidid was a particular case in point, while in a country like Afghanistan (since the Soviet withdrawal), old tribal ties, linked with religious ideology and commercial benefits, have resulted in the continuation of a vicious and pervasive civil war.

RESOLVING INTERNAL CONFLICTS – PROBLEMS TO BE ADDRESSED

1. Sovereignty

The principle of state sovereignty continues to be a major obstacle to addressing the problem of internal conflicts. While such conflicts are between the peoples of one state, the basis of the UN system is built on the integrity of the state and not of its peoples: it is the sovereign state which has the right to exist and remain inviolate. Notwithstanding the mechanism under Chapter VII of the UN Charter where there is a threat to international peace and security, the legal justification for closing the door to the UN or other government initiatives is always Article 2 (7) which protects matters essentially within the 'domestic jurisdiction' of member states. The principle of *consent* undermines the legitimacy of intervention by official third parties. It places constraints on political action and other measures across the whole spectrum of activities. NGOs, however, can intervene legitimately if they are invited by citizen groups or rebel communities to provide assistance and humanitarian aid.

Nevertheless, the agenda that state sovereignty is absolute is being increasingly challenged by a variety of forces. *An Agenda for Peace* asserted that the time of absolute and *exclusive* sovereignty had passed. Security Council resolution 688 facilitated the protection of the Kurds in northern Iraq through creating safe havens on sovereign Iraqi territory. In some cases, media attention presses for humanitarian intervention, and increasingly non-state organizations are focusing on the long-term benefits of good governance. But these inroads into the principle sometimes seem more the exception than the normal practice. Whether it is the death of over 30 000 people in Chechnia, or the unjust execution of one man in Nigeria, the international system reveals its frailties.

2. Access

If outside intervention is to occur, access to the parties in conflict must be achieved and in many cases this access is denied. This is a serious practical issue. Often the rebel leaders are difficult to contact and the changing theatres of war make radio and telephone contact impossible. In Sierra Leone, until the recent breakthrough which brought a cease fire to the civil war, three intergovernmental organizations experienced great difficulty in gaining access to the rebel group, the Revolutionary United Front.[8]

The problem of impartiality also arises. Gaining access to the rebel side is fraught with the danger of misperception. In the intensity of conflict, misunderstanding and misinterpretation of third parties is common. Contact with the other side is fraught with recrimination and demonization is usually caused. Third parties are frequently accused of providing legitimacy to the rebel side. Precisely because it is a state-centred body, the UN needs the approval of the government in power to intervene in the dispute. But this invitation by the national government can be seen by the other side as a sign of complicity. Non-governmental organizations have greater flexibility in gaining access, but traditionally their role has been providing humanitarian assistance. Their involvement in political matters is still viewed with scepticism. Yet, because they have the opportunity to make contact with rebel groups, NGOs can build trust and gain credibility. So, while NGOs may have difficulty gaining the trust of governments, IGOs have problems gaining access and the trust of rebels. By recognizing these limits and coordinating their efforts, each sector could add value and bring complementarity of action to the process.

3. Asymmetry

Internal conflicts are invariably caused by a challenge to the existing power relations in the state. Paradoxically, the inequality of power and resources between the two sides is compensated for by the tenacity of the 'rebel mind' which is reluctant to consider a compromise or identify a strategy other than violence. The effect of this asymmetry between the parties in an internal conflict in prolonging internal wars should not be underestimated. One recent study has analysed how the asymmetry of internal conflict rarely produces a stalemate needed for negotiations which function best under conditions of equality.[9] The rebel is not strong enough to overthrow the state and the state is not strong enough to crush the rebel. As one former US Secretary of State has commented: 'the guerrilla wins if he does not lose; the conventional army loses if it does not win'.[10] IRA hunger strikers, the suicide bombers of Hamas and the Tamil Tigers are all caught in the same trap – which produces no solutions to the conflict and an intensification of resistance on the opposing side.

This imbalance in power relations is itself a barrier to reaching a point of negotiation. Often the state enters dialogue only as a means of pursuing war by other means. By demanding the decommissioning of weapons for example, as a precondition for talks, governments are effectively asking for a surrender, which in turn is humiliating for the rebels. Negotiations work best when there is equality in the relationship, and where both parties have mutual veto power. In an asymmetrical conflict, however, the opportunity for negotiation arises when a mutually hurting stalemate occurs; in other words, both sides are locked in a situation where they cannot escalate the conflict with their available means or at an acceptable cost. However, both sides often attempt to force changes in the other's policy by playing on the element of cost.[11] Still the inequality remains; insurgents try to get the government to negotiate, while the government wants insurgents to surrender. The stalemate can only be broken if there is a process of mutual recognition and willingness to partake in dialogue; and even then, the internal dynamics of the insurgency can weaken the validity of their spokesmen, or the government's, and solutions may be inadequate or come too early in the life cycle of a conflict. The most effective situation, however is when parity is achieved and both parties are strong and legitimate enough to come to an agreement. This is a rare condition in internal conflicts.[12]

4. Political Will and Traditional Diplomacy: the Problem of Selectivity

Powerful governments are *selective* in their policies and frequently decide not to get involved in a long-running conflict because they see no domestic advantage accruing as a result. Strategic and national interests are usually the prerequisites for actual involvement although statements showing the 'deepest concern' can be made without cost. The fact that neither Burundi nor Rwanda possesses sufficient strategic interest has coloured the international community's response to the events which have taken place in both countries. The rings of friendship and convenience which tie countries together caused British reluctance to criticize French policy in Rwanda and Zaire. As a *quid pro quo*, the French have been hesitant in criticizing the British position on Nigeria. These compromises are the unwritten rules of international affairs.

Interest and involvement in internal conflicts often comes from neighbouring or regional states, who may fan the flames of conflict by supporting particular groups, or by attempting to increase their own sphere of influence. In Sierra Leone, for example, Nigerian and Guinean soldiers were sent in on behalf of the Sierra Leone government. India has had major involvement in Sri Lanka, while in Afghanistan Iran, Pakistan and Russia continue to bear influence, supporting opposing factions and fuelling the war. Regional concerns such as refugee flows and the spread of instability can also make neighbouring states more committed to bringing peace. Tanzania has been particularly concerned with the events in Burundi, and former President Nyerere has played a key role in the negotiations. Thus when focusing on a particular conflict, it is necessary to explore the regional context in which it is taking place, and build a framework addressing all the relevant features.

The issue of selectivity is further compounded by the propensity to treat internal conflicts as merely 'natural disasters' with the humanitarian industry ready to swing into action. The indignation that citizens feel at gross violations and killings is channelled into mercy missions so that humanitarian relief becomes a way of buying off political responsibility.

The question of political will needs to be analysed with greater vigour however because there is not a single, monolithic focal point in western democracies. Political will is the way that citizens shape the actions of their politicians and since the 1960s there has been a flowering of powerful lobby organizations which can develop around single issue causes. Amongst western nations different approaches to international issues are taken. Small- to medium-sized states such as Norway and Holland have shown an interest in low-profile interventions in internal conflicts. This is not strictly for strategic interests; rather it is a means of gaining credibility on the world stage, promoting values to which they adhere.

People outside the political process have made a difference and mobilized political will in such issues as landmines and nuclear weapons, so to some extent it is a fallacy to suggest that only strategic interests in the narrow sense determine political will. Strategic interests do not always preclude issues such as a good environment, the prevention of massive refugee flows, long-term trade potentials, and humane values. Of course, as far as short-term state interests are concerned, some of these have greater appeal than others.

5. Power of the Media

The media's role in the coverage of conflicts is an increasingly controversial and difficult one. Few broadcasting networks or newspapers want in-depth coverage of every war, and owing to financial constraints and competition, most cannot even provide proper in-depth coverage, even if they wanted to do so. Audiences and readers are becoming increasingly provincial in their scope of interest, and in an era where 10-second sound bites dictate attitudes, the complexity of war is impossible to explain. As one Nobel prize-winner has commented, 'we are always en route to the next shock. It is the agitation level that matters, not this or that enormity'.[13] In certain circumstances, the media is a powerful spotlight but there will always be areas of darkness where particular conflicts, and the potentiality for conflicts, are forgotten. Whether or not foreign-policy decisions to intervene can be explained by the CNN factor, public opinion has shown itself to be the most intangible and weakest of friends.[14] As the American correspondent Roy Gutman has stated, Bosnia 'will be recorded as the first genocide in history where journalists were reporting it as it was actually happening, and governments didn't stop it'.[15] As the events in Rwanda indicate, neither public opinion nor the media showed sufficient outrage to mobilize government action. Domestic pressures, re-election prospects, and the financial cost of sending troops to a distant land have combined to forge a new timidity and in some countries at least, an obsession with (its own) casualties.

6. Transforming a Culture of Violence

Perhaps the most intractable and complex issue to contend with, is the process of transforming a society from one which has become intrinsically violent, to one which has developed the socio-political institutions which can address and resolve civil disputes. The democratization of society is a key factor in conflict resolution, but it cannot stop at constitutional reforms and an election process. Democracy, in its widest sense, provides all levels of the population with a channel of communication, and participation in the socio-political arena. The government is held accountable for its actions, and in theory all sectors of society have equal rights under the law. Where that channel breaks down, then the danger of violence erupting increases. Since 1990 there has been a marked decrease in internal conflict in parts of Asia and Central America. In Nicaragua and El Salvador, peace accords were signed in 1990 and 1991 respectively, and elections ensued. Yet in June 1996, the number of violent deaths in El Salvador was still among the highest in Central America. This was predominantly due to the demobilization of state and guerrilla soldiers, without a proper rehabilitation process. With small arms still in their possession, many of the young soldiers became involved in criminal street gangs and drug dealing as a means of survival.

In Peru, Colombia and Guatemala, three new democracies, death squads still act with impunity and military and police backing. Still fighting a counter-insurgency, the government of Peru has effected changes to the 1993 constitution, thereby weakening democratic accountability and the independence of the judiciary. There is a fear for the future of democracy in the region, for so long as there is impunity for members of the past regime, a lack of accountability, and weak democratic institutions, there is also a destabilizing effect on the rule of law, which can lead to renewed violence. There may not be a categorical 'war' being fought, but the culture of violence which was engendered by years of civil war has not transformed either. Such issues which delve into the social psychology of a society, and relate to the innate sense of insecurity and fear that may exist, cannot be solved in limited periods of time, with limited personnel and resources. There is a need for long-term social, political and economic commitment, which the present international system is at times unwilling, and even unable, to give.[16]

TOWARDS AN EXPANDED FRAMEWORK FOR CONFLICT RESOLUTION

How can a state-based organization play a meaningful role in the internal conflicts of its member states? The UN is criticized as an unwieldy and increasingly flawed instrument for solving these issues. The agenda has been further altered by NGOs which are now taking over a large number of roles that were previously the preserve of the UN, particularly in the field of humanitarian action, development programs and the monitoring of human rights. Even the areas of peace making, preventive diplomacy and conflict resolution, which were the prerogatives and domain of the Security Council and the political office of the UN secretariat, have been opened up with new actors such as small states, eminent persons and NGOs developing and creating mechanisms to address these issues.

The international system today is much more than a system of states. With a variety of transnational actors from business corporations, academia, non-governmental agencies, civic groups and religious organizations, it is an ever-expanding network which cuts across the state system. The communications revolution has enabled greater communication world wide, and with regard to peace building and future security, there is a growing network of citizen-based groups which are willing to shoulder much of the responsibility.

However, the extended involvement of the non-governmental sector should not undermine the importance of the moral authority of the UN as a global organization, and its wide technical capacity and expertise. The fact is that the problems which face the world today require solutions which cannot be met by the UN alone. The United Nations can often provide the strategic frameworks for preventive diplomacy. At the very least, a better form of partnership is needed at every level between UN bodies, governments, NGOs and regional organizations. Drug trafficking and international terrorism demonstrate the willingness of governments in every part of the world to collaborate with each other in preventive action. The need is for this cohesion to move onto additional areas of concern.

A structured response to crises should be developed, whereby a division of labour based on the different comparative competencies of organizations is initiated. The aim is to ensure an increased coherence in the activities initiated by each organization. The UN is a suitable forum to advocate just such challenges. Indeed it is well placed to coordinate a number of initiatives so that complementary strategies can be developed. It can build the framework under which a wide range of other actors – eminent persons, NGOs, regional organizations – intervene in the cause of peace.

EARLY WARNING

The early warning of conflict situations is seen as a necessary element in conflict prevention. The failure of conflict management in recent years has been due in part to the tardiness of the actions employed. Protracted social conflicts have a determinable cycle and each phase of the conflict offers an opportunity for a particular kind of intervention. In most cases however, intervention comes during the stage when the conflict has escalated and the parties have entered a phase of attrition, when the spiral of violence and counter-violence has already begun.

An early warning system is one instrument to prevent the conflict from reaching this critical stage. When tensions and crises develop, the information which is available is fragmented, sometimes inaccurate, and this highlights the central problem of early warning. Warnings may be given by a number of organizations but they do not possess the ability to force the world's attention on these countries at risk. In April 1994, for example, when many of the world's journalists were congregating in South Africa for the elections the warnings which were coming from Rwanda were effectively ignored.

Early Warning Centres

The establishment of one or two official centres for early warning and preventive diplomacy which would produce regular and authoritative reports, warnings and recommendations would be of great value. These centres would be able to receive reports from NGOs and other agencies. Specific public and private recommendations could be made to all the different actors of the international community including the UN, particular national governments and NGOs. In Europe, the initiative at the European Parliament to establish an early warning observatory has received support. However, few practical steps have been taken, as a comprehensive study shows.[17] In examining the early warning and preventive actions of a number of intergovernmental organizations, the lack of effectiveness and cohesion in their operations was revealed. No well-developed early warning systems have *yet* been developed, although many organizations such as the OSCE, ASEAN, ECOWAS, and OAU are aware of the need for such a system. The lack of effective early warning in the past has, in part, been due to the inefficiencies of centralized governmental systems, whose response to an impending emergency is time-consuming and will often be delayed until the crisis has struck. Bureaucracies in the donor countries are not geared to the needs of the recipients, and as decision makers are only indirectly linked to the victims, there is little accountability regarding the efficiency and effectiveness of the response.

Amongst members of the Organization for Economic Cooperation and Development, the need for a division of labour and cooperation between donors and embassies within the region of conflict as part of an early warning system is increasingly acknowledged.[18] It is argued that with regular communication between these parties, the conflict situation could be diagnosed, and a 'common base of information' could be agreed upon which would then be used to formulate a coordinated strategy, which would be recognized by outside governments while being sensitive to the needs of the various factions involved in the dispute.[19]

The UN has also become more active in the area of early warning and rapid response. Under the direction of the UN Department of Humanitarian Affairs (DHA) the Relief Web project has been launched, the purpose of which is to provide updated, on-line global information for conflict prevention, preparedness and rapid response for the humanitarian community, so that relevant actors, particularly in regions of conflict or disaster, can make more effective use of information in developing complementary strategies for prevention and relief activities. Subject to following certain procedures regarding the collection and exchange of information, all organizations are welcome to join.[20]

Since sovereign governments do not take kindly to being informed that their country is on the brink of disaster, intergovernmental systems alone are somewhat limited in building a capacity for early warning. So their efforts need to be complemented by citizen-based and NGO systems, but here a number of practical issues must be taken into consideration. Firstly, many NGOs and international charities are limited by their mandates. For example, the ICRC has its own information-gathering system, but cannot share this openly with other NGOs, nor can it act on data provided by others. Secondly, every organization has its own priorities. So Amnesty's focus on Nigeria at a particular moment may not bear relevance to Oxfam's program focused on Tanzania at that same time. It is therefore necessary to develop a means through which all the organizations working in a specific region can coordinate their efforts and work towards a common agenda.

The creation of an early warning clearing house which could collect and disseminate regular early warning data to a network of early action agencies is a possibility today. With access to information databases world wide and a range of web sites on the Internet, the clearing house could synthesize the information gathered and offer a range of standardized reports on subjects such as countries at war, potential conflicts, minorities at risk, and thematic issues such as arms proliferation. The clearing house could also act as a referral system, pointing to recognized experts and information brokers who could provide more in-depth analysis.[21]

The search for a very effective early warning system is not an end in itself. A highly efficient early warning system will be useless unless it results in effective action. It must be tied to a structured multi-sectored response. Furthermore, early warning is not just the function of networks and the distribution of mandates, but also the empowerment of actors within the regions of conflict.

The early action network should also comprise human rights organizations, humanitarian agencies, development agencies, governments, regional and global intergovernmental organizations such as the OAU, EU and UN, the corporate sector and the academic community amongst others. The aim would be to ensure that a diverse set of organizations have access to regular and reliable information about ongoing and potential conflicts, upon which they could determine a coordinated plan of early preventive action.[22]

MULTI-TRACK SOLUTIONS TO CONFLICT

Multi-track diplomacy, defined as the application of peace making from different vantage points within a multi-centred network, reflects the different levels and variety of factors which need to be addressed. It highlights the combination of elements which can work together successfully to bring together a conjuncture of forces, thereby creating the ingredients for a successful peace process. It has recently been described as a 'web of interconnected parts (activities, individuals, institutions, communities) that operate together, whether awkwardly or gracefully, for a common goal: a world at peace'.[23]

The design of the multi-track approach is based on the idea that all efforts can be complementary to each other and part of a larger framework of initiatives.[24] The involvement of a variety of actors at different levels of a conflict is intended to bring greater accountability and adherence to human rights and humanitarian laws by all sides. For example, while NGOs may monitor human rights abuses at the grassroots levels, economic institutions such as the IMF or World Bank could press for a peaceful settlement, and national civic groups could form peace coalitions to bring pressure on the government and rebels to negotiate. Multi-track initiatives envisage a comprehensive, mutually reinforcing network with diverse actors intervening at different levels of the problem. It is clear that the world of conflict is multi-layered and different types of action must be used to address these different dimensions. Different organizations and groups, intervening at appropriate levels, can be used so that there is a division of labour based on the comparative advantages of each group.

It is argued that official diplomacy and unofficial 'second track' approaches should be complemented by a range of multi-track solutions. Official diplomatic manoeuvres are often circumscribed by political interests, a lack of trust concerning the intentions of the mediator, short-term domestic considerations, and an unwillingness to address the depth and complexity of social and economic problems that are caused by internal conflicts. Second-track approaches, such the Norwegian involvement in the Middle East, may stand greater chance of success, if it is intended to complement official negotiations, but cannot focus on all the other areas of concern which have affected the causes and duration of the conflict. Nongovernmental or unofficial diplomacy may be effective in creating dialogue, but does not have the necessary resources or political leverage to bring about change. Yet the combined force of these approaches can address the fundamental issues, and still bring the necessary political momentum.

1. Tools and Approaches

Within preventive diplomacy, multi-track diplomacy is gradually being developed through a series of parallel stages. On one level the development and analysis of theoretical approaches to peace building and preventive action are still taking place.[25] Studies are also being undertaken in building partnerships with international and local groups so that information about conflict prevention is shared and extended.[26] The next phase incorporates the development of regional working groups in the analysis of conflict scenarios by responding with practical initiatives.[27] The final stage is the establishment of a response mechanism that can respond during the early stages of the conflict situation, containing violence and making use of new opportunities to create peace initiatives with the help of NGOs, other institutions and local citizens.[28]

A distinction may be made between the tools used in the various stages of conflict, particularly during the pre-negotiation and the negotiation phases, when the challenge is firstly to bring the warring parties to the table, and introduce accountability. Amnesty International and Human Rights Watch conduct intensive monitoring of human rights abuses, and have been actively involved in holding non-state actors accountable. Local citizen groups can also create a framework to bring accountability amongst warring parties. The creation of peace zones and peace corridors in the Philippines, for example, did affect the actions of the fighters, as communities joined together to ban fighting in the zones. The objective should be to create opportunities for dialogue.

Most of the classical literature on conflict resolution deals with negotiations and how to achieve successful outcomes on win-win solutions during the negotiations process itself. In internal conflicts however, the major problem is how to bring the parties to the table.[29] As argued earlier, asymmetrical conflicts have a life of their own, and often the parties may want to prolong the war. Thus there is a need for more experience sharing and the development of new instruments through which the parties can be persuaded to come forward. Waiting for a hurting stalemate may be too costly and may prolong the war.

Listed below is only a selection of some of the methods and tools which may be useful in the expansion of multi-track diplomacy. Some are tried and tested approaches; however, often an organization will only use one method. For multi-track diplomacy to be effective it is important that a more integrative, 'multi-tool' approach is used. In other words a menu of options could be developed providing a range of activities which could be tailored to the needs of each situation.

- **Peace missions** – fact-finding missions to conflict area and citizens' missions to better define the problems.
- **Special envoys** – a group of experienced and credible emissaries sent to speak to all parties in the conflict, exploring negotiation routes. By involving respected international emissaries, more attention is given to the area of conflict and more people, both at a local and an international level, show interest in participating in the resolution process.
- **Peace monitors** – peace/human rights groups monitoring the safety of civilians, and offering recommendations for improvements. The development of a code of conduct for the adherence to human rights and humanitarian law is one step towards introducing

accountability. Special 'peace brigades' can be formed to monitor cease fires, secure the safety of peace corridors, and accompany human rights lawyers, acting as a deterrent against attacks.

- **Problem solving** – informal discussions with and between disputants, or those close to them, to encourage alternative routes to conflict resolution. These workshops can be conducted over a period of time, giving each group a chance to express their emotions and voice their fears in a non-adversarial setting. Furthermore, the methods used in problem solving workshops should be integrated into a wider public and political sphere.
- **Training workshops** – the objective is to transfer mediation and reconciliation skills and to encourage disputants, and others affected by the conflict, to consider alternative routes to conflict resolution. Each workshop can be designed to fit the needs of the participants, starting from the pre-negotiation phase. Using these workshops it would be possible to develop local, regional and national platforms for conflict prevention and resolution.
- **Capacity-building** – technical and logistical assistance for mediation efforts to the relevant actors and communities. This is linked to the above, but also refers to the provision of material goods such as computers, books, and general office equipment. Training in the use of computers and administrative matters is also important.
- **Peace conference or peace task force** – citizen-based peace groups or national peace conferences, bringing together different sectors of society and encouraging them to formulate a peace agenda. By establishing a forum for discussion, different working groups get the opportunity to exchange ideas and develop a common agenda and agreed plan of action.
- **Peace initiatives** – community-based initiatives such as 'peace zones' and 'days of peace' which facilitate the provision of food supplies to certain areas and strengthen confidence building in divided societies. These initiatives aim to galvanize local communities and villages into taking a more active role. They are also a means of bolstering people's confidence at a time when most feel despair and have no hope for change.
- **Linking differences** – informal settings where disputants can have a chance to understand opposing views. To avoid the embarrassment of official confrontation an informal gathering could be arranged through a neutral third party, where disputants have the chance to speak openly without fear of retaliation from their

own supporters or the enemy. It is part of the 'humanizing' process, in which disputants are encouraged to dispel stereotypical images of each other, so that they can once again talk as ordinary people relating to each other, not as soldiers and enemies.

- **Learning from comparative experiences** – experienced peacemakers can visit conflict areas and share their knowledge with local actors. By exploring the issues of conflict in an objective way, they can offer concrete examples of ways in which particular problems have been resolved in past conflicts.
- **Economic assistance or political packages** – economic incentives which draw attention to the advantages of economic cooperation between regions of conflict. By highlighting the advantages of reconciliation, such as investment and aid coming into the country, and opportunities for work and development, disputants can be encouraged to enter into peace talks and discuss a more balanced political and economic power-sharing base.
- **Human rights standard-setting** – campaigns stressing the importance of adhering to international human rights standards, and the need for a framework for international standards on issues relevant to internal conflicts. Amnesty International and Human Rights Watch are amongst the largest organizations monitoring human rights abuses world wide. By publicizing their findings they do put pressure on governments to change their treatment of political prisoners and inform the international community of the extent of abuse that exists. So they can have an enormous impact on the public's perception of a particular state, and thus also influence foreign and economic policy towards those states.[30]
- **Conflict resolution institution-building** – identifying and working with local and national partners and helping them to build links with international organizations and networks. The purpose would be to make conflict-resolution practice an inherent aspect of other civic groups. Additionally a network of conflict-resolution practitioners would strengthen the practical and conceptual developments, as new ideas could be explored and tested on a world-wide basis.
- **Police and military training** – retraining the military and law enforcement agencies to complement and support peace processes. Often the police and military are one and the same. The purpose here would be first to make distinctions between domestic policing methods and the role of armed soldiers in peacetime,

and to assist in the demobilization and rehabilitation of soldiers into civil society.

- **Computer networking for early warning and peace** – establishing computer networks between conflict areas and a wider international audience, so that information can be exchanged about the conditions of conflict, and the potential of escalation. In the former Yugoslavia, an e-mail network was used by civilians to relay messages between isolated areas and to dispel propaganda that was being broadcast by the governments involved.
- **Mobilizing the media for conflict resolution** – training the media to report events responsibly, and encouraging journalists to focus on the peacebuilding initiatives and positive elements within the conflict process. By informing the media of ongoing peace efforts and projects, the focus could be taken away from mere disaster and despair, to show that peace is possible and that local people are willing and able to make a difference. Images of starving refugees or gun-toting militias create in the rest of the world an imbalanced perception of many developing countries.

Finally, it is important to recognize the benefits and drawbacks of neutral outsiders in the mediation process. While the *outsider-neutral* model of third-party mediation has proved invaluable in resolving many conflict situations, it has also demonstrated serious flaws and clearly is not applicable in all circumstances. In a broader context, it is increasingly apparent that in dealing with specific or emerging conflicts it is necessary to incorporate the *insider-partial* approach into the development of comprehensive peace processes, and often a combination of both is the most advantageous. Examples of prominent local individuals exerting a strong influence on peace processes include Archbishop Desmond Tutu, Guatemala's Archbishop Quezada ToruZu and Senator Bobby TaZada in the Philippines.

The neutral outsider cannot by necessity stay in the country for a long time, they must often come and go. The committed insider, on the other hand, must live with the conflict, stay with the conflict and have day-to-day intervention with the conflict process. Such people are often well-known members of communities who, because of their roles as leaders, have access to those in power in their particular country, as well as within and outside their regions. Furthermore, these people are generally recognized by the grass-roots as well. Their positions are not based on political or military power, nor are they trying to secure it. Their position is unique also in the fact that they tend to have pre-existing bonds which cut across conflict lines. Drawing on the benefits of their unique position, along with the high degree of mobility they usually enjoy, middle-range leaders can harness all of these advantages to the benefit of the conflicting communities.

2. Citizen-based Diplomacy

Citizen-based peace making is the process of establishing peace constituencies within conflict areas, to create a common middle ground for dialogue. It is a necessary and vital ingredient of peace-building efforts for it gives the people directly affected by and involved in the conflict the opportunity to voice their concerns, fears and grievances. Peace processes which impose solutions on the population, without sufficient consultation of their needs' are likely to unravel at a later stage. Thus it is imperative that people are given the chance to reconcile their differences and partake in the resolution process. Within each country there is a huge reserve of skills and experience which can be tapped in pre- and post-conflict situations. Listed below are just some examples of citizen-based diplomacy.

- In Somaliland tribal elders have used traditional kinship networks to resolve conflicts. In Israel the PEACE NOW group have been an effective voice of Israeli and Palestinian people. Through the youth division they have made attempts at bridging the gaps between the two sides, making each aware of the others' history and culture. During the 1980s in the Philippines, rural villages, schools and universities took a stand against the army and rebel forces. Different sectors of society – the agrarian community, the fisherfolk, the urban poor – participated in the National Peace Conference, presenting their concerns and calls for social and economic reform.[31]
- Religious organizations can be effective at all levels of society. While the work of local church and religious leaders can complement the peace process at a grassroots level, international religious establishments such as the Quakers or the Catholic church can bring pressure and influence on a wider spectrum. In Mozambique for example, the Italian-based Catholic lay community of Sant' Egidio played a pivotal role in bringing the warring parties together. In Nicaragua in 1988 the Moravian Church and Protestant leaders facilitated the negotiations. In South Af-

rica too, the church played a key role in addressing people's fears and anxieties and encouraging them to take a peaceful route toward reconciliation.

- Women's movements have immense potential for establishing peace-building networks. In many parts of the world women already play a key role in rehabilitating refugees and providing food and shelter. In India and parts of Africa although women play a major role in the economy, their potential role in politics is still overlooked. In Burundi programs are under way to mobilize existing networks of women's groups and to introduce the concepts of conflict resolution and preventive action. By increasing the participation of women in peace making or conflict prevention, it is possible to reach a much wider grassroots base. Furthermore local women's movements can link with regional and international organizations to create a platform on which their concerns can be expressed and addressed.

- A focus on youth groups is also important as often it is young men who are the first casualties of war. By forming youth groups focused on the need for preventive action, it may be possible to create an anti-violence constituency amongst the young. Peer pressure to join a rebel army or to incite violence could then decrease. Furthermore, by establishing these networks now, future wars could be more effectively avoided.

- Community diplomacy through social movements is a broader form of the citizen diplomacy described above. The work of the Community Relations Council (CRC) in Northern Ireland has been noted. In Cambodia Buddhist monks started peace marches, in Sierra Leone villages declared areas of neutral territory, and in isolated parts of Bosnia, Christian and Muslim women exchanged their children overnight as a means of protest. These are all small acts of protest but symbolic of a deeper sense of frustration and despair about war. They are effective in that sectors of a society in conflict are in practice denouncing the political rhetoric and acting for themselves.

- There is a place for creative diplomacy through artists and personalities from the world of entertainment such as the British-based 'Comic Relief' charity. Using high-profile personalities with access to the media, it is possible to highlight the plight of war victims, and raise funds for projects. In addition since entertainers have mass audience appeal, they can be an effective means of informing the general public about conflict issues and the principles of preventive diplomacy.

In short, multi-track diplomacy advocates the involvement of every positive force within and outside the conflict arena in the resolution process. It is a means of including local communities and groups who ordinarily feel excluded from the peace process. The objective is an attempt to address conflict when it is still at its formation phase, and not stall until multi-billion-dollar emergency relief operations are needed. These operations provide governments with an excuse to avoid discussing the opportunities that existed in the earlier stages.

3. The Facilitating Role of NGOs

The UN charter has precipitated the development of human rights mechanisms and NGOs which have become a major feature of international affairs in the post-war period. Their development has progressed with a creativity and commitment to social causes which has often proved to be more effective than their slower official counterparts. In particular, development and humanitarian NGOs are in a continuous process of rethinking and revising their mandates to address the effects of war.

NGOs and other agencies can build issue-specific coalitions and national and regional platforms to advance preventive action. Working in coordination with IGOs and governments, NGOs can also provide the time commitment and low profile needed to build relationships with the parties and encourage progress towards negotiations. Since they can be categorized as 'unofficial organizations' they have the advantage of building trust and confidence between the two sides and using their resources to work towards a negotiated peace. In other words, with no strategic or political motivations, NGOs can initiate dialogue with the conflicting parties at times when there is a complete breakdown of communication. Furthermore, with the ability to provide long-term commitments to social programs and development projects, NGOs can act as catalysts nurturing the institutions of the state such as the judiciary, police, and civil service, and also civilian populations.

Alternative forms of diplomacy undertaken by NGOs have been particularly effective in South Africa, El Salvador and Northern Ireland but have rarely received public attention. South Africa's transition was a negotiated revolution where at every level of society, structures for the peaceful resolution of disputes were established. The National Peace Accord built local and national mechanisms to achieve this, and a wealth of NGOs were instrumental in developing a grass roots peace constituency. At the higher level, eminent persons and church leaders helped to facilitate negotiations when the discussions became deadlocked. Through the work of the Carter Center, the former President has also been involved in a number peace initiatives, including negotiations in Haiti in 1994, Bosnia and the Great Lakes Region.

AN UMBRELLA OF CONCERN

It is the argument of this chapter that multi-track solutions to conflict are the most credible and practical avenues available. A structured approach should promote complementarity of action, based on the comparative advantages of the widest circle of organizations, citizens and alliances as possible. A multi-track approach therefore achieves both a national and an international division of labour using not only NGOs, the UN, regional organizations, and independent governments, but also a network of businesses, the Church and citizens.

The strategic aim in the coming years must be to create an umbrella of concern which involves the participation of the whole international community. Whenever there is this umbrella of concern, these is a greater likelihood of reducing tension and resolving differences. Already a series of overlapping organizations such as the EU, OSCE, NATO and the High Commissioner for Minorities are focused on addressing European security issues in the future. With NATO membership expanding to include Eastern European states, and the continued evolution of the EU and the WEU (Western European Union), there is no single institution which has a monopoly on security matters. The objective now is to develop a system based on bilateral, subregional and regional levels. Within these structures the question of sovereignty, non-intervention in domestic affairs, self-determination and integrity of the state are being examined. Democratization and respect for a series of adopted principles and norms in relation to the domestic arena; the 1994 Code of Conduct between states; and arms control and arms reductions in the region, are additional issues which are being integrated and developed within the common security framework. This willingness to cooperate needs to be extended to other regional forums.[32]

The greater the burden is shared by the community, the greater there is a chance of resolution. In Cambodia, for example, the agreement between China, Japan, Australia, France, Britain and the United States to work under a common framework was of immense significance. In Mozambique, in addition to the Sant' Egidio community, the Italian government, the Vatican, the British-based company Lonrho, the UN and the American government were involved in reaching a peace agreement. The success was due to the influence that all the actors bore in keeping the peace process on two simultaneous and complementary negotiating streams. The conflicts in Burundi and Sierra Leone also show the influence of third parties. The Burundi NGO networks that exist in Europe and the United States have been effective in keeping Burundi in on the foreign affairs agenda, while in the country itself, local peace initiatives are being supported by NGOs, humanitarian aid is being provided, and small-scale development projects are under way.

The greater the concern that different levels of the international community show, the more it proves beneficial. Additionally, the more there is burden sharing between governments, human rights groups, regional organizations and the UN, the greater the degree of accountability of the parties to the conflict.

CONCLUSION

The range and diversity of mandates amongst intergovernmental and regional organizations, NGOs and grassroots civic groups will necessarily involve differences in opinion, resources, flexibility, knowledge, commitment, competence, location and availability. Yet when difficulties arise in the peace process – as they inevitably do – it is precisely the alliance and synergy between these different 'partners' which can play a critical role in sustaining the momentum for peace. A coordinated multi-track approach in preventive diplomacy aims to transform the handling of 'conflict systems' from a reactive one to a preventive one.

This is a new form of diplomacy, involving a strategic shift from purely state-controlled diplomacy towards a greater division of labour between governments, NGOs and other organizations. Peace in internal conflict can only come through a process which involves the very people who were at war with each other. Preventive diplomacy does not provide quick responses to spiralling tragedies; it is a matter of long-term approach requiring sustained financial, technical and personnel support. The objective is to eliminate the cycle of violence in internal disputes.

NOTES

1. Kaplan, 'The Coming Anarchy', *Atlantic Monthly*, February 1994.
2. 'Conflicts with over 1000 per year', Stockholm International Peace Research Institute (SIPRI). *1996 Yearbook*, Oxford University Press, Oxford, 1996.
3. Department of Peace and Conflict Research, Uppsala University, Sweden, *States in Armed Conflict 1994*, Report no. 39, with updates for 1995.
4. Since the research was conducted the Bosnian war has come to an end, despite continuing revenge attacks and other killings. The Chechen War has also reached an official cease fire.
5. The works of Ted Gurr at the Minorities at Risk project at the University of Maryland, USA; the International Peace Research Institute Oslo (PRIO); and the Interdisciplinary Research Program on Root Causes of Human Rights Violations (PIOOM) are particularly noteworthy.
6. I. William Zartman (ed.), *Elusive Peace – Negotiating the End to Civil War*, The Brookings Institution, Washington DC 1995.
7. Ibid.
8. Ed Garcia, *Sierra Leone Peace Talks, Report and Reflections*, International Alert (forthcoming).
9. I. William Zartman, *Elusive Peace*.
10. Henry Kissinger, The VietNam Negotiations', *Foreign Affairs* 47 January 1969, p. 219.
11. Zartman, *Elusive Peace*, p. 8.
12. Zartman, *Elusive Peace*, p. 333.
13. Saul Bellow, *Romanes Lecture*, Oxford, May 1990, Reprinted in *It All Adds Up – From the Dim Past to the Uncertain Future*, Penguin 1995.
14. Nik Gowing, Real-time Television Coverage of Armed Conflicts and Diplomatic Crises: Does it Pressure or Distort Foreign Policy Decisions? Harvard University 1994.
15. See Gutman, *Witness to Genocide*, Element 1993.
16. Rachel Sieder (ed.), *Impunity in Latin America*, Institute of Latin America Studies 1995.
17. Siccama, J.G. (ed.) *Conflict Prevention and Early Warning in the Political Practice of International Organizations*, Clingendael Report 1996.
18. M. Buchanan-Smith and S. Davies, *Famine Early Warning and Response – The Missing Link*, Intermediate Technology Publications, UK 1995.
19. Jacqueline Damon, *Conflict Prevention and Coordination in the Field of Development Cooperation*, UFW Report, Berlin 1996.

20. *Relief Web – Project Description*, DHA Relief Web, Geneva June 1996.
21. Rupesinghe, *Teaching the Elephant to Dance: Developing a New Agenda at the UN*, unpublished MS, May 1995.
22. Rupesinghe, 'The Role of International Alert in Advancing Early Warning and Early Action', London: International Alert May 1996, also appeared in *Refuge* vol, 15, no. 4, July/August 1996.
23. Rupesinghe, *Teaching the Elephant to Dance*.
24. Louise Diamond and John McDonald, *Multi-Track Diplomacy: A Systems Approach to Peace* (3rd edition), Kumarian Press 1996.
25. See M. Lund, *Preventing and Mitigating Violent Conflicts: A Guide for Practitioners*, USAID, Creative Associates International Inc. 1996.
26. For example, the Carnegie Corporation's Commission on Preventing Deadly Conflicts. *Final Reprint with Executive Summary*, New York: Carnegie Corporation of New York, December 1997.
27. H. Alker, T, Gurr and R. Rupesinghe, *Conflict and Early Warning Systems; An Initial Research Program*, Chicago 1995.
28. See H. Henderson and A. Kay, 'The Global Commission Fund for the United Nations – Information on Conflict Resolution Organizations', in a *Proposal to the UNSC for Anticipatory Risk-Mitigation, Peace-Building Contingents (ARM-PC)*, May 1996.
29. Ed Garcia, *Participative Approaches to Peacemaking in the Philippines*, UNU 1993.
30. Their impact may not be immediate, but persistent pressure on the government does bear fruit.
31. Ed. Garcia, *Participative Approaches*, p. 75.
32. See Chapter 7. *SIPRI Yearbook 1996*.

3 Multilateral Security: Common, Cooperative or Collective?

Raimo Väyrynen

THE CONCEPTUAL PROBLEM

The concept of 'security' has been used analytically in an ambiguous way' thus creating a problem of homonymy; the same word is used for different meanings. According to Barry Buzan, security has been 'a weakly conceptualized but politically powerful concept'. Politically, it has been used to legitimate very different external and internal policies depending on the internal structure of the state and its international position. This has fuelled controversies and made security, in Buzan's view, an 'essentially contested concept'.[1]

Now the needs of research and policy call for a reassessment of the security concept and the development of new policies which are appropriate in the post-Cold War era. Even this argument is contested, however, as some realist scholars believe that there is in fact no need to redefine either the concept or the field of security studies. Stephen M. Walt argues that the field as 'the study of the threat, use, and control of military force' has continued relevance and deserves to be maintained. The transition to the post-Cold War world has not obviated the need to analyse military challenges facing sovereign states. These challenges concern, however, more the means than the goals of security.[2]

This view has been countered by several different arguments. One type of criticism argues that security studies should be a more pluralistic field in which a broad view is adopted about the dimensions, means, and goals of security. Moreover, a broad view is needed on the historical and empirical aspects of security and its problems to provide an adequate basis for generalizations. The assumption that the international structure predominantly determines security policies should be relaxed and the variability of inter-, trans- and

43

intranational actors and their mutual relations should be admitted. Finally, security studies cannot be complete without an adequate normative theory.[3]

Such a methodological and substantive broadening is opposed by David A. Baldwin who wants to carry out a 'radical reform' by altogether eliminating security studies as a separate field and merging it with the study of international relations in general. In his view, the declining usability of military power leads to a further broadening of the dimensions, means, and goals of security, making security too broad a concept. This impedes, in turn, the policy relevance and muddles the academic role of security studies. Therefore, security studies, as a creation of the Cold War and nuclear weapons, does not have a meaningful academic role in the new international circumstances.[4]

The plan to eliminate security studies faces, of course, strong institutional and individual resistance. That is why it is likely to remain an influential field of research provided that it can reform itself by becoming theoretically and empirically more broad-minded as suggested by Edward Kolodziej. This suggestion is taken a step further by Paul Joseph who argues that the end of the Cold War calls for a drastic overhaul in the concepts of national security and approaches to its study. In his view, the principal threats to security have become more diverse, the use of force has become more collective and passive, security problems are conditioned by democracy and authoritarianism within states, and cultural attitudes towards peace and war are changing.[5]

Traditionally, the concept of security has been defined narrowly as the search of states for protection against external attacks. Now such a definition has turned out to be all too narrow. To remedy the problem, academic and policy communities have started to favour more comprehensive definitions of security. They refer, in addition to the military aspects, also to economic, environmental, and even cultural dimensions. Thus, security has come to mean also protection against social and economic fragmentation, environmental degradation, and the loss of cultural identity.

Another reason for the re-evaluation has been that the realistic concept of security is defined in negative, coercive terms and looks over the role of positive, non-violent efforts to enhance safety. The negative definition of security means that it is experienced as a burden; 'security after all is nothing but the absence of the evil of insecurity'.[6] This approach is framed in terms of territorial and

political division and exclusion which, in turn, may imperil the existence of constituent actors of the system, the states. The traditional
approach as been increasingly challenged by several new conceptions of security, only a few of which I will deal with here, namely
economic, environmental, feminist, and minority perspectives.

CHALLENGES TO TRADITIONAL CONCEPTS

Economic Security

Economic security is not a new concept as such, for it has also
been discussed in traditional contexts. However, in these, economic
factors have been seen primarily as components of national capabilities underpinning political influence and military performance.
If economic factors are viewed from the interdependence perspective, the security issue boils down to the problem of autonomy, i.e.
national security is threatened by the increasing interdependence
of and penetration into national economies. They create, in turn,
new constraints on domestic decision making and thus reduce the
freedom of national movement.

In current thinking, the problems of capability and autonomy
are often seen in the context of competitiveness. National economies have to become, through technological and institutional innovations, more competitive in order to accumulate cutting-edge
assets which enable them to survive in world-wide economic rivalries. The failure to compete economically translates over time into
a major problem of national security because capabilities and autonomy would be undermined.[7] Capabilities and autonomy can, of
course, be propped up by various national countermeasures, including stockpiling, substitution and diversification. Other approaches
include the creation of a national industrial policy which focuses
on the development of the economy's key sectors and the control
of foreign trade in strategic goods.[8]

As is well known, however, the protection of the economy on
security grounds can result in welfare losses because it is denied
benefits accruing from the international exchange of capital, goods
and ideas. It is true that while economic interdependence may promote peace between states, the dynamism of the international market
is also a constant source of uncertainty and anxiety. In the conditions of global capitalism, both national and individual security

become a multi-faceted and indirectly determined phenomenon.[9] This warns against over-stretching the concept of security to cover all uncertainties that the markets may produce.

The national emphasis on economic policy will probably have adverse consequences for security over the long term. In fact, there may not be any alternative to economic interdependence; even though it may increase domestic vulnerability, its direct economic and indirect security benefits are too important to be overlooked. Moreover, the adverse effects of vulnerability can be reduced by striking a proper balance between market-driven innovations and public allocation of resources and trying to control an increasing share of the world market. The combination of increasing vulnerability and the loss of market control is the most dangerous one for the defence industrial base and in that way for security.[10]

The emphasis on competitiveness as a precondition for national security may be, however, a misplaced idea. Paul Krugman in particular has argued that competitiveness makes sense only at the corporate and not at the national level. At the latter level it easily leads to a flawed analysis which considers international competition a major source of economic problems while their real roots are domestic. National countermeasures to competitive pressures may even escalate and lead to trade wars and political conflicts.[11] If Krugman is right, economic competitiveness should be retained as a corporate-level concept and thus separated from national security. Security should be sought by political means in an open world economy.

Environmental Security

Environmental security poses a different set of challenges to the concept of security. It leads to debate on whether risks to security have to be intentional (for example, the use of the environment for warfare) or whether unintentional threats (for example, depletion of the ozone layer) also qualify. If the existence of threat is considered a central identifying feature of security problems, then the focus should primarily be on the deliberate intent to produce harm. However, security would also be threatened if the source of threat knowingly violates international environmental norms, although the damage produced by this violation is not targeted to a specific individual or group.

Much like other risks, environmental threats can be either immediate and direct (such as the meltdown of a nuclear power plant) or long-term and indirect (as in global warming). In the latter case, one can speak of contextual threats which do not differentiate between individuals and groups, while the contaminating threats and the competition for natural resources have specific subjects and objects. The contextuality of threats has led some authors to subsume peace and security under a broad concept of environmental well-being. This creates almost a definitional relationship between environment and security where the former conditions the latter.[12]

If such a definitional relationship is ruled out, there remains, however, the possibility of instrumental and causal relations between environment and security. The instrumental relationship can be either negative or positive as the environment can be used by specific actors as an instrument both of warfare and of international cooperation. The causal relationship refers to the capacity of the deteriorating environment to result in premature deaths or new international interdependencies.[13] The mitigation or elimination of the environmental damage produced by human activities may require considerable efforts; the cleaning up of nuclear and other wastes after the Cold War is a telling example of that.[14]

The negative causal linkage between environment and security has been adopted, and the 'existential threat' approach squashed, by Marc A. Levy who suggests that 'environmental degradation constitutes a direct physical threat to US security interests when environmental damage results directly in the significant loss of life or welfare of US citizens, or otherwise impairs our most important national values'.[15] Levy's analysis comes close to the traditional view of military threats to national security. The difference is that he does not distinguish between national and individual security, but defines environmental security by direct, adverse health and welfare consequences of ecological changes for individual citizens as threats to 'national values'. This leads to the interesting implication that skin cancer caused by the ozone depletion is a national security risk.

Both economy and environment *per se* should be separated from the definition of security, that is their impact on it is an empirical rather than a definitional question.[16] Both economic competition and environmental deterioration create uncertainties and anxieties, but in spite of their unsettling effects they should not be equated with security. To qualify as a security threat, economic or environmental changes must have significant negative effects either at an individual or a collective level. This means that economic and environmental threats to security have to be layered and contextualized; they can manifest themselves at different levels, ranging from the individual to the global, and in different contexts, such as the competition for resources, migration and population pressures, and climatic changes.[17]

Women's Security

Feminist approaches to security differ from the military, economic and environmental approaches in at least one significant respect; they single out for attention the security concerns of a particular category of human beings – women. Obviously the security effects of military, economic, and environmental threats are not evenly distributed among the population but vary, for example by social class. The difference is that feminist approaches take a social criterion, gender, as the starting point of their analysis, while the differentiation in economic and environmental approaches is based on analytical categories.

To simplify somewhat, the feminist perspective observes that war and violence have always been heavily gendered and may now be increasingly so. Both the war itself and its practical conduct have a masculine character, crystallized in various hero myths, while it has gender-specific consequences for women, such as wartime rape and prostitution. When the civilian share of the victims has increased up to 90 per cent, the suffering of women from war has correspondingly increased, as the war in Bosnia so amply illustrates.[18]

While rape as a form of sexual exploitation is, in the first instance, directed at women, men can be secondary targets as rape can socially humiliate them as husbands. This, in turn, creates a pressure on women to hide the occurrence of rape and keep the knowledge of it inside themselves. On the other hand, the media may make efforts to publicize the rape and even identify the victims, offering women payment for their stories. Thus, by 'consenting to participate in the currently popular war coverage, these women are raped again'.[19]

It is clear that security, like most other social phenomena, is gendered and therefore a feminist approach to it is justified. It is also true that feminist perspectives on women's experiences broaden our understanding of what security really means. They also transcend social and political boundaries, for instance, by bringing in non-statist perspectives and new identities.[20] On the other hand, it would be wrong to gender all security problems; for example, a heavy gendering of the nuclear threat to security easily becomes artificial.

Minorities and Security

Ethnic, religious, and other minorities enter the security discourse in two different ways. If repressed, minorities may start seeking a greater autonomy and even secession from the political entity dominated by an alien majority. To promote their goals, minorities may also develop transnational ties to enhance the moral and material support for their struggles. Such processes are the stuff which civil wars, external interventions, and state terrorism are made of. Thus, the security of a minority is often jeopardized by the repression by the majority which, in turn, increases the possibility that force is used, and in that way everybody's security deteriorates. Ultimately, the repression and resistance of a minority can escalate into an interstate war.

Social and political marginality is always accompanied by insecurity, either latent or manifest.[21] Gurr's extensive empirical analysis shows that most of the 233 minorities he studied used non-violent protests to signal their grievances. However, although the minority status often correlates with violence, it does not necessarily motivate people to use force; less than half of the minorities started a rebellion; 35 minorities used terrorism as their weapon, while 79 were involved in guerilla or civil wars, especially in Asia, Africa, and the Arab world. Moreover, communal violence has been on the increase since World War II.[22]

The focus on minorities as the source and target of insecurity has some resemblances with the feminist perspective. They both shun the statist approach (although so do the economic and environmental perspectives to security). Both the gender and minority interpretations of security recognize that identity is an important ingredient of security. Its integrity reduces the sense of vulnerability and hence the need to fight for status and identity, while its violation fosters the sense of grievances and resistance. The identity formation and security are thus interrelated.

Methodological and Operational Issues

These reviews of various challenges to the traditional interpretations of security hint at an underlying *Methodenstreit.* Obviously all these four challenges and their effects can be studied empirically: how do external dependencies affect the defence industrial base; are population pressures leading to violence and insecurity; to what extent are women victimized by a war; or does minority secessionism lead to war? However, it is often asserted that the search for answers to such empirical questions leads to a myopic and curtailed understanding of security. Often the empirical approach is associated with the traditional, statist and military definition of security.

Alternative, 'critical' or 'utopian realist' approaches emphasize the need to go beyond the state, overcome statist divisions, and pay attention to the roles both of world order and of individuals in the security discourse. In critical studies the basic idea is to deconstruct the concept of security and reveal its theoretical and political commitments. By rethinking the security discourse and redirecting it from the geopolitical to the exploratory mode, political space can be created for new, non-military strategies to safeguard people's security.[23] Ken Booth argues that it is both illogical and unrealistic to make states primary referents of security studies. Rather than power and order in the state system, the emancipation of individuals and groups from the multiple threats facing them should have the priority.[24]

The enlargement of the scope of the security concept has moved attention from the state level both upwards, to regional and global levels, and downwards, to groups and individuals. The objective of this dual movement has been to free security studies from the perils of nationalism and statism and consider seriously both its individual and global dimensions. This has obviously complicated the field, depriving it of the parsimony of state-centrism and reawakening the debate on the level-of-analysis problem. Moreover, the recognition of the multi-dimensionality of the security problem has further increased the complexity of the concept.

In sum, the nature, sources and targets of security threats have all become more diverse than before. These changes have contributed to the diffusion of the security concept even to the extent that its meaning has lost much of its coherence. As a reaction, new efforts are being made to reconceptualize security and thus restore the concept's usability. Such a reconceptualization faces a dual challenge; on the one hand the concept of security has to be made more comprehensive, while on the other hand its analytical rigor should be retained. The use of the concept only as a medium and objective of discursive analysis does not necessarily help in enhancing security, by emancipation or otherwise.

More concretely, any effort to redefine the concept of security faces the need to specify the meaning of not only its military, but also its economic, environmental, and cultural aspects. These aspects are, in turn, affected by subnational, national, transnational and global actors and forces.[25] Efforts at the redefinition show immediately that the concept of security cannot be confined to the state level. The porosity of state boundaries and the increasing fragility of states hint at the importance of the individual and group security.

Traditional security risks, such as the threat of a military attack, were considered immediate and serious. The impact of new security risks is often delayed and indirect. For example, for peripheral nations security appears mainly as a problem of dependence and vulnerability rather than as a threat of a military attack. Especially in developing countries, rulers tend to respond to dependence and vulnerability by an outdated emphasis on the principle and practice of sovereignty. While sovereignty may be helpful in building up cooperative security arrangements among industrialized countries, it can become an element of insecurity in the Third World.[26]

Neither direct nor indirect threats to security can be managed adequately on the state level. On the one hand there is the need to strengthen the capacity and democracy of the state internally to make it more resilient against internal and external vulnerabilities and in that way more peaceful.[27] On the other hand the regionalization and globalization of international relations call for subsystemic and systemic arrangements to deal with both old and new threats to security. In sum, security studies has a major level-of-analysis problem to solve in order to keep its key concept relevant.[28]

From these vantage points one can develop a typology in which various *dimensions of security* (military, economic, environmental and cultural) are correlated with the *levels of security* and the types of actors characteristic of them (global, regional, state, group and individual actors). In addition, there are qualitative distinctions, most notably the distinction between *nuclear* and *non-nuclear* security, which are tackled neither by the dimensions nor the levels of security. While in principle these categories exclude each other, the dividing line is rather ambiguous, as the status of individual countries and their military strategies can contain both nuclear and non-nuclear elements.[29] The distinction between nuclear and non-nuclear security remains, however, both politically (as in the future of the Non-Proliferation Treaty) and ethically (for example the debate about the legality of nuclear weapons) relevant.

The diffusion of security concepts reflects the growing complexity and fragmentation of interstate relations and their closer intermingling with intrastate affairs. Comprehensive notions of security do not permit strong distinctions between 'domestic' and 'foreign' affairs. The stretching and proliferation of security concepts should not be permitted to go too far, however, because 'security' could then lose its analytical value. To avoid this pitfall, the concept of *threat* has to be retained as the main unifying element in the study of security.[30]

AN OPERATIONAL SOLUTION

For the purposes of the present analysis, threat can be operationalized as a product of the probability of value deprivation (immediacy), value salience (priorities), and value proportion at stake (severity). The highest threat is then one which poses an immediate and severe risk to the most important values of the target. The realization of threat is defined, in turn, as the product of the actor's capability and intention to deprive the target of specific values. Capability has to be understood in relative terms and, in the end, is more important than the intention as without it there would be no threat.[31] The reverse argument is also true, but intentions can change more quickly than capabilities and that is why they are more central.

This formal operationalization of threat can, in principle, be applied to all types of threats to security. Moreover, it provides a framework for comparing different types of threats and their effects. However, before an effort is made to develop such a framework, a critical issue needs to be revisited: should the concept of security be applied only to intentional threats or should one also include unintentional and indiscriminate risks, such as natural disasters and plant diseases which are either beyond human control or are due to ignorance and negligence?[32]

This analysis focuses only on intentional threats purporting to produce deprivation and harm in the target; this choice does not mean, of course, that unintentional risks cannot jeopardize the safety, well-being, and identity of people affected. The point is rather that in unintentional dangers, the dynamics of the escalation and resolution of conflict are quite different because the source of risks is either unknown or an actor has not deliberately carried out adverse acts. Nuclear power accidents, epidemics, global warming, and other similar hazards jeopardize human life, but neither for analytical nor political reasons should they be considered security risks in the first place.

The problem of intentionality is particularly vexed in environmental threats. An instrumental conception of threats makes sense in this area only when ecological resources are used directly to harm the target or when they are used to promote international peace and cooperation. In most cases it is difficult to imagine that ecological resources have 'agentive functions' in the same sense as weapons are constructed to have in defending national security. Environmental threats are seldom targeted at a particular actor, but the environment shapes the conflict propensity in an indirect way; for example, population growth increases resource scarcity, migration and inter-group clashes, or ecological marginalization fosters violence through changes in social structures.[33]

The indirect nature of environmental threats does not necessarily make them unintentional, however. There is an intentional element in them to the extent that the producer of harm is aware of the violation of national or international environmental standards. In this approach the threats to security and violation of norms are considered in the framework of common morality instead of according to a utilitarian approach.[34]

Efforts to develop a comparative framework for the analysis of threats should, first, define the values that are threatened by intentional acts. In this regard I will follow a conventional classification of values into *survival*, *well-being* and *identity*. They correspond, respectively, to such norms as the respect for life, access to adequate material entitlements and clean environment, and the right to human self-realization. Intentional acts to deprive these values are threats to individual and collective security. Such threats to security can be materialized on different dimensions and levels. A simple classification of levels distinguishes between *individuals, groups/ nations, states* and the *global system*. Since the origins and the impact of threats can be on different levels, in discussing threats one has to make a distinction between their sources and targets. By focusing on the targets of threats, a typology can be developed as shown in Table 2.1.

Table 2.1   A Typology of Intentional Threats to Security

	Survival	*Well-Being*	*Identity*
Individual	Homicide, murder	Unemployment, ozone depletion	Deportation, lack of civic freedoms
Group	Ethnic cleansing	Economic discrimination, desertification	Deprivation of minority rights
State/Nation	Armed aggression	Economic boycott, nuclear power accident, acid rain	Loss of national sovereignty
Globe	Nuclear war	Global economic breakdown, environmental catastrophe	Global cultural confrontation

Survival here refers to physical safety, well-being to economic and environmental quality of life, and identity to an independent cultural existence. These three types of threats to security challenge different aspects of it which are, however, interlinked. Survival has the highest priority, because the loss of life makes other dimensions of security irrelevant. The preservation of well-being or identity is conceivable even if the other is threatened. In reality economic/environmental and cultural threats are, however, conditioned by each other. For example, the deprivation of a political group of its rights usually also has adverse economic consequences, while economic discrimination undermines its political rights and influence.

As suggested above, the dynamics of threats and reactions to them vary from one dimension and level of security to another. In the following, I will mostly concentrate on the nation, state and group levels of analysis which are reproduced on all three dimensions of security. There can be three types of responses to threats to survival: submission to overwhelming power in the hope to retain one's safety, resistance to threats in the effort to reach an equilibrium which will thwart an aggression, and the escalation of the confrontation to a riskier level. Typically, threats to survival, as a high-priority value, lead to counterthreats, an increase in hostilities, and in that way further threats to security.[35] In other words, an action-reaction spiral develops between the parties.

If the state, nation or group submits itself to external threats, the national or group identity and possibly also the economic well-being would be jeopardized because of the loss of autonomy. If the parties can create an equilibrium or a stalemate in their mutual relations, the economic and cultural values of the nation or the group can be better safeguarded and a basis for resolving the conflict created.[36] Such equilibria are, however, seldom stable and easily degenerate into mutual rivalries threatening further the security of actors involved.

The dynamics of security problems are quite different when physical safety is not in jeopardy, and threats are focused on well-being and/or identity. Then, threats are seldom immediate, but often accumulate over time, creating vulnerabilities to which responses are needed, but less urgently. As a result, the escalatory dynamics are slower and less sensitive than in the case of threats to survival because one's material well-being and identity can, to only a limited degree, be enhanced by countermeasures. The amelioration of material and cultural threats calls for reforms to increase economic, environmental and cultural resilience and self-confidence rather than active countermeasures.

MULTILATERAL SECURITY SYSTEMS

There are basically three different approaches to multilateral security: common, cooperative, and collective. This section outlines the main elements of these approaches and compares them with each other. Section Five will then scrutinize the extent to which they can be effectively used to solve various security problems specified in Table 2.1.

Common Security

Common security was a concept conceived by the Independent Commission on Disarmament and Security Issues (ICDSI, the Palme Commission). It was aimed, in the first place, against unilateral politics, manifested in the INF deployment and SKI initiatives in the early 1980s, which not only undermined common security, but ultimately also the national security of the adversaries.[37] According to the Palme Commission, 'nations must come to understand that the maintenance of world peace must be given a higher priority than the assertion of their own ideological or political positions.'[38]

The report of the Palme Commission emphasized the need to create a living practice for common security in which states would consider not only the first- but also the second- and third-order consequences of their unilateral military decisions and especially give up any plans to fight a nuclear war. The Commission also made a good number of specific recommendations such as the establishment of nuclear-weapons-free and chemical-weapons-free zones in Central Europe, mutual control of strategic space defences and the strengthening of the ability of the United Nations and regional organizations to maintain peace.

The idea of common security provides a metaphor for a reformed international security system in which the concern with the impact of one's own decisions on those of the others would ameliorate the security dilemma and make all parties better off. 'Common security' suggests that the consideration of the 'shadow of the future' in security decisions is, ultimately, in everybody's interest; cooperative and reciprocated rationality is the best foundation for a sound security system. The critics of the concept noted the lack of credible deterrence and other effective guarantees in the common security scheme. According to them, it would be ineffective against states which deliberately pursue a unilateralist strategy to reap gains.[39]

Common security was originally a political and military concept. True, the report of the Palme Commission contained a chapter on its economic aspects, but this focused almost entirely on the material costs of the nuclear arms race. The World Commission on Environment and Development (the Brundtland Commission) adopted more self-consciously a comprehensive definition of security, but even in its case the focus was rather narrow: the environmental risks of nuclear weapons, competition for resources, and environmental stress as a source of security risks.[40] There was practically no conceptual analysis of what common security could mean in this broader environmental context.

The Commission on Global Governance, co-chaired by Ingvar Carlsson and Shridath Ramphal, took a long leap towards expanding the notion of security, stressing the global 'security of people and the planet'. While states have the right to security, this cannot take precedence over people's rights to a safe and rewarding life. The Commission lists several threats to planetary security: global environmental problems, biodiversity, resource scarcities, nuclear weapons and hazardous chemicals; population growth adds to pressures on life-support systems, especially in developing countries.

The 'bottom line' of the Commission's recommendations is that 'the primary goals of global security policy should be to prevent conflict and war and maintain the integrity of the planet's life-support systems by eliminating the economic, social, environmental, political, and military conditions that generate threats to the security of people and the planet, and by anticipating and managing crises before they escalate into armed conflicts'.[41] The Commission on Global Governance has adopted a very broad definition of security by considering several levels and dimensions of it. Its work clearly expands and specifies the notions of comprehensive security incipient in the reports of the Palme and Brundtland Commissions. None of them reaches out, however, to the security problems stressed by the feminist and minority approaches.

Cooperative Security

The concept of cooperative security has been used much, and in different senses, in the first half of the 1990s. One dominant usage has been in the European context where the CSCE (now OSCE) has been seen as harbinger of a new, cooperative security system. Cooperation between diversities cannot be enforced from above, but must be based on common institutions and norms with which the governments are expected to comply. Institutionalized, cooperative security must be transparent and accountable to convince the parties of its impartiality and predictability.[42] Cooperative security, based on institutions and norms respected by the parties, seems to have taken root in European interstate relations after the Cold War. At the same time its limitations in the control and management of civil violence have become clear.[43]

A somewhat different type of usage has been coined by a working group of the Brookings Institution. The group assumes that international disputes can occur, but the best way is not to escalate these by countermeasures. Instead, a regime to prevent and manage conflicts within an agreed framework of norms and procedures should be established. 'Cooperative security is designed to ensure that organized aggression cannot start or be prosecuted on any large scale'. For this purpose the contesting parties should set up strict controls of nuclear forces, convert defence industries, stress defensive configurations of military forces, monitor military developments effectively and develop a legitimate concept of intervention. These measures do not need to lead, however, to 'a single, all-encompassing legal regime or arms control agreement, but would probably begin with a set of overlapping, mutually reinforcing arrangements'.[44]

In practice, American advocates of 'cooperative security' are particularly concerned with the diffusion of nuclear weapons and other military or dual-capable technologies to uncontrollable nations. The overall internationalization of economic activities, the shrinking military budgets and the disarray in the former Warsaw Pact force the arms manufacturers and military experts to seek markets in countries that may have plans to accumulate new destructive military power. These concerns have been particularly pronounced in the case of the former Soviet Union in which 'cooperative engagement' and 'more sophisticated forms of collaboration' are deemed to be needed to stem the spread of military technologies.[45]

While 'cooperative security' stresses the need for joint actions in setting limits on acceptable behavior and reducing armaments, it does not emphasize the commonality of security interests and the importance of collaboration as much as 'common security' does. The Brookings usage of 'cooperative security' relies on an asymmetric approach seeking justification for the US intervention into the former Soviet Union to prevent the spread of nuclear and other military technologies. The concept does not confer on Russia and Ukraine a reciprocal right to monitor the US production of nuclear weapons and the safeguards on their international proliferation. Thus, 'cooperative engagement' becomes a part of the US world-order policy rather than a symmetric and comprehensive international strategy to reduce nuclear weapons and stop their future development.[46]

'Cooperative security' stresses the need to accommodate interests and policies of (potential) rivalries and maintain a stable world order under the guidance of great powers. Most versions of 'cooperative security' have little to say on any level but that of state security. The politico-military dimension of security dominates, and while economic security gets some attention, cultural and environmental dimensions are hardly noticed at all. Feminist and minority perspectives to security are not considered at all in this tradition. Some interpretations of 'cooperative security' add to its standard definition the need to resolve conflicts peacefully and restrict unilateral interventions, but even then the conception of security remains very limited.[47] Thus, 'cooperative security' differs from the traditional, state-based notion of security only by its stress on the mitigation of political and military rivalries.

Collective Security

The principle of collective security, according to Hedley Bull, 'implies that international order rests not on a balance of power, but on a preponderance of power wielded by a combination of states acting as agents of international society as a whole that will deter challenges to the system or deal with them if they occur'.[48] Collective security aims to create a putative international coalition that will deter potential aggressors and punish them if they resort to the use of force. Neither the aggressor nor the victim has been defined in advance.

Collective security rests on joint efforts to maintain the status quo by representing and mobilizing international society. It does not rely on just any coalition of powers which decides to act together but calls for a broadly acceptable and representative form of collective action. Thus, a viable system of collective security requires a framework of established institutions, norms and procedures which helps to mobilize an international response at the moment of need.[49]

Critics of the collective-security theory argue, while recognizing the relevance of military power in international relations, that it makes unwarranted assumptions on the willingness of states to cooperate even at the expense of their unilateral interests.[50] In a more theoretical vein one may query what impact the prevailing distribution of power, the tendency of states to free ride variations in threat assessment, or the absence of threat altogether have on the structural characteristics and operational performance of collective security.[51]

In reality, the effectiveness of collective security calls for a concert of powers, such as the UN Security Council, which is given a mandate to decide and launch a collective-security operation. A concert is an arrangement in which the interests of major powers are not opposed enough to prevent cooperation in managing regional or global international relations. In exploring the nature of concert, a distinction must be made between the mandating and the implementing agent. The United Nations has retained its role to confer legitimacy on collective security actions and humanitarian interventions, but its operational role is increasingly taken over either by *ad hoc* coalitions (as in the Gulf War) or by NATO (as in Bosnia). It is doubtful whether either of these two operations can be considered a genuine collective-security action.

⌐The traditional interpretation of collective security provides advice on how states can be defended against external military threats.⌐ Economic aspects are included in this interpretation in the sense that economic sanctions may be used to punish the aggressor or that the victim of an attack is supported economically by the international community. One reason why neither cooperative nor collective security is able to tackle the non-military dimensions of security is that they consider only threats and not vulnerabilities, which are key problems in broader definitions of security.

If economic, environmental, and cultural vulnerabilities are considered, it is possible to expand the traditional notions of collective security. Both state and non-state actors can defend themselves collectively against environmental threats and vulnerabilities. Reactions to environmental threats should lead by mutual agreement to cut back harmful activities in order to prevent the deterioration of the situation. This requires that the actors recognize that their well-being hinges on collective commitments and sacrifices by everyone. Collective defence against vulnerabilities demands far more ambitious cooperation; in addition to limiting harmful activities, collective environmental defence requires cooperation to enhance joint capabilities (for example the international food security system).[52]

One can also think in terms of a collective defence against cultural threats of marginalization and discrimination. Transnational cooperation between, for example, indigenous people or Muslim groups is intended to defend their cultural heritage and identity as well as their social position and political influence. One may, of course, argue that the use of the security concept in such a connection is artificial and stretches the concept beyond recognition. On the other hand, if the scope of a concept is expanded at all, it is bound to acquire new meanings and applications.

These new meanings and their concrete references may contradict, however, the original ideas of security. This is even the case when the principle of collective security, based on the principle of state-centric sovereignty, is used to deter and manage profound changes in the internal affairs of states. To be theoretically meaningful and politically relevant, the concept of collective security has

Table 2.2 Parameters of Multilateral Security Systems

	Common	*Cooperative*	*Collective*
Threat	Unilateral measures	Instability	Aggression
Principle	Common interests	Order	Status quo
Response	Reciprocity	Institutional control	Deterrence, Punishment
Outcome	Compromise	Regimes	Use of force

to be defined in such a situation in a flexible way; for example, cooperation between major powers can take a number of forms and political and economic instruments of influence should be emphasized at the expense of the military intervention.[53]

The tensions become even more obvious if the concept of collective security is applied to economic, environmental and cultural areas. There the defence against vulnerabilities requires both transnational cooperation between non-state actors and deep economic and cultural changes which both undermine the state-based status quo in international relations. The same is largely true for cooperative security, although its emphasis on rather unstructured joint actions probably makes it more amenable than collective security to develop strategies against economic, environmental and cultural threats.

A Comparison

The three systems of international security can be compared along four parameters that identify the nature of the dominant threat to multilateral security, the principle on the basis of which the response to it is generated, and the outcome of this response as shown in Table 2.2. In the conventional definition of a common security system, the threat of destabilizing unilateral measures is countered by a rational and forward-looking effort to identify common interests and develop a compromise that removes the threat to security. To be viable, common security has to be institutionalized, but over the short term it can also be based on tacit and informal coordination of security interests. While informal agreements cannot be formally binding, they provide a temporary means to reduce impediments to cooperation.[54] In fact, Cold War history is filled with informal agreements and understandings, especially between the United States and the Soviet Union.

In a cooperative security system, the threat lurks in the instability that the unhindered spread of destructive weapons and the offensiveness of military forces can create. The prevention of instability from spreading requires collaboration on the basis of common interests, but it must also derive some strength from the preponderance of power by the leading state, institutional and normative resources embedded in international regimes. The case of *non-offensive defence* (NOD) is of some interest here. Its advocates have placed the NOD metaphor and policy in the context of common security as it requires a mutual adjustment of military postures and strategies. On the other hand, NOD can also be considered a cooperative security strategy, because it relies also on unilateral measures which common security cannot.[55]

Finally, a collective security system is intended to deter an aggression by the preponderance of collective military power which can be used in the common interest if deterrence fails. While common and cooperative security have multilateral aspects, bilateral relations also matter, especially between great powers. The efforts of these powers to adjust their competing interests and control sources of instability are, pivotal for both common and cooperative security. In collective security, the multilateral element is stronger in assessing threats and making and implementing decisions. This is due, among other things, to the fact that collective security is not primarily dependent on a balance of power which forms a basis of common security. One cannot meaningfully speak of the mutual adjustment of interests in an asymmetric relationship.

THREATS TO SECURITY AND MULTILATERAL RESPONSES

The above analysis rests on the assumption that the concept of security, even if it is confined to intentional threats, has become more complex and diverse. Therefore, threats to security cannot be repelled or managed only by traditional, state-centric and military-oriented measures which have predominantly been bilateral in character. New approaches both to the definition and defence of security are needed. This section makes an effort to relate to each other the two typologies developed in Tables 2.1 and 2.2 and the conceptual discussion at the beginning of the chapter. In that way one can try to ascertain whether any new interpretations of reality and policies can be created.

The principle of common security does not have much to offer in defending groups against threats to their survival, well-being and identity. Conflicting interests could be adjusted, however, in the early phases of the conflict, when common sense still prevails, or after a stalemate when parties are too tired to continue fighting. In these two situations a compromise can be struck in which interests in mutual security, well-being and culture are traded on a reciprocal basis. In the intense phases of the conflict, inter-group prejudices and tensions usually run so high that a common-security approach cannot provide adequate instruments to mitigate them effectively. If the group conflict threatens to escalate so as to jeopardize the security of states, then the mutual fear of pre-emptive and unilateral moves may foster cooperation between the states involved.

If the concept of common security is to be made relevant for the environmental, feminist and minority aspects of security, it has to be significantly redefined. First it must give up its state-centricity and consider the security of subnational and transnational actors. This conceptual move is implausible in the cases of feminist and minority interpretations of security. An emphasis on the security of a subgroup in society hardly qualifies as common security. The case of ecological security is different, since people have common interests in a healthy environment. If we add the developmental dimension to the concept of security, it may be said that 'security is common when it ensures that the poor have access to resources, freedom from environmental degradation and the pollution of others' economic activities'.[56]

The implementation of cooperative security in group conflicts requires the recognition of the right of another country to be interested in your internal affairs. It should permit a constant monitoring by the countries involved of each others' activities and their efforts to act in a preventive mode if signs of disorder emerge. Monitoring can aim to prevent, by a combination of incentives and punitive measures, 'ethnic cleansing', economic deprivation and the suppression of minority rights. The enforcement of these norms requires both an investment of resources to make it effective and a degree of consent in the target country. The consent briefly existed in the Soviet Union/Russia in 1989–92, but has been now withdrawn and the preconditions for cooperative security have become more precarious. Another test case for cooperative security is the US-Chinese relationship where the prospects for US monitoring and enforcement are scant.

States frequently cooperate also in new fields to strengthen their mutual security, especially against environmental threats. It is also conceivable that cooperation will increase to protect the security of minorities and the vulnerable by mutual monitoring and implementation of international norms. Such group-focused collaboration in bilateral relations between governments is in its infancy, however, and can be stopped simply by referring to the principle of sovereignty. It is also unlikely to succeed if one or more of the parties to a relationship have autocratic governments.

There is, however, a trend towards more intrusive intergovernmental cooperation with a view to strengthening mutual security. The agreement between Argentina and Brazil on mutual nuclear inspections to make sure that neither side develops nuclear weapons is a concrete example of this trend. Another example is provided by bilateral and multilateral agreements in the 1970s and the 1980s to avert the nuclear danger (hot lines, preventive agreements, and arms control treaties) and incidents at sea. These were efforts to control the potential of military instability and escalation in interstate relations.

Various systems of multilateral collective security have been established to deal with the threats to survival. Opinions on the feasibility of creating a workable system of collective security to assure the survival of states, not to speak of groups and individuals, are divided. The divisions not only concern the political credibility and effectiveness of collective security but also whether it can be legitimate and democratic enough to respect the rights of small states as well. It looks as though we have to live, in the foreseeable future at least, with a situation which combines the United Nations as a mandating organization with regional bodies, such as NATO, as implementing agents. In other words, collective security has to be married with cooperative security.

Collective security to safeguard group rights exists, for instance, in the human rights regime of the Council of Europe: such an arrangement is possible. It becomes feasible, though, only when strict interpretations of the sovereignty norms are relaxed and the intervention into internal affairs of states – provided that they have violated basic norms of human rights, democracy and environment – becomes legitimate. While world society as a whole has not yet reached this phase, it is possible to speak of the emerging universal norms of human rights, democracy and environment, and of the growing recognition that in the case of their serious violations external intervention is warranted. The establishment of war crimes tribunals for the former Yugoslavia and Rwanda, intervention in Haiti, and the growing concern with democratic rights in Myanmar are examples of this tendency.

Humanitarian intervention is, both as a concept and policy, different from the traditional notion of collective security. In spite of that, it is possible to think in terms of a new system of collective security which protects the material and cultural security of intra-state groups by international intervention. This obviously requires a re-definition of collective security. Rather than being a preponderant collective reaction to an aggression against the violation of state sovereignty, collective security could be defined as a joint action to protect individuals and groups against starvation and deprivation of human rights. This is also a more realistic option because such protective operations ('micro-enforcement') usually requires less force than extensive collective security operations of a more traditional type ('macro-enforcement').[57]

It has to be realized, though, that the collective protection of group rights as a security issue calls for measures, such as economic sanctions and humanitarian intervention, which jeopardize the sovereignty and security of states. It is probably difficult to reconcile the collective protection of the sovereignty and security of states on the one hand with the defence of survival, economic well-being and cultural group rights by collective international measures on the other. These two aims are, ultimately, incompatible and one has to choose one way or the other. In the long term, this may mean that the traditional idea of centralized collective security has been replaced by a combination of common and cooperative security systems which gives precedence to the mitigation of tensions by mutual accommodation on the one hand and a limited regime of humanitarian intervention on the other.

All these concepts of security suffer, however, from the same weakness of being state-centric. Their application to defend security as a group right or against collective threats, such as the environmental ones, requires a fair amount of conceptual stretching, however. This creates a real dilemma: the old concepts of multilateral security struggle to encompass the new meanings of security, but on the other hand new concepts either do not exist or are so general that they have hardly any meaning at all (for example human security).

NOTES

1. Barry Buzan, *People, States and Fear. An Agenda for International Security Studies in the Post-Cold War Era*, Hemel Hempstead: Harvester Wheatsheaf 1991, pp. 5 and 7.

2. Stephen M. Walt, 'The Renaissance of Security Studies', *International Studies Quarterly*, vol. 35, no. 2, 1991, pp. 211–39.

3. Edward A. Kolodziej, 'Renaissance in Security Studies?: Caveat Lector?', *International Studies Quarterly*, vol. 36, no. 4, 1992, pp. 421–38.

4. David A. Baldwin, 'Security Studies and the End of the Cold War', *World Politics*, vol. 48, no. 1, 1995, pp. 117–41.

5. Paul Joseph, *Peace Politics. The United States Between the Old and New World Orders*, Philadelphia: Temple University Press, 1993, pp. 6–11.

6. Arnold Wolfers, 'National Security as an Ambiguous Symbol', in his *Discord and Collaboration*, Baltimore: Johns Hopkins University Press, 1962, p. 153 (first published in 1952).

7. Hanns W. Maull, *'Wirtschaftliche Dimension der Sicherheit. Entwicklungslinien in den letzten drei Jahrzenhten'*, *Europa-Archiv*, vol. 44, no. 5, 1989, pp. 135–44; Michael Borus and John Zysman, 'Industrial Competitiveness and National Security', in Graham Allison and Gregory F. Treverton (eds), *Rethinking America's Security. Beyond Cold War to New World Order*, Lanham, MD: University Press of America, 1992, pp. 136–75.

8. Brian McCartan, 'Defense of Opulence? Trade and Security in the 1990s', *SAIS Review*, vol. 11, no. 1, 1991, pp. 133–45.

9. Barry Buzan, 'The Interdependence of Security and Economic Issues in the "New World Order"', in Richard Stubbs & R.D. Underhill (eds), *Political Economy and the Global Order*, New York: St. Martin's Press, 1994, pp. 89–102.

10. Beverly Crawford, 'The New Security Dilemma Under International Economic Interdependence', *Millennium*, vol. 23, no. 1, 1994, pp. 25–55; and Beverly Crawford, 'Hawks, Doves, But No Owls: International Economic Interdependence and Construction of the New Security Dilemma', in Ronnie D. Lipschultz (ed.), *On Security*, New York: Columbia University Press, 1995, pp. 149–86.

11. Paul Krugman, 'Competitiveness: A Dangerous Obsession', *Foreign Affairs*, vol. 73, no. 2, 1994, pp. 28–44. Krugman's view that international trade matters less than often suggested has been extensively criticized; see, e.g., Ernest H. Preeg, 'Krugmanian Competitiveness: A Dangerous Obfuscation', in Brad Roberts (ed.), *New Forces in the World Economy*, Cambridge, MA: MIT Press, 1996, pp. 107–18.

12. E.g. Patricia Mische, 'Ecological Security in a New World Order: Some Linkages Between Ecology, Peace and Global Security', in *Non-Military Aspects of International Security*, Paris; UNESCO, 1995, pp. 155–95.

13. These distinctions are made by Lothar Brock, 'Peace Through Parts: The Environment on the Peace Research Agenda', *Journal of Peace Research*, vol. 28, no. 4, 1991, pp. 407–23 and Lothar Brock, 'Security Through Defending the Environment: An Illusion', in Elise Boulding

(ed.), *New Agendas for Peace Research. Conflict and Security Re-examined*, Boulder, CO: Lynne Rienner, 1993, pp. 79–102.

14. Stephen Dycus, *National Defense and the Environment*, Hanover, NH. University Press of New England, 1996, ch. 4.
15. Marc A. Levy, 'Is the Environment a National Security Issue?', *International Security*, vol. 20, no. 2, 1995, pp. 35–62 (the quotation is on p. 46).
16. The view that environment should not be 'securitized' is gaining increased support; see Daniel Deudney, 'The Case Against Linking Environmental Degradation and National Security', *Millennium*, vol. 19, no. 3, 1990, pp. 461–76 and Barry Buzan, Ole Wæver & Jaap de Wilde, 'Environmental, Economic and Societal Security', *Working Papers No. 10*, Copenhagen: Centre for Peace and Conflict Research, 1995.
17. A similar approach has been advocated by Nina Græger, 'Environmental Security', *Journal of Peace Research*, vol. 33, no. 1, 1996, pp. 109–16.
18. These and related issues are discussed by Cynthia Enloe, 1994, *The Morning After: Sexual Politics at the End of the Cold War*, Berkeley, CA: University of California Press. See also Marysia Zalewski, 'Well, What is the Feminist Perspective on Bosnia?', *International Affairs*, vol. 71, no. 2, 1995, pp. 339–56.
19. Maria B. Olujic, 'The Croation War Experience', in Carolyn Nordstrom and Antonius CG M Robben (eds), *Fieldwork Under Fire: Contemporary Studies of Violence and Survival*, Berkeley, CA: University of California Press, 1995, pp. 186–204 (the quotation is on p. 197).
20. J. Ann Tickner, 'Re-visioning Security', in Ken Booth and Steve Smith (eds), *International Relations Theory Today*, Oxford: Polity Press, 1995, pp. 185–97, esp. pp. 190–3.
21. Sam C. Nolutshungu, 'International Security and Marginality', in Sam C. Nolutshungu (ed.), *Margins of Insecurity: Minorities and International Security*, Rochester, NY: University of Rochester Press, 1996, pp. 1–35.
22. Ted Robert Gurr, *Minorities at Risk: A Global View of Ethnopolitical Conflicts*, Washington: The United States Institute of Peace Press, 1993, pp. 89–122.
23. See Simon Dalby, 'Security Modernity, Ecology: The Dilemmas of Post-Cold War Security Discourse', *Alternatives*, vol. 17, no. 1, 1992, pp. 95–134; and Ronnie D. Lipschultz, 'On Security', in Ronnie D. Lipschultz (ed.), *On Security*, pp. 1–23.
24. Ken Booth, 'Security and Emancipation', *Review of International Studies*, vol. 17, no. 3, 1991, pp. 313–26.
25. See Robert Mandel, *The Changing Face of National Security: A Conceptual Analysis*, Westport, CT: Greenwood Press 1994. For a more popular analysis, see Joseph J. Romm, *Defining National Security: The Non-Military Aspects*, New York: Council on Foreign Relations Press 1993.
26. This perspective is stressed by Mohammed Ayoob, *The Third World Security Predicament, State Making, Regional Conflict, and the International System*, Boulder CO: Lynne Rienner, 1995.

27. See Ayoob 1995, pp. 165–88 (n. 7) and K.J. Holsti, 'War, Peace, and the State of State', *International Political Science Review*, vol. 16, no. 4, 1995, pp. 319–39.
28. The levels of security have been most systematically discussed by Buzan 1991. See also Ole Wæver, 'Securitization and Desecuritization', in Ronnie D. Lipschutz (ed.), *On Security*, pp. 46–86.
29. Harold Müller, 'Maintaining Non-Nuclear Weapons Status', in Regina Cowen Karp (ed.), *Security With Nuclear Weapons? Different Perspectives on National Security*, Oxford: Oxford University Press/SIPRI, 1991, pp. 301–39.
30. This is the approach adopted by Buzan 1991.
31. For a more detailed presentation of this approach, see John Jacob Nutter, 'Unpacking Threat: A Conceptual and Formal Analysis', in Norman A. Graham (ed.), *The Impact of Military Spending and Arms Transfers*, Boulder, CO: Lynne Rienner, 1994, pp. 29–51.
32. A detailed classification along these lines has been developed by Dietrich Fischer, *Non-Military Aspects of Security: A Systems Approach*, Aldershot: Dartmouth, 1993, ch. 2.
33. For a more detailed discussion of the indirect effects of environmental factors on violence, see Thomas F. Homer-Dixon, 'Environmental Scarcities and Violent Conflict: Evidence from Cases', *International Security*, vol. 19, no. 1, 1994, pp. 5–40.
34. Terry Nardin, 'Ethical Traditions in International Affairs', in Terry Nardin and David R. Mapel (eds), *Traditions of International Ethics*, Cambridge: Cambridge University Press, 1993, pp. 14–18.
35. This well-known process has been formalized in, for example, Nutter 1994.
36. The relevance of stalemate is stressed especially by I. William Zartman, 'Negotiations and Pre-negotiations in Ethnic Conflict: The Beginning, the Middle, and the Ends', in Joseph V. Montville (ed.), *Conflict and Peacemaking in Multiethnic Societies*, New York: Lexington Books, 1991, pp. 515–16.
37. This has been, of course, noted by earlier authors, such as Wolfers 1962, p. 158, who observed that 'every increment of security must be paid for by additional sacrifices of other values usually of a kind more exacting than the mere expenditure of precious time on the part of policy-makers. At a certain point, then, by something like the economic law of diminishing returns, the gain in security no longer compensates for added costs of attaining it'.
38. *Common Security: A Programme for Disarmament*, The Report of the Independent Commission on Disarmament and Security Issues, London: Pan Books, 1982, pp. 6–7.
39. For various viewpoints on common security, see Raimo Väyrynen (ed.), *Policies for Common Security*, London: Taylor and Francis/SIPRI, 1985; Raimo Väyrynen, 'Common Security: A Metaphor and a Doctrine', in Yoshikazu Sakamoto (ed.), *Strategic Doctrines and Their Alternatives*, New York: Gordon and Breach, 1987, pp. 164–88; and Dieter S. Lutz, 'Gemeinsame Sicherheit: Das neue Konzept: Definitionsmerkmale und Strukturelemente im Vergleich mit Anderen Sicherheitspolitischen

Modellen und Strategien', in Egon Bahr and Dieter S. Lutz (eds), *Gemeinsame Sicherheit: Idee und Konzept, Band I*, Baden-Baden: Nomos, 1986, pp. 45–82.

40. *Our Common Future*, Oxford: Oxford University Press, 1987, pp. 290–307.

41. *Our Global Neighborhood: The Report of the Commission on Global Governance*, Oxford: Oxford University Press, 1995, pp. 78–85.

42. Kari Mottolc, 'Prospects for Cooperative Security in Europe: The Role of the CSCE', in Michael Lucas (ed.), *The CSCE in the 1990s: Constructing European Security and Cooperation*, Baden-Baden: Nomos 1993.

43. Janie Leatherman, 'Making the Case for Cooperative Security', *Cooperation and Conflict*, vol. 31, no. 1, 1996, pp. 108–15.

44. Janne E. Nolan *et al.*, 'The Concept of Cooperative Security', in Janne E. Nolan (ed.), *Global Engagement: Cooperation and Security in the 21st Century*, Washington, DC, 1994, pp. 3–18 (the quotations are from pp. 5 and 7).

45. Janne E. Nolan, *et al.*, 'The Imperatives for Cooperation', in Janne E. Nolan (ed.), *Global Engagement: Cooperation and Security*, pp. 19–64.

46. The Brookings reader, however, contains some articles which conceptually emphasize the importance of balanced institutions and reciprocal norms in promoting cooperative security; see Antonia Handler Chayes and Abraham Chayes, 'Regime Architecture: Elements and Principles', in Janne E. Nolan (ed.), *Global Engagement: Cooperation and Security*, pp. 65–130.

47. Randall Forsberg, 'Creating a Cooperative Security System', *Boston Review*, vol. 17, no. 6, 1992, pp. 1–3.

48. Hedley Bull, 1977, *The Anarchical Society: A Study of Order in World Politics*, New York: Columbia University Press, pp. 238–40.

49. Different aspects of collective security are discussed in, for example, Inis, Claude Jr., *Swords into Plowshares: Problems and Progress of International Organization*, New York: Random House (4th ed.), 1971 pp. 245–85 and Andrew Bennett and Joseph Lepgold, 1993, 'Reinventing Collective Security After the Cold War and the Gulf Conflict', *Political Science Quarterly*, vol. 108, no. 2, 1993, pp. 213–38.

50. For an extended criticism of collective security, see John Mearsheimer, 'The False Promise of International Institutions', *International Security*, vol. 19, no. 3, 1995, pp. 26–37.

51. George W. Downs and Keisuke Iida, 'Assessing the Theoretical Case Against Collective Security', in George W. Downs (ed.), *Collective Security Beyond the Cold War*, Ann Arbor: The University of Michigan Press, 1994, pp. 17–39.

52. Marvin Soroos, 'Global Change, Environmental Security, and the Prisoner's Dilemma', *Journal of Peace Research*, vol. 31, no. 3, 1994, pp. 321–5.

53. Stephen M. Walt, 'Collective Security and Revolutionary Change: Promoting Peace in the Former Soviet Union', in George W. Downs (ed.), *Collective Security Beyond the Cold War*, Ann Arbor: The University of Michigan Press, 1994, pp. 169–95.

54. Charles Lipson, 'Why Are Some International Agreements Informal', *International Organization*, vol. 45, no. 4, 1991, pp. 495–538.

55. Björn Möller, *Common Security and Nonoffensive Defense: A Neorealist Perspective*, Boulder, CO: Lynne Rienner 1992.
56. Dalby 1992, pp. 116–17.
57. These issues are discussed in greater detail in Raimo Väyrynen, 'Enforcement and Humanitarian Intervention: Two Faces of the Collective Action by the United Nations', *Joan B. Kroc Institute for International Peace Studies*, University of Notre Dame, 1995, Occasional Papers 8:OP:2.

Part II

Economy and Ecology

4 Back to Heterodox Questions: Progress with Regress Through Competition

Javier Iguiñiz-Echeverria

In the field of international relations, and more specifically, when dealing with human rights, national security, environmental protection, peace and democracy, economics has to be considered. Aggregate economic movements and structural transformations influence perceptions, hierarchies in values and priorities for action. There is no clear and direct connection between economic status and other aspects of human relations but, determinisms aside, economics in its narrowest meaning of production and trading of things, matters. It is clear that it is not true that the traditional world of economics can be the starting point of social analysis, *the* independent variable; but it is also clear that it has some internal coherence even though it is embedded in a more complex and deep set of human interactions. Yet it is also true that the way some problems are conceived and defined, and also confronted, depends partly on the place a society, a group or an individual occupies in the global economy. However, that 'place' has to be defined and explained as precisely as possible to make of the economic reality something useful in the analysis of those and many other related topics. In this chapter I am going to suggest one way of introducing the economic factor, but without attempting any causal relation with the other aspects studied in this volume.

In this world of globalization, opening of national markets, privatization, deregulation and several other methods of extending the reach of the rules of the game of the human interactions that we call 'market' it is interesting to note that the specific nature of market interactions is not usually introduced in a systematic way. Many times we find either a definition of market where nobody

73

competes, as in the neoclassical approach, or one in which con-
spiratorial strategies by individual business leaders define outcomes.
The economic place an individual or group occupies in the global
economy is usually described in terms of his or her income *per
capita*; that is, of one of the results of economic activity. But it is
less common to define the economic status in terms of the complex interaction between facts that, being social, are out of control
of economic agents, and decisions by these same agents. Either
'laws' or 'strategies' dominate unilaterally most of the analyses, and
it is paradoxical, to say the least, that in a world that is becoming
more difficult to control, it is the strategic aspect of the economic
process that acquires pre-eminence in the theoretical literature. That
is the new power of microeconomics. Regulation in this context is
becoming the regulation of individual agents' behaviour and not of
market structures and processes that, in a significant measure, escape them. A multilateral approach to regulation has to consider
seriously this point.

PROGRESS WITH REGRESS

The objective of this chapter is to present in a non-technical manner some basic ideas behind new mainstream models that constitute a healthy reaction to the current unsatisfactory state of theoretical
affairs. Heterodox thinkers, among them Schumpeter and Marx,
but also Myrdal, Prebisch, and many others, are directly and indirectly inspiring sophisticated neoclassical theoreticians in their effort to make theory relevant in a world of general unemployment,
and I would add widening inequality. This inequality is not only
the result of differences in velocity, of 'backwardness', but also of
the regress of those that lose in competition, once this process became
more aggressive as in the 1980s. In Latin America, the number of
poor doubled in the 1980s; many non-poor became for the first
time poor. It is perhaps this impoverishment of previously not poor,
(which is occurring in developed countries also, see Towsend 1993,
p. 15) that has made the inequality problem a more sensitive one.
Inequality is now more of a problem among culturally homogeneous
human beings. In fact, homogeneity in non-economic aspects of
life and inequality in the economic ones move together. As several
forms of oppression recede, inequality moves ahead. As the World
Bank had to recognize in its report on workers: 'Divergence in

incomes per capita is the dominant feature of modern economic history.'[1] The United Nations Development Program some years ago presented impressive figures about changes in the 1970s and 1980s.[2] In Latin America, most of the countries studied by the Economic Commision for Latin America and the Caribbean (CEPAL) show the same trend (CEPAL 1994, 35–45), and many of the best observers and analysts of Latin America have recognized the importance of such extreme inequality (Sheahan 1987, 23; Cardoso and Helwege 1992,19).

My belief is that, although these models are far from constituting, separated or put together, a theory of the capitalist development process, they recognize the economic crisis, and the regressive component intrinsic to capitalist economic progress. Future debate will show how coherent they are, and how much explanatory power of current trends they have. In the context of the present volume I hope this chapter will help provide materials to describe and understand some of the underlying structural justifications for multilateralism. If I am near what such multilateralism means, it has to regulate unplanned but systematic results of economic competition; among them, inequality at the regional and world levels, and not just individual behaviour of governments, firms or individuals.

This need for regulation of results is even more important because in the economy success begets success, and failure, regress; and most of the time, poverty.[3] Academic answers to this cumulative causation problem have been there for decades but they are now appearing within the core of mainstream economics. I hope to show that future debate within economics will become more interesting. A leading example of recent facts, recognition, and theory adaptation to deal with them is the new endogenous growth theory.

> Although all less developed countries are affected by the worldwide economy, the effects are not uniform. For our purposes, the key observation is that those countries with more extensive prior development appear to benefit more from periods of rapid worldwide growth and suffer less during any slowdown. That is, growth rates appear to be increasing not only as a function of calendar time but also as a function of the level of development.
>
> Romer 1986, 1012

Wealth and poverty, progress and regress are the type of realities usually related on moral grounds. Scientifically serious causal economic relations are not so easy to find. Moral criteria do not require scientific proof of causality. But this search for causal links is also important to reduce the impact of structural factors on human behaviour. Probably most of the times in a specific social structure creation of wealth implies a reduction in poverty. It is one *or* the other. However, both can also be seen as independent, and should be analysed as parts of different processes. In that sense, it would be a question of one *and* the other. Finally, it is also found that, under some circumstances, progress, accompanied by increasing wealth for some collectivities and individuals' can be analytically related to regress,[4] and many times increasing poverty for other groups and individuals. It is progress *with* regress; that is regress actively created by progress, not just by default. The models presented below add new members to the group of theories that have attempted an analysis of these twin features of the competitive process. In other words, how many are regressing and become poor because they are losers, and not because they have not played, are not or have not been in the game?

All this is important in order to answer seriously questions that are not being asked in spite of their obvious importance: How easy is it to 'make markets work for the poor'? How convenient is it to 'improve markets'? or to 'extend markets'? Under what conditions is a market deepening better? In what kinds of markets? Markets embedded in a complex set of components of the human dimension can accept a different question: how to regulate the competition?

The objective of this summary is not to provide a precise answer to this global problem but to select some of the competition mechanisms that help us to understand the inner processes which make it difficult to extend the benefits of growth and technical change to the whole population.

HETEROGENEOUS COMPETITORS IN A MOVING FIELD

Three aspects of the economic process are being recognized more and more as important in mainstream economic theory. First, is the heterogeneous power of competitors within an activity or market. Success and bankruptcy, entry and exit are part of reality with the same status. Second, the asymmetric effects on equality of the cyclical economic process. The worsening of equality in a recession is more important than the improvement, if any, in the recovery.

Third, the reallocative dynamics of the growth process and the asymmetric nature of the job-reallocation process.

In what follows I will touch upon three classic themes in heterodox thinking.

1. Heterogeneity Among Competitors

One of the most interesting developments in economic theory is the questioning of the relevance of homogeneity of firms within industries to understand competition. Cycles could be studied neoclassically by relying on the 'representative firm' paradigm but at great cost when analyzing unemployment in recessions. In terms of the empirical analysis influencing contemporary theory, one of the most important studies is the Timothy F. Bresnahan and Daniel M.G. Raff papers about the effects of the Great Depression on the motor vehicle industry.

> The partial diffusion of mass-production technology and related organizational changes formed the initial conditions for motor vehicles competition in the Great Depression. Those firms whose plants and organizations embodied mass production had a competitive advantage.   Bresnahan and Raff 1991, 330

Another data-intensive work influencing model-intensive papers is presented by Davis and Haltiwanger. Here again, but looking to the problem of job reallocation along the cycle, a crucial feature is heterogeneity. For instance, behaviourally speaking:

> The magnitude and cyclical variability of gross job flows differs systematically across plants with different observable characteristics. On average, job reallocation rates are substantially higher among younger, smaller, and single-unit plants. At the same time, job reallocation rates among these plants show no systematic cyclical variation; whereas job reallocation rates among older, larger, multi-unit plants show pronounced countercyclical variation.[5]

At the theoretical level, this heterogeneity is being considered a critical feature of market competition (Diamond 1994). In countries with very high and fluctuating inflation rates, the adjustment at the firm level happens to some extent automatically, that is, as a consequence of macro-developments. Although future analyses of

job reallocation will certainly be quite important, it would be necessary to consider changes in real wages as an alternative adjusting
mechanism.[6]

Without heterogeneity there is no true capitalist competition.
Obviously, it is only 'when firms' costs differ [that] competition can
play an important role in selecting more efficient firms from less
efficient ones' (Vickers 1994, 14). Ruin is a common outcome and
may lead to extreme poverty in many of those cases where the
competitor is already poor. Regress, and maybe ruin, is part of a
selection process. 'Competition also provides the basis of selection, of deciding who has a comparative advantage in performing a
particular task' (Stiglitz 1994, 161).

Contests are processes of selection, and are based on incentives;
what matters is relative, not absolute, performance (Stiglitz 1994,
111–12).[7] Odagiri summarizes the contrasts between theories in the
following way:

> While the neoclassical school has mostly confined its analyses to
> competition in terms of quantity, in the short term, by exit, and
> with incentives given according to absolute levels of merit, com-
> petition in the real world has increasingly operated in terms of
> non-quantity variables (such as Schumpeterian competition in inno-
> vation), in the long term (that is, through an evolutionary pro-
> cess of competition), by the use of voice option (reinforced by
> the threat of exit), and with incentives given according to rela-
> tive merits (namely, rank-order tournaments). All these are forms
> of competition because they involve one person or firm striving
> against existing or potential rivals.' ...'The increasing prevalence
> of these forms of competition coincides with an increasing specifity
> of assets, both physical and human.
>
> Odagiri 1992, p. 18.

That selection process is part of a substitution strategy (Zamagni
1987):

> In everyday language competition is synonymous with contest and
> rivalry. The many different meanings which have been attributed
> to this term in economics have a common feature which can be
> identified with this everyday concept of competition. What are
> the constituent elements of the economic concept of competition?
>
> Firstly, there must be a contrast of interests between economic
> agents.... Secondly competitors must be able to substitute each
> other.[8]

This is why the competitiveness of a firm is associated with the share of a market possessed by such firm. The competitive struggle has to be viewed from two perspectives: that within a market, and the competition between producers in different markets. In the first case a key economic result is the collective formation of a natural, long term or production price; in the second, the trend toward a never achievable uniform or natural rate of profits (Shaikh 1990).

However, competitive struggles do not concentrate on just replacing the competitor from a market, either from the inside or as a result of the entry of others into that market. Competition, at its best, involves the destruction and creation of existing markets, not only of competitors in a particular market. As is well known to Schumpeter: '.... this process of creative destruction is the essential fact about capitalism' (Schumpeter 1947 p. 42). In general, the behavioural aspect of competition relates that process to those practices typical in war. 'The oligopoly-theorist's classical literature can neither be Newton and Darwin, nor can it be Freud; he will have to turn to Clausewitz's *Principles of War*.' (Rothschild 1947, 29)

A key term in most of the newest theory is *strategy*; it makes explicit that individual's decisions matter when trying to understand outcomes. It is, as Krugman reminds us, a business-minded view of the economic process as opposite to a true economist's view. True economic thinking includes more than describing fights. The neoclassical option was to forget that competition meant direct conflict. To arrive at an idyllic general scene of universal harmony they simplified the *homo economic* behaviour to the extreme, and abandoned competition.

2. The Non-intended Effects of Human Action

Most of the new theory on competition develops this general perspective. It deals with the structure, performance and conduct of a direct and explicit confrontation. Now everybody in the economic profession recognizes that competition is an activity for those directly involved, and not just a state or structure; but in addition it is becoming important that it is also a process resulting in outcomes that often depart from the wishes of both competitors. The literature on externalities is just an example of such awareness. We can talk of a behaviour of individual entities, and of a process that generates outcomes out of control. The classic and most sophisticated theory in the twentieth century concentrated in one of these non-intended effects of competition.

During the two centuries since the publication of *The Wealth of
the Nations*, the main activity of economists, it seems to me, has
been to fill the gaps in Adam Smith's system, to correct his er-
rors, and to make his analysis vastly more exact. A principal theme
of *The Wealth of Nations* was that government regulation or centralized planning were not necessary to make an economic system function in an orderly way. The economy could be coordinated
by a system of prices (the 'invisible hand') and, furthermore, with
beneficial results. A major task of economists since the publication of *The Wealth of Nations*, as Harold Demsetz ... has explained, has been to formalize this proposition of Adam Smith

                                                              Coase 1992.

There is wide agreement on what the classic economists wanted to
show. As Harris (1988, 140) synthesizes:

> The classical conception of competition is that it is a process,
> not a state. Moreover, it is a turbulent process. It has as its con-
> spicuously observable outward character that it is associated with
> booms and busts, economic crises, financial panics, bankruptcies
> and the like. This turbulence is predominantly an aspect of the
> process of circulation, where it takes the form of price wars and
> trade wars, and not so much of the production process, except
> in Marxist analysis, where it takes the form of a constant press-
> ure of the individual capitalists to innovate under penalty of
> ruin.

However, classical economic theory went further than the description of the competitive process. Concretely,

> ... the central problematic of the classical conception ... [was]
> to demonstrate how, if at all, such a process of competition,
> correctly conceived as a turbulent process or as 'creative destruc-
> tion', may be considered to converge or gravitate towards a state
> of uniform profit rates as a condition for continuity and repro-
> duction of the economic system as a whole and, in the longer
> term, to generate a continuing decline of the overall profit rate.[9]

The question they studied is not, therefore, competition as such,
but how that kind of battle was compatible with the expanded reproduction of the economy as a whole.

But this preoccupation with processes that escape the will of the participants allows us to distinguish between the description of individual behaviour and the social outcomes of myriads of individual contests taking place every minute. Competition can, then, be analysed in impersonal terms, as a process of social reproduction that is quite independent of the conscious objectives and strategies of individuals and firms or nations, and of their particular achievements. These two aspects, subjective and objective, are both important. Actually, the problem of analysing competition through these two approaches is not easy to solve, and it is not a question of introducing microeconomic reasoning into aggregate processes in order to understand them. The micro-foundations of macroeconomics will not stretch to the point at which classic and general equilibrium theorists want to arrive.

3. Cycles and Technology

Another convergence in approaches occurs in the way cycles are being studied. It is well known that heterodox economists such as Marx and Schumpeter questioned the world of equilibrium, and stressed permanent disequilibrium as a crucial feature of the capitalist economies. One of the best-known instabilities is the cyclical one. In general, growth is associated with a more important presence of progress than of regress, and the other way around in recessions.

The conventional analysis of fluctuations has been typically undertaken with the help of a separation between short and long term that was mainly based on the absence or presence of technical change. This division was explicitly used by Keynes, within the neoclassical tradition of the 'given technology' analysis: to understand short-run evolution of poverty and inequality there was, according to him, no need to introduce technical change into the analysis.[10] It has been, perhaps, the furthest such a neoclassical assumption has gone to explain such a structurally important topic. It reminds us of the analysis by Marx of cyclical processes assuming no technical change and 'absolute surplus value'. Although useful in many respects, it served to hide behind aggregations the competitive aspect of the economic process. In any case, that separation between short and long run has recently been questioned with better analytical tools. As Aghion and Howitt say (1995, p. 113):

The tendency for temporary shocks to become embedded into the economy's long-run growth path calls into question the traditional division of macroeconomic theory between trend and cycles, and calls for a return to the Schumpeterian view of growth and cycles as one unified phenomenon. The other side of this unified view is the short-run effect that can be exerted on the economy by random economy-wide changes in technology.

This unification of cycles and trends has a long tradition. In a classical perspective there are models that produce that connection between the short and the long run, between technological change and distribution of income. One of them relates variations in poverty to changes in technology, and is presented by Anwar Shaikh:

> Smith, Ricardo and Marx typically abstract from supply/demand and supply/capacity variations in order to focus on the long term patterns produced by the effects of factors such as technical change, population growth, and fertility of land, on the relation between the wage share and the normal rate of profit (Shaikh 1991, p. 291, N. 5).

The link between short-run evolution and long-run trend is also obtainable by extending the Keynesian and Kaleckian framework to solve the 'knife-edge' problem posed by the Harrod-Domar view of growth (Shaikh 1989, 1991).

As we shall see below, the new awareness in the cyclical nature of the economy is becoming crucial to an understanding of the production of unemployment and inequality.

CREATIVE DESTRUCTION

The process of creative destruction has several channels. Techno-logical (and organizational) process innovations are both crucial and well known in the theory of development. The research process in itself, and the product innovation that it brings about is an interesting area where simultaneous progress and decay of competitors appears to be quite common. The effects of faster growth on unemployment has also been included in some of the most recent models. Obviously, recessions are extremely important when analysing bankruptcies and unemployment. In this section we will present some synthesizing summaries showing this variety of mechanisms relating stagnation and crisis to growth, job destruction to job creation, obsolescence to novelty – in general, regress to progress.

1. Cost Reduction and the Treadmill

The first type of connection between progress and regress which should be mentioned is indeed quite old. In an always interesting little book Cochrane (1965) summarized the simplest process of competition as follows (p. 66):

> ... the innovators reap the gains of technological advance during the early phases of adoption, but after the improved technology has become industry-wide, the gains to innovators and all other farmers are eroded away either through falling product prices or rising land prices or a combination of the two, and in the long run the specific income gains to farmers are wiped out and farmers are back where they started – in a no-profit position. In this sense, technological advance puts farmers on a treadmill.

In a study by Caballero and Hammour (1994) the price mechanism also operates to increase the damage to the laggards. The explanation presented is that most modern firms have more influence on prices and this adds to the destruction process resulting from recession and the entry (i.e. creation) of new firms.

> ... if creation declines only mildly in response to a sharp contraction, the equilibrium price falls more sharply, which induces additional destruction. This is the reason why destruction not only preserves, but *amplifies* the asymmetries in demand: it must 'make up' for the symmetry in creation.
>
> Caballero and Hammour 1994, pp. 1361–2

In an important work on wages from a Marxist viewpoint the same idea is presented, this time related to the changes in the level of wages and their differences.

> Marx shows that workers who are unfortunate enough to be employed in the more backward firms will generally find that their wages and working conditions will deteriorate both absolutely and relatively to workers who are employed in the more advanced firms.
>
> Botwinick 1993, p. 120

In any case, the new importance assigned to heterogeneity within an industry is essential in order to present one of the most important market mechanisms that helps to explain the progress-poverty relation. 'Thus, differential conditions of production will be continually reproduced within industries as new capitals enter with the latest techniques and older capitals continue to depreciate their aging fixed capital stock' (Botwinick 1993, p. 120).[11] As Cochrane concludes, 'Cruel as it may seem to the displaced farm people, it is part of the growth process of the national economy' (Cochrane 1965, p. 71).

2. Innovation/Obsolescence: Deterring Creation

Knowledge is considered the main tool for competition. The new theory of economic growth is improving the mathematical models that introduce this fact into economic models.[12] Let us look at some of the most interesting polarizing effects of research.

First, in one recent paper, Aghion and Howitt present one aspect of competition among firms: competition through research expenditure. Research in this model has one main effect: improvement of the quality of products. As the authors say: 'This channel introduces into endogenous growth theory the factor of obsolescence. Obsolescence exemplifies an important general characteristic of the growth process, namely that progress creates losses as well as gains' (Aghion and Howitt 1992, p. 323).

The process by which the progress of one is not necessarily the progress of the other competitor is based on the dissuasive effect of the leading researchers on those that are less powerful. If some of the firms announce more expenditure on research, that in itself will reduce the expenditure of the rest of the competitors.

> The more research people expect will occur following the next innovation the shorter the likely duration of the monopoly profits that will be enjoyed by the creator of that next innovation, and hence the smaller the payoff. This introduces a negative dependency of current research upon the amount of expected future research.   Aghion and Howitt 1995, p. 109.

In this model, two factors produce this negative dependency but the most interesting one is that if a competitor knows that more expenditure in research is going to be done by others in response to his or her innovation, that competitor knows that obsolescence will arrive sooner, and the monopoly profits that will be received will last less long. As a consequence, the decision to invest in research could be postponed.

Second, the relationship between average growth and research is not unambiguous.

> ...the average growth rate of the economy is not necessarily increased by an increase in the productivity of research. In particular, a parameter change that makes research more productive in some states of the world can discourage research in other states, by increasing the threat of obsolescence faced by the product of research in those other states, to such an extent that the average growth rate is reduced.
>
> Aghion and Howitt 1992, p. 325.

3. Reallocation of Resources and Jobs

The mere fact of reallocating resources is now considered important in explaining the costs of the normal market process. In a recent paper Aghion and Howitt reminded us of one of the possible consequences of reallocation of resources.

> ... as Corriveau ... has shown, endogenous growth-models based on uncertain competitive innovation can rationalize a phenomenon that constitutes an awkward fact for existing real business cycle theories: negative shocks to aggregate GNP. In the Corriveau model these occur when the random arrival of new technological information leads society to reallocate resources to take advantage of the new possibilities implicit in this information but no immediate fruits in the form of enhanced output arise to offset the costs of reallocation.
>
> Aghion and Howitt 1995, p. 113

Answering the question about the effect of growth on long-run employment, these same authors in another paper summarize their model (1994, p. 479).

> The source of unemployment in the model is labor re-allocation across firms. More specifically, any production unit has to incur a fixed overhead cost in human capital whose price in terms of

final consumption rises at the economy-wide rate of growth. Thus
a production unit whose technology is fixed eventually becomes
unable to produce enough to cover its fixed costs, at which point
it is shut down by the firm that created it, forcing the worker
into unemployment until matched with a new machine.

The consequence is that unemployment is not only a result of recession but, under some circumstances also of growth.

> In the long run, faster economic growth must come from a faster
> increase in knowledge. To the extent that the advancement of
> knowledge is embodied in industrial innovations it is likely to
> raise the job-destruction rate, through automation, skill-obsol-
> escence, and bankruptcy associated with the process of creative
> destruction. In short, increased growth is likely to produce an
> increased rate of job-turnover, and the search theories of Lucas
> and Prescott (1974) and Pissarides (1990) imply that an increased
> rate of job-turnover will result in a higher natural rate of unem-
> ployment. This conclusion is also consistent with the empirical
> results of Davis and Haltiwanger which show that periods of high
> unemployment tend to be periods of high job-turnover at the
> establishment level. It suggests the possibility of a positive long-
> run tradeoff between growth and unemployment, at least over
> some range.   Aghion and Howitt 1994, p. 477.

In general, as experience shows, ' . . . productivity increases are
embodied in new jobs at the expense of old jobs' (Aghion and Howitt
1994, p. 478). Thus, growth has its own effect on unemployment.
But obviously, recession does most of the damage.

4. The Cleansing Effect of Recessions

After analysing several empirical studies, two leading economists
summarize the position thus:

> The view that emerges from interpreting the greater cyclicality
> of job destruction along creative-destruction lines is one of re-
> cessions as times of 'cleansing', when outdated or relatively un-
> profitable techniques and products are pruned out of the productive
> system.   Caballero and Hammour 1994, p. 1352.

Along the cycle, 'the rate of job destruction is more responsive to changes in sectoral activity than is the rate of job creation . . .' (p. 1359).

The question is: how, and when, do the cyclical fluctuations impact on the competitive relative advantage of every competitor? It is well known that recessions are critical periods for many firms. In a recent article Caballero and Hammour produced a new model isolating and organizing some of the main factors explaining the ruin of the least productive competitors when demand declines in the economy. Their main interest there is to analyse the effects of the macroeconomics evolution on the interaction of competitors in a determined market.

The nature of the process is interesting and should be clarified eliminating other (also important) factors. In this model, we are not, indeed, facing a technological innovation process at the firm level as in the treadmill case. New firms entering at the most advanced end of the industry's structure embody the already existing best technology. They do not create new technologies or increase supply while being part of the industry and competing. This is not, therefore, a paper on technology creation and supply increases by firms as a result of competition. That is why the authors establish that '[o]ur emphasis here is on variations in demand as a source of economic fluctuations, and on the way a continuously renovating productive structure responds to them' (Caballero and Hammour 1994, p. 1350). It is structural change which matters, and it has a double source: entry of firms with ever more advanced technology, and their impact on the already existing less advanced ones.

It is not, therefore, that some of the existing firms will accommodate those variations in demand innovating faster and destroying the less innovative ones in that industry. This would be, exactly, destructive creation, intra-industry competition at its best. We are in a case of destructive entry determined by 'the rate at which production units that embody new techniques are created'. The creative activity in the paper refers to the creation of new firms, and not to the creation of new technologies. That is why I prefer to use the term 'entry' rather than the term 'creation' used in Caballero and Hammour's paper.

The cleansing effect or rate of destruction of outdated firms depends on two main factors: the level of demand for those industries' products and the rate of entrance of new firms through the most competitive extreme of the industry. This entrance affects those firms that are obsolete at the time of this most recent entrance, but also those that have become obsolete due to the shortening of the age of the oldest unit allowed by competition to remain in operation. Thus, obsolescence depends in two ways on the destruction process, first on the competitive situation of the firm *vis-à-vis* the already existing more efficient firms, and second on the new members in the industry, for '. . . the age at which units become obsolete is determined by the destruction process' (Caballero and Hammour 1994, p. 1352). It is not, strictly speaking, a new technological fact that matters but the relative place of competitors.

PRODUCTIVITY DIFFERENTIALS AND INTERNATIONAL COMPETITION

In this chapter I want to illustrate how competition at the firm level can have unintended effects (positive or negative) on a global level. The debate on the impact of competition on underdevelopment and poverty is important, since it influences the decision makers of all countries. The new version of the old debate on the effect of international relations among different countries is more sophisticated but better substance has not always been incorporated. As Matsuyama summarizes:

> Many argue that, incorporated into a larger market area, small economies can enjoy all the benefits of economies of scale, and become main beneficiaries of economic integration. Others believe, however, that economic integration and the free movement of labor and capital lead to a concentration of economic activities into the center, leaving the periphery underdeveloped.
>
> Matsuyama 1995, p. 713

Let me present some examples of these divergent views of international interaction.

Development of Underdevelopment Once More

A well-known article by Krugman has been presented many times as an example of how we can model an underdevelopment process through de-industrialization. The key point is that differences at the starting point become irreversible and accumulative. The concrete mechanism is simple, and quite classic:

> As manufacturing capital grows, the relative price of industrial goods falls, until eventually a point is reached when the lagging region's industry cannot compete and begins to shrink. Once this starts, there is no check, because costs rise as the scale of industry falls; and the lagging region's manufacturing sector disappears.
> Krugman 1990, p. 99

The 'crucial assumption' is 'that there are external economies in the industrial sector' and that therefore 'a small "head start" for one region will cumulate over time ...'; and the consequence is that ' ... trade with developed countries prevents industrialization in less developed countries' (Krugman 1990, p. 93).

From a quite different perspective, Anwar Shaikh (1980, 1990) arrives at a similar conclusion. The question is: if two countries both produce two commodities and one is more productive in both of them than the other, will these countries specialize each in one of the two commodities? The typical answer in the textbooks is: yes. The reason is that both countries will benefit if instead of producing both, they specialize in that product where their productivity is relatively better compared to the other product. But, Shaikh argues, the mere fact that some outcome is better for everybody does not ensure that it will happen. However, the separation in trade theory between the real sector and the monetary sector does not allow any explanation about why what is best should happen. The key element that transforms an absolute or competitive advantage into merely a comparative advantage is the theory of money (Shaikh 1980, pp. 215–6; 1990, p. 194). The basic idea is that any theory which asserts that a trade deficit in one country will result in a price reduction relative to that of the superavit country will do the job of converting both countries to greater competitivenesss in the product in which each one is relatively less disadvantaged. 'Any monetary theory that which translates the initial trade deficit of the backward country into falling price levels (falling relative to the price level in the advanced country) will do the trick' (Shaikh 1980, 216).[13]

Different theories of money are then presented to relate deficits to prices.

The classical quantity theory argued that an outflow of gold from a country would lead to a fall in the money supply and hence in the price level.... [In the case of the cash balance approach] a decrease in the money supply implies a decrease in the cash balances of individuals and firms; in order to 'not let their cash balances shrink too far,' people in the deficit country curtail their consumption and investment spending, and this drop in aggregate demand in turn leads to lower prices and wages ...

An alternate path to this same result is made possible by tying the price level to the level of money wages. In this version, since the competition of cheap cloth and wine from abroad means a reduction in domestic wine and cloth production in the backward country, the resulting trade deficit will be associated with a rise in unemployment. Money wages in the backward country will consequently fall, and with them, money prices....

Shaikh 1980, p. 216

The same relation is established with devaluation initiatives. But if there is no such price-effect, as for instance in Keynes' view, and also in Marx's analysis, the process is completely different. As Marx is reported to have said:

But in fact, a decrease in the quantity of gold raises only the interest rate, whereas an increase in the quantity of gold lowers the interest rate; and if not for the fact that the fluctuations in the interest rate enter into the determination of cost-prices, or in the determination of demand and supply, commodity-prices would be wholly unaffected.

Marx 1967, III, p. 551; in Shaikh 1980, p. 224

The consequence of this difference in monetary theory changes the whole outcome of the free trade competitive struggle when a country starts interacting with disadvantages in both commodities. Instead of protecting the less productive country through the relative cheapening of its commodities due to price changes, the rising interest rates in the deficit country increases the cost of capital, and aggravates its competitive situation in both products. The country that started with a competitive (absolute) disadvantage in both commodities will continue non-competitive in each one of them. Underdevelopment will become a process, not just a situation, an easily reversible starting point.

For a while, higher interest rates attract speculative capital, and direct foreign investment may also be attracted by lower wages. However, sooner or later, interest payments and profit remittances will change the course of capital: ' ... in free trade, the absolute disadvantage of the underdeveloped capitalist country will result in chronic trade deficits and mounting international borrowing. It will be chronically in deficit and chronically in debt' (Shaikh 1980, p. 226).

This debate about the pertinence of monetary theories continues in recent analysis about integration initiatives such as NAFTA.

Universal Harmonies Once More

According to Paul Krugman (1992), what is essential to countries is not so when we deal with international competition. On the one hand, in any country, '[P]roductivity isn't everything, but in the long run it is almost everything. A country's ability to improve its standard of living over time depends almost entirely on its ability to raise its output per worker' (Krugman 1992, p. 9). However, when we deal with the market relation between different countries the importance of productivity to determine the living standards of the population is nil. 'So, while low productivity is a problem, low productivity relative to other countries is not only not a disaster; it is irrelevant' (Krugman 1994, p. 274).

This view is decisive when we try to understand the process of underdevelopment, since what the quoted author is saying is that competition between economically powerful and weak firms of different countries does not lead to any difficulty in the weakest competitor.

There are two kind of arguments in this debate. One is related to the relative importance of trade for a country like the USA; the other, most important to us, refers to the price mechanisms that counteract the eventual impact of trade deficits in the country with less competitive firms. The reason for this lack of importance of productivity in the international competition between firms is that national economies react to the deficits and superavits in trade and isolate themselves from the impact that such competition could have on them. That is why ' ... productivity and competitiveness have very little to do with each other and, indeed, ... the whole concept of 'competitiveness' is at best problematic, at worst misleading' (Krugman 1994, pp. 268–9).[14] But, indeed, the topic under debate is the consequences of international trade on relatively low-productivity activities located in countries with a different currency from that in the countries where relatively high productivity activities are located.

The starting point in Krugman's argument is a situation where East and West produce both autos and buses. East is more productive in both than West. The question is: 'What will happen if these two countries trade with each other?' (Krugman 1994, p. 271). This is, by the way, the same question Shaikh used to challenge the relevance of the comparative advantage approach to international trade. Krugman's answer is that the relative productivity of countries is irrelevant.

There are two basic views in this respect. One is supported by Krugman's recent work and by most of the establishment in economics, stressing that the most probable outcome of competition is insignificant; the other considers that there may be significant negative effects of trade on the weakest competitors. Let us illustrate an important part of this author's argument when there is a relative increase of productivity in other countries.

> Now suppose that productivity growth in the rest of the world accelerates to three per cent. How does this change the picture?
>
> Obviously something has to give. If US wages were to continue to grow at the same rate as foreign, and if the exchange rate were to remain unchanged, then U.S. goods and services would rapidly be priced out of world markets.
>
> Krugman 1994, p. 275.

But this time, contrary to his model on uneven development, that option is not allowed to happen. As we summarized above, all theories that relate national trade deficits to national prices through wages, exchange rates, real balances or directly thanks to the more simple monetarist view will do the job of transforming the absolute advantage in both commodities by one country into an advantage by each country in one of the two products. And that is what Krugman does (continuing the previously quoted paragraph).

> Either US wages must grow more slowly, foreign wages grow more rapidly, or the dollar start declining. It makes no difference to our point which happens; so let's suppose that the dollar begins to slide on average by 2 percent per year to offset the two-percent-per-year lag in US productivity.[15]

This is the mechanism that impedes the pricing-out-of-the-market of the deficit countries' less competitive industries, and ends up benefiting the country that is less productive in both goods. In this way, what is best will become real; but we know that there is no easy way to ensure that the convenience of some pattern of international trade becomes true practice.[16]

We are back again in the middle of a debate about universal harmonies or underdevelopment processes. Obviously, empirical work is needed to choose among theories and models. All we can say is that the universal-harmonies world needs to be supported with research and not just with internally coherent models.

CONCLUSION

The new theory is producing an ample set of new tools capable of helping to explain growing divergences between countries' long-term evolution. Empirical work is also presenting growing inequalities. There is not, in fact, much novelty at the conceptual level but new tools allow us to manipulate them coherently. Many of these mentioned above were already present in heterodox development theorists but models of cumulative causation not only legitimize it professionally, but also help us in a more rigorous analysis of current general trends.

> ... the standard neoclassical paradigm, exemplified by Kenneth Arrow and Frank Hahn (1971), emphasizes the self-adjusting mechanisms of market forces with its efficient resource allocation. As different activities compete for scarce resources, expansion of one activity comes only at the expense of others, which tends to dampen any perturbation to the system. Imperfect competition and incomplete markets (through an endogenous change in the range of products offered in the market), as departures from the standard paradigm, leave more room for complementarities, and make the system more conducive to circular and cumulative causation, as complementarities help the system break away from the stabilizing forces of resource constraints.
>
> Matsuyama 1995, p. 702

Even more, '... complementarities arise as an outcome of the internal mechanisms of the market system. . . .' (p. 703).

These complementarities were part of the heterodox development thinking, and are obviously important to analyse in a more sophisticated way 'perturbations' as growing long-term inequalities at the world level. At the same time, this suggests that a view of the economy based on 'given' resources and technology does not allow us to understand the evident absence of internal economic mechanisms capable of controlling environmental damage; yet neo-classical theory will remain relevant as far as 'one activity comes only at the expense of others'.

Having said that, we are learning that new activities do not compete for the same resources the old ones were using; scarcity is not the best starting point. New products call for new resources and these are often created from 'nothing' as a chip or from knowledge.

If during the twentieth century mainstream economic theory has dealt with the task of showing how the system was kept together,[17] and in harmony, in the twenty-first century the task will probably be the understanding, and to a few, the justification, of the social and geographical concentration of the benefits of technological and organizational transformation. At least three quarters of the population of the planet will be asking that question. The World Bank has shown recently it is aware of the problem: 'There is a substantial risk that inequality between rich and poor will grow over the coming decades, while poverty deepens' (World Bank 1995, p. 80). 'There can be no guarantee that the poorest workers will see their living standards rise' (World Bank 1995, p. 9).

What are the theoreticians saying about inequality? Cumulative causation and inequality reproduction is related to 'history' and 'expectations'.

> On one side is the belief that choice among multiple equilibria is essentially resolved by *history*: that past events set the preconditions that direct the economy to one or another steady state. In the traditional literature this view is the preponderant one; indeed, as I shall emphasize later there is a strong tradition arguing that history matters precisely because of increasing returns. On the other side, however, is the view that the key determinant of choice of equilibrium is *expectations*: that there is a decisive element of self-fulfilling prophecy.
>
> Krugman 1991a, p. 652)

Indeed, his own work points to the side of history. In his *Geography and Trade* proposal, he says: 'In particular, I want to show two things: that increasing returns are in fact a pervasive influence on the economy, and that these increasing returns give a decisive role to history in determining the geography of real economies' (Krugman, 1991b, p. 10). He summarizes another previous work in the following manner:

> I have used external economies to formulate an 'uneven development' model in which the division of the world into rich and poor nations takes place endogenously, and a model in which a variety of heterodox views are justified by a framework in which patterns of specialization generated by historical accident get 'locked in' through learning effects.
>
> Krugman 1991a, p. 651

The pessimism about equality present in the 1995 World Bank Report (World Bank 1995) is the result of facts, and also of theories, the best of which is that rescuing economies through self-fulfilling expectations cannot be ruled out. Indeed, facts suggest that expectations are more relevant to case studies than to general trends.

> The possibility of self-fulfilling expectations cannot be ruled out. In particular, the economy may be able to escape from a 'bad' state only if expectations of agents are somehow coordinated. 'History' alone may not be enough to dictate the long-run behaviour of the economy with externalities.
>
> Matsuyama 1991, p. 619

NOTES

1. *World Development Report 1995. Workers in an Integrating World*, Oxford: Oxford University Press 1995, p. 53. The text continues in the same page: 'By one estimate, the ratio of income per capita in the richest to that in the poorest has increased from eleven in 1870, to thirty-eight in 1960, and to fifty-two in 1985. This divergent relation between growth performance and the initial level of income per capita not only applies to those extreme cases but is empirically valid on

average over a sample of 117 countries. Statistical analysis of growth in income per capita confirms the importance of initial levels: on average, countries that started richer grew faster.'

2. *Human Development 1992....* Previous work on this international inequality can be seen in Senghaas 1985, 28–9, Bairoch and Lévy-Leboyer 1981, and Kuznets 1966 among others.

3. It must be obvious that I am leaving aside the crucially important environmental and other regressive aggregate effects of individuals' economic progress in an industrial world. In this chapter, and in spite of them, I am assuming that this type of progress is, indeed, progress. Not industrial goods, but industrial competition is still, I think, the most decisive fact of activity relating economic interaction to inequality and poverty.

4. Regress does not necessarily mean impoverishment. It happens that failure in competition and obsolescence of human 'capital' occur in contexts where a safety net is powerful enough to support a reduced but still a decent life. But in many underdeveloped countries failure to compete in a more aggressive context deepens already-existing poverty levels and impoverishes many members of the 'middle class'.

5. Also plants that produce durable goods. (Davis and Haltiwanger 1992, 855).

6. We have shown that in Peru, the employment behaviour of firms is very heterogeneous along the cycle, and that such heterogeneity is commonly found within industries and within firms of the same institutional characteristics (state, private and cooperatives). (See Iguiñiz and Montes 1994; Iguiñiz and Vilcapoma 1993).

7. Competition also provides the basis of selection, of deciding who has a comparative advantage in performing a particular task (Stiglitz 1994, p. 161).

8. Zamagni 1987, p. 293. That same idea is presented in the following fashion: ... cada capital individual lucha para capturar la mas grande porción posible del mercado, suplantar a sus competidores y excluirlos del mercado ... (Shaikh 1990, p. 83).

9. Harris 1988, p. 142. For a summary, see also Zamagni (1987, p. 294).

10. 'The outstanding faults of the economic society in which we live are its failure to provide for full employment and its arbitrary and inequitable distribution of wealth and income' (Keynes 1964, p. 372). Keynes' message was that inequality was not needed in order to create employment.

11. The old (worst producers) vs new (best producers) has to be analysed better. Empirical works do not seem to show that firm's age is a problem. Increasing returns are considered positively related to experience.

12. 'The main contribution of the literature on endogenous growth pioneered by Romer (1986) and Lucas (1988) has been to endogenize the underlying source of sustained growth in per capita income, namely the accumulation of knowledge' (Aghion and Howitt 1992, p. 323).

13. For instance, Kindleberger describing a debate in the United Kingdom in the 1920s presents one of the arguments in this way. 'The argument evoked a proposal, which had been seriously put forward in 1923, deliberately to ship $100 million in gold to the United States to

cause inflation there and relieve the pressure on the British balance of payments. The idea was rejected by Montagu Norman in November 1923 as impractical. The Federal Reserve system could too readily sterilize the gold, that is, take it into the monetary base but sell off an equal amount of government securities to leave the total base, and the prospect of inflation, unchanged' (Kindleberger 1993, p. 327).

14. We will not deal at this time with the concept of 'competitiveness'; only a reference will be used to determine one of its most important and classic meanings. 'In the final analysis, competitiveness is determined by relative prices, for given products, between countries pairs' (Klein 1988, p. 309).

15. Krugman 1994, p. 275. The same argument is presented in Kindleberger (1993, p. 3320) '... the price level was still out of line. If prices and wages would not go up in the United States, they would have to go down in Britain ... Prices and wages did not rise in the United States, and it became necessary to force them down in Britain.'

16. Suboptimal outcomes of free competition are not, after all uncommon. See, for instance in Matsuyama (1995, p. 723).

17. And, we should add, how we could impede recessions.

REFERENCES

Aghion, Phillip and Howitt, Peter 1992, 'A Model of Growth Through Creative Destruction', *Econometrica*, 60, 2, March.

Aghion, Phillip and Howitt, Peter 1994, 'Growth and Unemployment', *Review of Economic Studies*, 61.

Aghion, Phillip and Howitt, Peter 1995, 'Technical Progress in the Theory of Economic Growth', in Jean-Paul Fitoussi (ed.), *Economics in a Changing World*, New York: St Martin's Press.

Backus, David K, Kehoe Patrick and Kehoe, Timothy J, 1992, 'In Search of Scale Effects in Trade and Growth' *Journal of Economic Theory*, 58, 2, December.

Bairoch, Paul and Lévy-Leboyer (eds) 1981, *Disparities in Economic Development since the Industrial Revolution*, New York: St. Martin's Press.

Boltwinick, Howard 1993, *Persistent Inequalities: Wage Disparity under Capitalist Development*, Princeton: Princeton University Press.

Bresnahan, Timothy F. and Raff, Daniel M.G. 1991, 'Intra-Industry Heterogeneity and the Great Depression: The American Motor Vehicles Industry, 1929–1935', *Journal of Economic History*, 51.

Caballero, Ricardo J. and Hammour, Mohamad L. 1994, 'The Cleansing Effect of Recessions', *The American Economic Review*, vol 84, no. 5, December.

Cardoso, Eliana and Helwege, Ann 1992, *Latin America's Economy*, Cambridge (USA): MIT Press.

Coase, Ronald 1992, 'The Institutional Structure of Production', *American Economic Review*, vol. 82, no. 4, September.

Cochrane, Willard W. 1965, *The City Man's Guide to the Farm Problem*, Minneapolis: University of Minnesota Press.

Comisión Económica para América Latina y el Caribe (CEPAL) (1994) *Panorama social de America Latina*, Santiago de Chile: CEPAL.

Davis Steven J. and Haltiwanger, John 1992, 'Gross Job Creation, Gross Job Destruction, and Employment Reallocation', *Quarterly Journal of Economics*, 107, no. 3, September.

Dennis, Kenneth G. 1977, *'Competition' in the History of Economic Thought*, New York: Arno Press.

De Soto, Hernando 1986, *El otro sendero*, Lima: Editorial El Barranco.

Diamond, Peter 1994, *On Time*, Cambridge (UK): Cambridge University Press.

Figueroa, Adolfo 1984, *Capitalist Development and the Peasant Economy in Peru*, Cambridge (UK): Cambridge University Press.

Harris, Donald J. 1988, 'On the Classical Theory of Competition', *Cambridge Journal of Economics*, p. 12.

Hunter, Alex, 1969, 'Welfare Analysis and Monopoly', in Alex Hunter (ed.) *Monopoly and Competition*, Penguin. England.

Iguiñiz, Javier and Montes, Noemí 1994, *Pluralismo empresarial, representatividad y empleo*, Lima; DESCO.

Iguiñiz, Javier and Vilcapoma, Leopoldo 1993, 'Institucionalidades, industrias y la "firma representativa"', Lima: *Economía*, xvi, 32, December.

International Labor Office (ILO) 1972, *Employment, Incomes and Equality: A strategy for increasing productive employment in Kenya*, Geneva: ILO.

Keynes, John M. 1964, *The General Theory of Employment, Interest and Money*, New York: Harbinger.

Kindleberger, Charles P. 1993, *A Financial History of Western Europe*, New York and Oxford: Oxford University Press (second edition).

Klein, Lawrence R. 1988, 'Components of Competitiveness'. *Science*, vol. 241, 15 July.

Knight, Frank 1946, 'Inmutable Law in Economics: Its Reality and Limitations', *American Economic Review*, XXXVI, May.

Krugman, Paul 1990, *Rethinking International Trade*. Cambridge (USA): The MIT Press.

Krugman, Paul 1991a, 'History versus Expectations', *Quarterly Journal of Economics*, vol. CVI, May, issue 2.

Krugman, Paul 1991b, *Geography and Trade*, Cambridge (USA): The MIT Press.

Krugman, Paul 1992, *The Age of Diminished Expectations*, Cambridge (USA): The MIT Press.

Krugman, Paul 1994, 'Productivity and Competitiveness', appendix to Chapter 10, in Paul Krugman, *Peddling Prosperity Economic Sense and Nonsense in the Age of Diminished Expectations*, New York: Norton.

Kuznets, Simon 1966, *Modern Economic Growth*, New York: Feffer and Simmons.

Lucas, Robert 1988, 'On the Mechanics of Economic Development' *Journal of Monetary Economics*, 22, 1, July.

Marshall, Alfred 1891, *Principles of Economics* vol. I.

Marx, Karl 1967, *Capital* III, Moscow: International Publishers.

Matsuyama, Kiminori 1991, 'Increasing Returns, Industrialization, and Indeterminacy of Equilibrium', *Quarterly Journal of Economics*, vol. CVI, May, issue 2.

Matsuyama, Kiminori 1995, 'Complementarities and Cumulative Processes in Models of Monopolistic Competition', *Journal of Economic Literature*, vol. XXXIII, June.

McNulty, Paul J. 1968, 'Economic Theory and the Meaning of Competition', *Quarterly Journal of Economics*, vol. 82, November.

Morstensen, Dale T. and Pissarides, Christopher A. 1994, 'Job Creation and Job Destruction in the Theory of Unemployment', *Review of Economic Studies*, 61.

Odagiri, Hiroyuki 1992, *Growth Through Competition, Competition Through Growth*, New York: Oxford University Press.

PNUD (UNDP) 1992, *Desarrollo humano: 1992*, Tercer Mundo Editores, Santa Fé de Bogota.

Portes, Alejandro 1994, Interview by Amparo Armas in *Gestión*: Ecuador, Agosto, n. 2.

Romer, Paul 1986, 'Increasing Returns and Long-Run Growth', *Journal of Political Economy*, vol. 94, no. 5, October.

Rothschild, K.W. 1947, 'Price Theory and Oligopoly', *Economic Journal*, 57, in Hunter (1969).

Schumpeter, Joseph A. 1947, 'The Dynamics of Competition and Monopoly', excerpt from: *Capitalism, Socialism and Democracy*, in Hunter (1969).

Senghaas, Dieter 1985, *Aprender de Europa*, Barcelona and Caracas: Editorial Alfa.

Sethuraman, S.V. 1981, *The Urban Informal Sector in Developing Countries: Employment, Poverty and Environment*. Geneva: ILO.

Shaikh, Anwar 1980, 'The Laws of International Exchange'. In Nell, Edward (ed.) 1980) *Growth, Profits, and Property*. Cambridge (UK): Cambridge University Press.

Shaikh, Anwar 1989, 'Accumulation, Finance and Effective Demand in Marx, Keynes, and Kalecki', in William Semmler (ed.) *Financial Dynamics and Business Cycles: New Perspectives*. New York: M.E. Sharpe.

Shaikh, Anwar 1990, *Valor, acumulación y crisis. Ensayos de economía política*, Tercer Mundo Editores. Santa Fé de Bogota.

Shaikh, Anwar 1991, 'A Dynamic Approach to the Theory of Effective Demand', in Dimitri B. Papadimitrou (ed.), *Profits, Deficits and Instability*, London: Macmillan.

Sheahan, John 1987, *Patterns of Development in Latin America. Poverty, Repression and Economic Strategy*, Princeton: Princeton University Press.

Stiglitz, Joseph E. 1994, *Whither Socialism?*, Cambridge (USA): The MIT Press.

Stoneman, Paul 1988, *The Economic Analysis of Technological Change*, Oxford: Oxford University Press.

Sylos Labini, Paolo 1988, *Las fuerzas del desarrollo y del declive*. Oikos-Tau. Barcelona.

The Economist, 5 November 1994.

Thomas, J.J., 1992, *Informal Economic Activity*, Ann Arbor: The University of Michigan Press.

Townsend, Peter 1993, *The International Analysis of Poverty*, New York: Harvester/Wheatsheaf.
United States of America Attorney General's Committee on Anti-Trust Laws (1955), 'Workable Competition', in Hunt 1969.
Vickers, John 1985, 'Strategic Competition Among the Few. Some Developments in the Economics of Industry', *Oxford Review of Economic Policy*, vol. 1, no. 3, Autumn.
Vickers, John 1994, *Concepts of Competition*, Oxford: Clarendon Press.
World Bank 1995, *Workers in an Integrating World*, World Development Report 1995, Washington and Oxford: Oxford University Press.
Zamagni, Stefano 1987, *Microeconomic Theory. An Introduction*, Basil Blackwell: Oxford.

5 A Signal Failure: Ecology and Economy After the Earth Summit

Peter Harries-Jones, Abraham Rotstein and Peter Timmerman

It is very difficult to awaken someone who is pretending to be asleep.
African proverb

Save us from single vision and Newton's sleep.
William Blake

INTRODUCTION

Coming Down From the Summit

Six years after the 1992 Rio Summit, it is perhaps time that we came down from the Earth Summit, and looked around at the landscape stretching out before us.[1] At the conceptual level, we see that 'sustainable development' has become enshrined as the working language for everyone from environmentalists to real-estate speculators. At the international level, environmental accords that were reached at Rio – the Climate Convention, the Biodiversity Convention and Agenda 21 (the extended blueprint for common international action) – have been ratified and are beginning to be incorporated into the international bureaucracy, not without some backing away from the original commitments. The international environmental movement is in substantial disarray, seemingly unable to rearticulate its vision into a new politics for the late 1990s. Nationally, environmental issues have taken a back seat to the problems of an economic system that is steadily diverging from the old certainties of growth as the promise of full employment and security for the middle class.

101

At the same time, the deterioration in the ecological conditions of life continues, masked by local improvements in some developed countries, while intensifying elsewhere. We are still faced with a number of problems:

- The extinction of upwards of 140 plant and animal species each day. There are observed declines in the global populations of amphibians, bird species (75 per cent of which are declining or threatened), primates (66 per cent of the world's species threatened with extinction).
- World human population is growing by over 90 million a year.
- 17 million hectares of forest are disappearing each year.
- The Antarctic ozone layer recorded its greatest extent of loss in spring 1995, with 40 per cent less ozone than in the 1960s.
- While the rate of increase of greenhouse gas emissions to the atmosphere has slowed slightly, the absolute contribution continues to grow (three billion tons a year). The warming trend, which was slowed for two years by the effects of the eruption of Mount Pinatubo, has reasserted itself.[2]

Before 1992, we might say that we were concerned that this kind of phenomenon was not being recognized by the international power structure. Now we are more concerned that these phenomena, though recognized, are being incorporated into a higher-order justification for the intensification of the status quo. One outcome of Rio, as we understand it, was that although NGOs had more influence on the process than at any previous effort, they were ultimately co-opted under the banner of 'sustainable development'. The environmental movement, which had characterized itself as operating from a set of assumptions that were fundamentally different from those of Western industrial society, found itself unable to be anything other than a mirror of its adversary, or turning out to be one more variant of the continuing internal critique of modernity.

The unexpected legacy of Rio was that mainstream interests have captured the debate about the future of the earth, and framed it for their own purposes. Among the most poignant examples of this was the ratification by the representatives of Southern countries of the Northern development model, which appears in the Rio Declaration as the highest principle of all, even before the environment (see Sachs 1993 for further discussion). Another legacy, which is currently being played out in the international negotiations around climate change and biodiversity, is a form of neo-ecological colonialism whereby technology transfer and joint implementation agreements between developed and developing countries are being instituted along the old power lines (for example the Netherlands and the old Dutch East Indies; the French and West Africa, and so on).

Ecology, Economy, Epistemology

These factors all suggest that the momentum of the current world economic dynamic is so powerful that it has been able to deflect or co-opt the opposition of the environmental movement, which, whatever its flaws, seemed to us to provide at least the possibility of a stronger critique of our situation than whatever else was on offer among the broken shards of the Left, the neo-Left, and the ironies of post-modernism.

Our suggestion – sketched out more fully in the rest of this chapter – is that one of the reasons for the weakness of the environmental critique has been that it did not go deep enough, and even that it lost its way fairly early in its progression. We believe that the relationship between the environment (the ecology) and the economy has been misconstrued by both the environmental movement and the practictioners of the economic order, and that this misconstruing is both a cause and a product of a flawed epistemology. In the next section of this chapter we begin by looking again at the critical issue of the relationship between the economic system and the ecological system. The role of the modern economic system, its epistemology and its method of integration are discussed. The practitioners of industrial order have managed to avoid wrestling with this relationship through the use of a number of rhetorical ploys, such as arguing that economic growth is the only method of obtaining enough resources to repair the damage caused by economic growth.

Below, drawing on Polanyi (Rotstein 1988) we argue that the 'self-regulating' market as a synthetic institution usurps all other forms of institution, and in so doing 'gives rise to new and unexpected phenomena proliferating as an autonomous network [and] acquires inadvertently a runaway existence'. It is therefore 'natural' that before Rio, Nature was categorized as a factor of production, as land, or resources. What is clear after Rio is that the environmentalist vision of a global ecosystem made it all the easier for Nature now to become categorized as a factor of *global* economic production.

We make the case here that Nature cannot be treated as a mere factor of production. Quite the reverse. The ecology generates the economy. Since the economy has been cut loose and has run roughshod over the ecology in recent times, we need to begin to re-embed the economic system within the ecology; and we argue that a start to this process of re-embedding begins with the retrenching or intelligent downsizing of the global economy, rather than the downsizing of the ecology. This retrenching goes against the imperatives of the economic system, and presents us with a series of novel conceptual challenges. However, failure to retrench will present us with some harsh physical consequences, of which the case study we present on the East Coast fisheries is only a Canadian example.

In the rest of this introduction we provide a background to the most difficult and controversial of our discussions, concerning the interplay of the ecological system, the economic system, and the epistemological issues at stake.

The Tightrope Walker

The economistic world view within which we live is so powerful that we have great difficulty in seeing past it to the ecological realities beyond. There are two different versions of this difficulty. One is that the unmodified ecological system of Nature is opposed to or unapproachable by human activities, because Nature and culture are separated by epistemological barriers. All that we can know is what we give ourselves as meaning. We are therefore licensed to 'develop' and modify Nature at will. This is the standard package of modernity, as handed down from Descartes, through Kant, and into contemporary theory and practice.

The second version – in some ways more insidious than the first – argues that the ecological system is actually or potentially continuous with the economic system. It can be redefined and redescribed economically in a way that will allow it to be managed and 'sustained' to meet our needs. It is a factor of production, or an 'externality' whose days external to the economy are numbered. It is this second version of how the economy and the ecology relate to each other that has gained substantial momentum in the debate over 'sustainable development', and bids to be taken seriously as an 'environmentally friendly' economics, or an 'economically friendly' environmentalism.

In this chapter, we set forward a third position. We argue that although the economy and the ecology are quite different systems, with many fundamental incompatibilities, the economic system is ultimately dependent upon the ecological system, and is wholly dependent on it for its continuation. We suggest that to deny this dependence, to ignore it, or to redefine it for purposes of later colonization are dangerous tendencies which imperil the sustainability of the economic system.

Polanyi noted that a disembedded economy, that is, an economic order whose elements are disembedded from their original multi-layered context – including the values associated with social justice – is always vulnerable to runaway escalation; because the dampening mechanisms required to control this runaway are no longer the rich, multiple reciprocities of social order, but a single quantitative measurement of social value: money.

By analogy, we suggest that there is a special danger in the continuing effort to replace or redirect ecological system characteristics by the disembedding of ecological forms of organization through the single valuation of market price, or by replacing natural systems with human-constructed substitutes. We argue that ecological systems are characterized by extremely complex weaves and cycles which not only adjust to each other but also re-enter their own domains in order to reproduce themselves as interconnected organized entities. We call this their *recursiveness*. Their recursive patterns are unknowable in detail, and likely to be unpredictable in perpetuity. Although human beings can cut into ecological recursion and construct some substitutes – for example humans are already harvesting for their purposes something like 40 per cent of the world's net primary productivity from land-based sources – these local successes lead us to believe that we have some managerial control over the complex cycles of ecological production. We are essentially stalemated by the problem that the signalling system of the economy (for example prices) and the signalling systems of the ecology are radically different.

To discuss what we may use to protect us against single valuations deriving from a 'single vision', we draw upon the work of Gregory Bateson and Niklas Luhmann, who have tried to articulate what it would mean to deal properly with two systems that are fundamentally discontinuous, and have different communicative structures. As we later discuss more fully, the communicative structure within which we as human beings operate does not allow us to speak directly to Nature, but only about Nature. Also, because of the way in which social systems operate, this kind of logic leads us into both ethical and epistemological traps that are impeding our ability to respond to the environmental dangers we face.

The socio-economic dynamic based on a 'single vision' of the gradual economization and rationalization of the earth renders us susceptible to 'Nature's revenge' – the convulsions of a natural system struggling away from our grasp. The most familiar example of this, as we go on to describe further, is the collapse of managed fisheries in Canada. The case illustrates the danger of the ecosystem as mere purveyor of a resource capable of being extracted for 'maximum sustainable yield'. The obsession with locking into a single number (or set of numbers) representing 'throughputted fish resource', however obtained, seems to have driven the ecosystem into wild oscillations as one element of it was forced to be held steady. This is rather like a tightrope walker who is forced to keep his or her balancing pole perfectly horizontal no matter what the wind or his or her own body motions may do. Rather than protect the walker, the fixation of the pole forces the walker to overcompensate, and fall.[3]

Similarly, market signals may propel decision makers in many arenas (not just fisheries) into harvesting the profits from a system that 'on paper' looks healthy, but is in fact on a downward ecological spiral. How this is possible – that is, how the market recasts and reduces social and ecological phenomena into economic indicators, and thereby removes itself from these other versions of reality – is the subject of our next section.

ECONOMY

With the coming of the industrial revolution, traditional economic life in all its social diversity was replaced by a powerful new social invention to match the steam engine and the power loom. The industrial revolution itself was rooted in the adoption of elaborate and expensive machinery along with new sources of power in order to produce the consumption goods of everyday life. The economy was recast into the autonomous network of institutions known as the self-regulating market economy. This reorganization of the

economy was at least as significant a factor in the subsequent ecological crisis as was the technological rush into steam engines and
the social creation of 'dark satanic mills'.

A bird's-eye view of economic life in the pre-industrial era may
throw the characteristic features of our present economic system
into high relief. Such a flashback may also help us to uncover a
long legacy of other forms of social and institutional arrangements
associated with economic activity other than the ones we have come
to accept as the norm.

Some simple propositions may help elucidate the crucial differences between the traditional and the modern economy. In the past,
the 'rules of the game' of economic life were typically subordinated to the goals and aspirations of the society, whether barter
trade or feudal; and to its main political authority, whether chief,
lord or monarch. The economic process was also at the behest of
the periodic obligations of religious rite and the intermittent ur-
gencies of war. The 'economy' as such was hardly distinguishable
as a discrete process or 'system' within its broad social milieu. 'Economic man' may have existed at the margin as merchant or banker
(surrounded by extensive regulations), but there had yet to appear
the stereotype that was to be emblematic of the market economy.
Such a traditional setting was best summed up in Karl Polanyi's
phrase that 'the economy was embedded in society'. Economic life
comprised a dense network of continuous transactions mandated
by the mutual obligations of social status.

Two general patterns stand out within this closely woven network. First were the unceasing rituals of give and take, the 'quid
pro quo' where goods moved back and forth between symmetri-
cally related individuals or groups. This economic pattern is known
as 'reciprocity', where personal status and its accompanying social
obligations govern the social and economic interchanges of daily
life. The 'transactions' within such a pattern turned on what was
appropriate to the occasion and the status of the transacting parties, rather than to the strict monetary or quantitative valuing and
balancing characteristic of the modern economy. Yesterday's good
turn was followed by today's reciprocal gesture: equals were – over
the shorter or longer term – exchanged for equals according to the
mutually understood local rules and expectations.

The second pattern of the pre-modern period consisted of the
flow of goods to the central political authority and the redistribution of these goods by a leader for recognized purposes of his own

or those of the larger society. For example, the acts of fiefdom performed by peasant and serf for the feudal lord included obligations of periods of unpaid labour and delivery of a specified share of the harvest. In return, the feudal lord was to protect his people from danger, but it was also expected that he would glorify his status role, dispense largesse, and otherwise act 'nobly' to sustain his fiefdom.

By contrast to these socially embedded patterns of reciprocity and redistribution, the principles and practices that underlie market activity have emerged in a sharp rupture with such a past. The economy has been cut loose from the many ties that bound it into the larger social fabric. The modern mode of economic operation has been articulated in highly sophisticated fashion by the discipline of economics. Several schools of thought contend with each other, and we can only address here the mainstream or neoclassical premises, ignoring more recent variants (we shall deal later with some Keynesian postulates).

We begin with what is assumed to be a certain cast of mind, which Max Weber summed up in the term, 'rationality'. Its practical application (following the economic theorist Menger) has become the fundamental axiom or existential premise (so to speak) of modern economics, known as the 'scarcity' postulate. In this view, it seems to be self-evident that there are not enough material goods in the world to give everyone as much as he or she would wish to have. Hence goods have to be partitioned in some orderly way, or 'allocated' among us, as economists are fond of saying. They must be rationed rationally.

In practice, this framework of thought emphasizes choice, and the range of choices in decision making based on achieving the optimum result from the alternatives at hand. Such choices have been highly refined by the process of measuring and quantifying all inputs into the economic process. The instruments of money and of accounting are able to equate with great precision diverse items that have no intrinsic connection with each other. This casts a wide net of rational calculation over the choices of all possible inputs.

It is further assumed in this process of choice, allocation, and reallocation that factor inputs are substitutable for each other based primarily on their relative cost and productivity. This creates a world of interchangeable bits and pieces that are constantly in flux in their combinations and recombinations.

At one master stroke, this shift from the broad give-and-take of social life to precise quantification and the exact 'balancing' of transactions between buyer and seller has dissolved the traditional economy and turned it on its head. Ecology, located broadly within this schema as the factor input, 'land', makes its appearance as an identical piece of the grand jigsaw puzzle open to the same manipulation as the other bits and pieces. Here lies the root of the ecological crisis.

The central institution of the modern economy, the market, plays a pragmatic role in coordinating and directing this flux of diverse inputs into the economic process. In due course it marshalls everything in accordance with the price signals it receives and transmits. Such markets for diverse goods and services combine together in linked and cellular fashion to create a network of markets or a market system that is in principle self-balancing or self-regulating through the signals sent by price fluctuations. Eventually this network covers the entire range of economic activities. Price changes act as a spur to, or a brake on producers and consumers respectively, and manage in the end to balance the entire economic system (at least in theory).

Monetization, apart from creating a 'relation' among the hitherto unrelated, depends in turn, as noted, on two prior features: a system of quantification of all factors of production (standard units of length, volume, and weight) and precision in recording these units for both accounting and production purposes. Quantification, precision, and monetization create, in aggregate, a distinct process or *modus operandi* that encompasses the operation of the entire economy.

When viewed from an ecological perspective, the cast of mind and the economic process sketched out here creates certain striking dissonances. The 'alchemical' or transformative power of money is the first feature that comes to mind. All goods and services have their price or monetary equivalent in a market economy, thereby creating an artificial common denominator for the most diverse or intrinsically unrelated items. This dissolves their specificity in an acid bath of 'equivalent monetary value': a woodlot is worth a new car is worth one-half of a child's education is worth two tickets to Bali.

This institutional process plays a further role in the realm that mainly concerns us here: the genesis of the ecological crisis. While we have already talked of the distinct process relating to the deployment of commodities in the economy, a further 'fiction' operates in a market economy. The factors of production – labour, land, and capital – are treated in the same way as the inanimate goods that are produced for sale, that is, the genuine commodities of everyday life. Yet 'labour' as such is inseparable from the person who is hired. Moreover these persons have certainly not, like commodities, been 'produced for sale'. Thus the market creates a pretence or fiction in treating labour as a commodity.

'Land', moreover, (using the term in the broadest sense to encompass the entire ecological system) has not been 'produced' at all, and is devoid of any real basis for its status as a commodity on the market. Labour and land are the abstract names attached to people and their habitat – the two basic ingredients of community – but they are treated in a market economy as if they were indeed genuine commodities like all the others. (Polanyi refers to them as 'fictitious commodities'.) At the margin, all factors are indiscriminately regarded as substitutable for each other in the search for the mix that would produce the optimum output.

This equation of the unlike through monetization serves as the basis for mobilizing a modern economy: the drive for efficiency or increasing productivity cannot be achieved without these central features. But the artificiality of such a process comes sharply into view when contrasted with the indigenous processes of the natural or biological world – the world in which we are required to survive.

The rational (and even ethical) drive for efficiency means that economic analysis focuses on the allocation problem to the exclusion of other issues that are deemed to be 'external' to the economist's world. So for example, we find that the role of economic analysis in the international negotiations over what to do about climate change and biodiversity is to redescribe issues of justice, equity and the possible undermining of earth support systems in terms of cost/benefit analysis.

While there is nothing wrong with determining what is the best use of scarce resources, there is also no route from this kind of analysis to raising the question of what to do about a culture of rational monetization! Issues of overconsumption of natural resources, the lack of real choice, the global maldistribution of resources, and so on, are described as 'givens' and are not a normal part of the official discussion.

It is at this point that the environmentalist (and the non-neoclassical economist) begins to make his or her entry on the scene as an alternative voice.

ECOLOGY: THE CRISIS OF THE ENVIRONMENTAL MOVEMENT

The changing role of the environmentalist and the environmental movement provides another important entry point for some of the themes of this chapter. The modern environmental movement began in the 1960s as a hybrid between old-fashioned conservationism and a new sensitivity to a hitherto unnoticed victim of industrialization, i.e. the natural world. Except by romantic analogy, this new victim did not easily fit into the standard political categories of either Left or Right, although environmentalists quite early took on board parts of the New Left agenda of the late 1960s.[4]

Beginning in the late 1960s environmental organizations began to appear on the national and international scene as part of a proliferation of NGOs. Historically, the interplay between the international, national, regional and local organizations was somewhat complicated. Roughly speaking, in the 1960s there were a number of national and international institutions that were quite conservative and narrow in their focus (for example World Wildlife Fund, Sierra Club) but which provided a seedbed within which a larger movement could find language and models for emulation. A myriad of smaller organizations grew up within the shadow of these larger groups, and the larger groups were in turn altered by the issues and visions of what had become a mainstream cultural force.

By the 1990s the smaller local, regional, and national groups had joined into uneasy coalitions with their larger partners on the international scene, and were pressing for major changes to the international landscape. As noted in the introduction, the Rio Earth Summit represented a high-water mark in that effort, which has since become stalled. Environmental organizations, especially in developed countries, have been unable to sustain and build upon their earlier successes, in spite of the mounting evidence of a fundamental deterioration in the conditions of global environmental well-being. This is in part due to the lack of responsible and responsive political structures at the global level to which the populist base of environmental concern can apply pressure – real power to mandate serious change still resides (if at all) in the senior environmental groups, with their access to the corridors of international diplomacy. One problem with these senior groups is that, as they have become more successful and have themselves necessarily become bureaucratized, the tension between their radical roots (as well as their grassroots constituencies) and their contemporary influence as lobbyists and knowledge brokers has grown.

Simultaneously, certain conceptual contradictions within the environmental movement have now come out in the open. Among these contradictions, we can single out the already mentioned uneasy mix of political and philosophical sources to be found in early Green politics. In particular, we can single out New Left politics and the general background of nineteenth-century romanticism.

First, New Left politics, like all modern political theories, has an inherent bias towards metaphors of progressive development. We can locate the origins of these metaphors in the potent mingling of images of biological development with the idea of incessant improvement of industrial processes at the turn of the nineteenth century. This romanticism of progress can be seen at its most potent in the simultaneous Gothic delight and horror at the spectral processes of capitalist development as painted in Marx's *Das Kapital*.[5]

Second, because of the direct poetic heritage of romanticism that feeds into environmental thought, environmentalists have regarded a kind of individualist wilderness experience as foundational. In the United States, this has fed into a social-anarchic politics which can as easily be right wing as left, such as barricading oneself into a pure mountain fortress.[6] It has also complicated relations with 'Third World' environmental and development organizations which operate from quite different principles. In Canada, for example, some environmentalists who are advocates of an intensely pure wilderness life clash with native peoples whose relationship with Nature is more casual and negotiable, yet remains profoundly spiritual as well.

Third, this romantic heritage of 'oneness with Nature' presents us with the other side of the economy erasing the separateness of the ecology: the environmentalist vision very easily slips into using the ecology to erase the economy. The unifying thrust of 'ecological oneness' is as imperial as the economistic interpretation of 'sustainable development'. Not only does this often hamper the 'green political' handling of the complexities of human social interaction; but it has also made it hard for environmentalists to engage with contemporary cultural theory and practice. The predominant view of 'culture' and 'nature' presupposes that there is a barrier or filter between ourselves and the natural world, without agreeing on the characteristics of that boundary – where it comes from (consciousness, intelligence, or technology?) and what it entails. In this and the following section, we offer an extensive discussion of this very point.

It has therefore hitherto been very difficult for the environmental movement to articulate more effectively (for instance through the example of environmental deterioration) how this situation relates to the inchoate global concern of many people for the overall trajectory of current development patterns. In part this is because there is something of a contradiction in developing a globally unified vision of protecting global diversity. There have indeed been recent complaints (from postmodernists such as Jean-Francois Lyotard) that 'saving the planet' is merely the flip side of global corporatism, and derives from a similar drive to create a single narrative structure within which all future diversity will have to operate.

Of the important narrative forms to which environmentalists do subscribe, sustainability is obviously the most familiar, and something of a meta-narrative. It is not simply that there is a commitment to keep 'the story of life on earth' going; but more profoundly, there is a commitment to keep the capacity for generating new stories available in this place called earth. This narrative form has within it a spiralling rhythm of ethically open recursion, best captured in the old Biblical phrase: 'Seedtime and harvest shall not fail'.

It is this recursive ethical rhythm that may be more radical than the usual calls for 'sustainable development', because it brings into the foreground the fact that natural systems have quite different operating rules than economic systems – and presumably different replacement times, investment rules, and so on (speaking in the language of natural-resource accounting); all of which need to be respected and their integrity maintained. As we point out in the next section, the signalling system is also quite different between the ecology and the economy, and requires a different epistemology to respond appropriately to these patterns of difference.

Environmentalists have, however, been unable to articulate this epistemology. Another contributing factor to environmentalist disarray is the ambiguous theoretical development of the discipline of ecology, which has been very susceptible to being co-opted by the social model of the day. For instance, in the 1950s and 60s, the most famous ecological models (by the brothers Odum) were deliberately patterned on the economic market, even to the point where energy was seen to be the equivalent of cash flowing through the system (see Rapport and Turner 1977 for a promotional review of this process).

Where then should we look for the sources of a renewed environmentalism? One potential basis for such a revival would be the return to the earliest sources of the movement's strength, before it became hostage to professionalization and managerialism. Of special importance is the fact that one of the early threads of the environmental movement, which became mislaid during the 1970s, was the drive to reduce what may be called 'threats to the intimate' associated with the infiltration of radiation, DDT and other micro-poisons into natural and human systems. These threats were simultaneously brought to public consciousness in 1962–3 by the movement towards an international test ban treaty, and by Rachel Carson's *Silent Spring*. These unsettling threats re-emerged again in the late 1980s with the breakthrough of concerns over species loss, ozone depletion, and climate change. These global threats to the underlying fabric of life have coincided with a myriad of new ways in which risks to the local integrity of the person are appearing, ranging from health risks to human genome research.

An important new threat is the movement of 'information' into a central metaphoric role in our culture. A widespread, understudied phenomenon is what the sociologist Anthony Giddens has called 'disembedding mechanisms' for an emerging bio-industrial complex. He argues that embedded or embodied information (such as traditional practices or genetic codes) is being leveraged out of its original context, translated into symbolic tokens, and thereby made universally available as 'information' for exploitation. An interesting current example of this is the Human Genome Diversity Project, which is supposed to be taking samples of all the relevant racial strains of humanity for storage in gene banks.[7] This use of 'information' is the latest incarnation of the infinite substitutability we saw come to life in the market system.

Our sense is that one of the most unsettling aspects of globalization is the threat to personal uniqueness, first brought about by the turning of the person into a commodity (i.e. labour, as described above); and now more profoundly into a form of usable disembedded information, which is, in turn, the new commodity of commodities. One other locus then, for environmental revisioning, is the exploration of 'threats to the intimate' to probe this new range of global threats with local impacts, thus moving beyond the stale formulation of 'Think globally, act locally'.

EPISTEMOLOGY

The Problem of Levels

Managerial environmentalism is based on a belief in the precisely calculable dyanamics of the relationship of economic activity to ecological degradation. Linked to the economic world view we have already sketched out it further believes in the continuing substitutability of resources, artificial for natural, on the occasions when human activity depletes the latter. But this continuousness or seamlessness is challenged by (among other things) the myriad examples of discontinuity in ecological systems, scenarios of 'flip' in ecological stabilities – the wild oscillations on the tightrope we have already described.

A good place to begin critical enquiry is at the boundaries – or interface – of the conjoined ideas inherent in the phrase 'sustainable development' and ask whether (or to what extent) the *order* of ecology (sustainable) and the *order* of economy (development) can, in fact, be conjoined or balanced.

Immediate questions arise. In what ways are these orders comparable? If comparable, what are the characteristic patterns of their interface? If the two orders are in some ways incompatible, does the managerial framework put forward in Agenda 21 (and elsewhere) have a fateful blindspot? Management theories of knowledge are well equipped with models and scenarios about a 'balance of factors' approach to sustainable development, but are generally not equipped to deal with the implications of 'levels of order' or 'metalevel' approaches.

Meanwhile, among the most radical 'Deep Green' environmentalists there is clear understanding of levels of order between ecology and economy, and a clear comprehension that Nature is 'meta-' to the economic order. This has been the principal statement of all Deep Greens, and they are unified around this general principle (Naess and Rothenberg 1989). The most notable characteristics of the meta-order – its interconnectedness, its autonomy, its quality of emergence, its self-production – become the way through which human economy must become restructured. The conclusions that these environmentalists draw from such an ecological perspective are, however, open to question.

The problems arise in translation of some of the characteristics of Nature's order to economy and society. Generalization 'down' –

that is from the characteristic forms and processes of Nature to formulations about optimization – leads to as many false trails as generalization 'up' – managerial theories translating principles of economic order to ecological order. In the 1980s, for example, there was a brief flurry of excitement around the social and political possibilities inherent in Varela and Maturana's concept of *autopoiesis*, that is, the way in which living organisms 'bootstrap' themselves at a molecular level and constitute viable organizations through their own 'self-production'.[8] Both authors (Maturana and Varela 1980) carefully noted that the phenomenon of *autopoiesis* could be satis-factorily translated to premises about language and cognition, but they were not prepared to say anything about the translation of their notions to society or politics. The response of others such as Edgar Morin, to *autopoiesis*, was far less careful (Morin 1977, 1980); and a number of authors began to claim that Maturana and Varela's cybernetic notions of self-production, and of autonomy through self-organization, were fundamental to social interaction, social order, politics and economy (Dobuzinskis 1987, provides a survey of this literature).

Notions of biological autonomy – parts that mutually specify them-selves – are particularly attractive to Deep Greens. Though Maturana and Varela occupy only a small slot in the Deep Green literature because their cybernetics is complicated, the demonstration of bio-logical order as self-productive and self-organizing through its interconnectedness articulates a key notion in the Deep Green 'ecocentric vision' or Deep Ecology. Thus, in Deep Ecology, Na-ture has its own characteristic structures and potentialities to un-fold. Human beings, unaccustomed to look at the *telos* of Nature as anything other than as an extension of human *telos*, fail to see Nature's intrinsic values. Instead humans adopt an ideology of chauvinism or, perhaps, human imperialism, to account for their apparent control of natural wealth.

The *telos* principle in Nature serves as a basic reason for the Deep Greens' respectful treatment of natural entities and natural systems. The very recognition of a different *telos* in Nature sup-ports their view that Nature has an array of intrinsic qualities which exist in addition to any *telos* derived by humans concerning their own agency. It also provides a criterion for alternative courses of permissable action in an uncertain universe. That is, the guiding value of a Deep Green vision must be the productive optimization of good ecological effects. An ecocentric sensibility always seeks to optimize those qualities that enhance interdependency and mutual constraint in ecological order. When priorities must be set by environmentalists working to protect Nature against the bulldozer and the chain saw, the priorities that must prevail are the intrinsic qualities of ecological order in support of sustaining Nature's *telos* – integrity, stability, diversity (Rodman 1995, pp. 253, 254).

Nevertheless, it is precisely at this point, when Deep Ecology promotes conversion from the perspectives of industrial production in market economies to a new ecological order, that epistemological difficulties arise. For the ecocentric perspective is locked into its own conundrum about the specification of intrinsic qualities. If all biological organization is autonomous, self-organizing and self-productive, that is, what we have called *recursive*; and if we as humans are part of this recursive system of life (in other words part of a natural *telos*), how can we know that what we are doing in destroying the so-called 'intrinsic qualities' of Nature is something other than just being part of a self-perpetuating organization of the production of the living? In short, how can any recursive system provide the means for evaluating its own recursive properties of life and death, stability and degradation? This is a more sophisticated version of the old dilemma that either whatever human beings do is natural, because we are ourselves creatures of Nature; or alternatively, that our consciousness separates us fundamentally from the natural order.

Surely the worst answers that any Deep Green ecologist could provide for the evaluation of how human beings should evaluate their interference with Nature would be along the lines that recognition of intrinsic qualities is self-evident or that human beings have a genetic propensity to recognize beauty – and thus intrinsic qualities – of natural order.[9] This is an argument from a distorted aesthetics or a misapprehended idea of the sacred. And, as Gregory Bateson pointed out, with our known historical capacity for supporting pathologies about gods and national characteristics, what guarantee do we have that there can be no pathological disturbances in aesthetics? Pathologies of culture will promote pathologies of aesthetic perception which in turn generate monsters of aesthetic creation (Bateson 1991, pp. 253–7), like Hitler's turning Germany into a theatre of blood.

Ecology as Communicative Order

An important step towards a better understanding of the human-ity/Nature interface was achieved by Gregory Bateson, and by the German sociologist Niklas Luhmann. The latter drew heavily on the Maturana-Varela theses for his conclusions.[10] Both Bateson and Luhmann explore how, and under what conditions, society can come to a recognition of environmental danger given its tangential at-tachment to its ecological surroundings. That is, from the perspec-tive of ecological communication, society holds a very peculiar 'mirror' up to Nature. Humanity is not able to communicate directly with Nature, any more than it is able to manage Nature. Society can only ascribe and communicate to itself what it perceives as en-vironmental signals about change, or environmental degradation. It can only communicate *about* its environment within itself, no more than this – for 'more' would violate the condition of its own autonomy. But these signals are internal to the communication system itself. How then do they 'reach out' beyond the bounds of culture?

Bateson employs a memorable metaphor to describe the sort of knowledge that the peculiar 'mirror' does in fact permit. He dis-tinguishes between a sighted and a blind person (Bateson quoted in Harries-Jones, 1995, p. 52):

> A seeing man on entering a room will use his eyes to obtain spot-for-spot images of what is in the room. The blind man, us-ing wind currents and echoes, will get much of the 'same' infor-mation but in very different form. If a sofa has been moved to a new position under the window since the last time he visited the room, the *difference* between the room then and the room now will be perceptible to him, wherever he is in the room
>
> Bateson, cited in Harries-Jones, 1995

These differences are non-locatable – that is, they are not any-where; they are the registering of the change where something was and is not any more – and are not registered by sighted individ-uals. But the systemic properties of non-locatability within a system of differences make it possible for the blind person to learn about the system of which he or she is a part and to detect change within it. But this can only occur recursively over time, that is, the blind person must enter the room twice. Similarly, Bateson argues that we can never step into the river of experience once. All communication looks as if we are registering things for the first time, but in fact information is the perception and registering of *patterns* of differences.

But does this solve the problem of internal self-referencing? Bateson and Luhmann suggest that this kind of communication – the registering of patterns of differences through their recursion – is the only available form that simultaneously permits communication within one system, and is yet able to retain and detect the differences of the other with which it is conjoined as part to whole.

Applying this to ecological evolution, Bateson and Luhmann would argue as follows: if recursive forms were realized *only* as physical embodiments of the process of evolution, that is, as specific objects – trees, tigers, lakes – we are presented with the spectacle of humanity as wandering on its perverse maladaptive journey through a world of changing ecological settings, as if history were a play in which a new painted backdrop is occasionally rolled down for each act. But if both ecology and ecological evolution are regarded as ongoing communicative processes about 'adaptation', and not just physical processes, then, in addition to physical embodiments of adaptation we must consider adaptive and maladaptive communicative embodiments as well.[11] Says Luhmann (1988):

> The theory of self-referential systems [in ecological communication] alone has realized that the classical instruments of the acquisition of knowledge, namely deduction (logic) and causality (experience) are merely forms of simplifying self-observation. Methodologically, this means that the point of departure has to be the observation of self-observing systems and not the assumed ontologic of causality.

This means that our ideas of causality – I push this and it moves – are actually precipitates of our sense of the world as a collection of objects and not as systems of relations, mediated by the communication of differences. Recognition of this should effect all classical instruments for the acquisition of knowledge. The direction in which an epistemology of ecological communication leads is towards investigation of the communicative gap between humanity and Nature, and to the formal aspects of intercommunication across this 'gap' or discontinuity. The objective of this approach is to have a clearer perspective of what processes actually constitute the distinctions between social systems and the environment of which it is a part and how we do – or rather do not – monitor these.[12]

In his 1989 work, *Ecological Communication*, Luhmann argued that one cause of the failure of the environmental movement has been that it subscribes to a set of fixed moral and ethical rules that derive from the 'ontologic of causality'. This underestimates the variety of the environmental movement – surely a Taoist approach would not be too far from an ecological epistemology, and there are many environmental Taoists. Nevertheless, the movement was driven originally by a more complex response to environmental issues than became the case more recently as some NGOs moved into mirroring management.

One familiar way in which this 'ontologic of causality' appears in dealing with the management of environmental issues has been the problems associated with updating the Anglo-Saxon legal systems where cause-effect relationships of harm must be proved. This approach worked well in the 1970s and 80s when it was easy to find 'point-source' polluters, and to separate out polluters from pollutees. But an issue like climate warming due to greenhouse gas emissions is different, since in this case the question arises: Who are we to indict? There are, of course, energy barons and others who could be cited; but essentially we are dealing with a situation where the polluters and the pollutees are the same people. Virtually every activity in modern society adds to the greenhouse gas burden.

In 1988, following the ontologic of causality the nations of the world signed an agreement to eliminate chlorofluorocarbons from industrial processes, in order to protect the ozone hole. Because there were only nine manufacturers of CFCs in the world, it was fairly easy to make this accord work, and it has in fact gone from strength to strength. It was optimistically expected that the same kind of process could be used for climate change, and in 1992, at the Rio Summit, a similar accord was reached. However, in this case, the ontologic of causality has been hopelessly stymied by the fact that one is dealing with an all-pervasive systemic issue. There is no single causal mechanism. This has bedevilled all attempts to develop a consistent and coherent strategy for dealing with greenhouse gas emissions.

This is the kind of pervasive, systemic issue which illuminates what we see as the struggle to come up with a new way of responding to the challenge of 'Nature's Veto'.

The Case of the Fish Wars

We are able to cite a dramatic example of the failure of the 'ontologic of causality' in the case of the recent round of 'fish wars' off the coast of Canada. This example also confirms our notion of signal failure – that is, perversities which arise because of failure to understand both the disjunction of principles governing economic performance *vis-à-vis* ecological order, and yet that they remain in a joint communicative relationship.

These 'fish wars' flared between Canada and the European Union, together with Spain, in March of 1995; and also between Canada and Alaska a few months later. While Canada argued for the need to limit turbot fishing off the Grand Banks in order to save the species' existence, both the Spanish ambassador and the European Union retaliated by calling Canada 'pirates' because the Canadians were boarding foreign trawlers outside their 200-mile jurisdiction. In other words, territorial limitation of jurisdiction on the high seas was morally prior, in the view of Spain and the European Union, to any argument about species' survival.

The 'fish war' phenomenon is becoming global and the fishing industry around the world is *en route* to producing a total breakdown of marine ecosystems. International treaties over fishing quotas face breakdown every fishing season, the most recent example being that of Northwest coastal salmon in North America. As the Alaska-Canada salmon disputes demonstrate, the problem is not simply that of taking too many fish, but of fishing in a depleted ecological setting where salmon cannot thrive. What happens to spawning grounds in dammed-up rivers, and in clear-cut forests next to rivers, and to river-water pollution and to the temperature of the water, is as much a part of 'overfishing' as the actual trawlers out at sea, fishermen, and their wall of nets.

A total collapse of the sea fishery, let alone marine ecosystems, will be devastating, since fish is the major source of protein for more than one billion people in East and South East Asia, and one fifth of the people on the continent of Africa. And that total collapse is a very distinct possibility. The United Nations Food and Agriculture Organization (FAO) warned in 1996 that nine of the world's 17 major fishing grounds had been devastated by overfishing with four more under serious threat. So, the oceans are stretched to the breaking point. This is so despite the puzzling fact that the 'economics' of fishing leading to this state of affairs makes no economic sense.

The term commonly used during the Canada-Spain crisis was 'overfishing' or 'overexploitation'. But this is a euphemism. 'Overfishing' leads us to believe that if fishery 'management' is implemented globally, through treaties creating quotas for fish of all species, this will provide a 'solution' to the problem of overfishing. In fact owners of the world's trawler fleets are happily engaged in a madhouse economics of too many boats chasing too few resources; fishers their employees do not care about conservation of resources and will catch any sort of fish, immature along with adult. This state of affairs is subsidized by national governments, and governments subsidizing the fishing fleets are reluctant to stop overfishing because there are too many vested interests at stake. Thus an eighteenth-century notion of national vested interests, unevenly supported by rationales of twentieth-century notions of 'ecological management', frames discourse in the sea-fleet fishing industry.

Sea-fleet fishing is being accompanied, in turn, by massive economic debts in the fishing industry. Instead of debt discouraging further fishing, it seems to be triggering even more frenetic activity. The FAO estimates that in 1992 the global fishing industry was subsidized to the tune of $54 billion and yet still managed to lose $50 billion. Almost half (46 per cent) of the income from the catch that the fishing fleets did manage to pull in was spent paying back capital investment on the costly high-tech super trawlers – fish factories (*Guardian Weekly*, 15 April 1995, p. 8).

In Newfoundland, to which we will pay particular attention, the major events leading to the crisis of 'overfishing', that is the killing-off of Northern Cod, were accomplished in the name of conservation by the Canadian ministry responsible for 'fisheries development' (Finlayson 1994). So-called conservation began in the years 1977–89 after Canada extended its zone of jurisdiction on the high seas to 200 miles beyond its territorial shores. The Canadian government believed that it was applying expert management principles to the cod fishery, based on scientifically accurate assessments of stock abundance in the cod fishery.

If asked during these years how those estimates were arrived at, marine fishery scientists and bureaucrats at the Department of Fisheries and Oceans would have agreed that estimates were based on 'fish mortality'. If asked how they estimate fish mortality, they would have said that they made estimates through fish catch. And if asked how that data was obtained, they would have replied that their largest source of data is from the commercial fishery. In the commercial fishery fish catch is reported by weight, and weight is converted into estimates of biomass. As Finlayson reports, the management task was to ensure that there was no sharp drop in biomass from year to year. By this means, the Federal DFO had convinced itself that there were increases in the annual rate of growth of cod, as much as 15 per cent annual rate of growth during the 1980s, in spite of increased fishing effort on the part of high-tech trawlers (Finlayson 1994, p. 42ff).

In fact, cod was being fished at levels which ensured its precipitous decline. In 1989 an independent review panel on the state of the Northern Cod fishery reported this fact,[13] but it took three years before the Minister of Fisheries declared a temporary ban on commercial fishing for Northern Cod. The temporary moratorium was then lengthened to an indefinite moratorium in 1994. The 1989 report noted that while the use of weight of catch configured as biomass was a common and accepted global practice for virtually all fish stocks, this choice to treat stock as biomass was fallacious for a number of reasons. The most obvious is that 200 000 10 kg fish have the same biomass as one million 2 kg fish, although the two equations have very different implications for fish population. Essentially what happened was that the system became reoriented around and locked into a single set of numbers representing the predicted flow-through of 'fish resources': what was important was maintaining the numbers – how they were achieved and at what levels of intensity was irrelevant.

The management of fish 'resources' also proceeded from the perspective of assumed causal relations between the intervention of technology and the size of the stock of fish. These were related to an accounting device, the economists' inflation-corrected discount rate. Even at a minimal level, treating fish as part of a living ecology instead of a discounted financial figure would have brought a host of other factors into perspective such as cod migratory patterns, a highly variable physical environment, the numbers of young fish annually recruited to the stock, and incompletely known interactions among different species occupying similar territories, for example harper seals and cod. Moreover, it is hardly ever recognized that the term 'maximum sustainable yield', which has 'sustainable' in it, depends upon a whole range of assumptions of interference with the natural system. The simplest example is that the removal of one year's harvest of fish is often predicated on the assumption that the remaining fish will over-reproduce to replace the missing fish. This is designed to pump the ecosystem towards producing a higher surplus ('the maximum sustainable yield'), and this emergency replacement is then taken to be the new norm.

Taken together, the whole parade of mistaken assumptions acted to maximize the rate of extinction of Northern Cod and produce a runaway 'tragedy of the commons' in the seas off Newfoundland. At the height of the 'fish war' an unnamed British mandarin of fish stock management was quoted as saying:

> Officially, I would say that the UN and Europe are working hard to manage fish stocks better and that we'll come up with the answer in time . . . Privately, I think it's all over . . . We'll fish the seas out, then – when there is nothing left – we will sit back and consider the folly of our ways while we wait for 10 or twenty years for stocks to recover.   *Guardian Weekly,* 10/5/95:8.

The mandarin's comments could be taken as the sort of cynicism expected from diplomats were it not for the panoply of advice stemming from models about 'best harvesting strategies' that led to this barren statement.

In *Nature* two groups of authors ponder the dynamics of species extinction, and the mistaken assumptions that continue to increase rates of liquidation of species, including fish. For one author, what is called 'overexploitation' in the jargon of the accountants, that is inflation-corrected discount rates on an annual or periodic basis, is 'the cited cause of endangerment for about one third of the plants and animals on the Red List' (May 1994, p. 43).

For the other authors, the surprising conclusion of their research is that if population and environmental factors are taken into account in forecasting models, and incorporated into models of harvesting strategies, the use of discount rates leads to even more devastating results than before. From a purely economic perspective, acknowledgement of variation in population levels or of natural environmental fluctuation (environmental and demographic stochasicity) in a situation in which the overall catch is declining evokes a 'rational' economic response to liquidate the stock in a much quicker period of time. The only possible conclusion, they say, is that 'for the common good, economic discounting should be avoided in the development of optimal strategies for sustainable use of biological resources' (Lande, Engen and Saether 1994, p. 89).

Consider what happened in Newfoundland. Decisions by entrepreneurs of the fishing fleet were based on their own discounting
of future returns in the increasingly difficult process of harvesting
fish. For the captains of the fleet both Canadian and non-Canadian,
the 'optimal' result, the greed of present value, was to cash in the
entire stock of Northern Cod and invest realized capital elsewhere.
As the difficulties of harvesting fish in overfished waters increased,
so 'a tragedy of the commons' emerged on a massive scale. Lande,
Enge and Saether argue that an alternative harvesting strategy is
required that sets discount rates to zero and at the same time recognizes the necessity for high variance in annual harvest. Thus a
more 'optimal' outcome would include frequent years of no harvest.[14]

Though Lande, Enge and Saether on the one hand, and May on
the other, are too careful to say it, they have sketched an end game:
the absolute necessity for a global institutional response that cannot, in fact, be put into place. That is why we argue that social and
political policy has to rid itself of its reliance on the 'ontologic of
causality' represented so profusely in the economistic forecasting
of exploitation of ecological resources. Ecological 'solutions' are
primarily epistemological. The case of the fish underlines this: what
happened was a failure to understand the type of relation between
the two orders – the economy and the ecology – and the paralysis
of survival chances which always occurs following such communicative failure.

It is imperative to stop ecological systems from being radically
redescribed and foreshortened to conform to the signalling mechanisms of the market. Further, we must abandon, because we have
to abandon, fallacious suppositions of how we can control ecosystems.
We now *know* – even by statistical measurements – that fallacies
of control result in 'harvesting strategies' that drive ecosystems crazy.
Is it 'rational' to pursue an economics of extinction?

Instead we must begin with an alternative epistemology. Humanity
must have a clear understanding that the recursive patterning of
ecological systems are unknown now and unpredictable in perpetuity.
And we live within a larger ecological system, many of whose processes are beyond us and of which we are only part. We must begin
with these characteristics of ecology of living forms and treat them
ecologically, as a multi-level phenomenon. The 'solution' is not an
immediate sojourn in the nearest monastery, Buddhist, Christian
or otherwise. On the contrary, following Bateson, it require us to
take seriously issues those premises about ourselves that we have

previously categorized as belonging to the realm of the transcendent, the 'sacred', and therefore untouchable (Harries-Jones 1995, pp. 212–34). Among the most important of these issues to think about are those of self-reference flowing from the recursiveness of ecological order. We are both the fishers and the fished-out.

Summary

To summarize this section, our epistemological approach emphasizes the discontinuity between ecology and economy, rather than the continuity and balance as emphasized in the concept of 'sustainable development', and put into operation by managerial environmentalists. We have argued that the alternative, recognition of the discontinuity in the two orders, does not necessarily produce solutions. Indeed there are still great problems translating this notion of discontinuity of levels, and the subsequent inversion of levels of order (in other words, putting the economy back inside the ecology), into appropriate social models. And, we have noted, Deep Green social movements may have erred in their translation of ecological concepts into viable social ones.

Nevertheless our approach offers a new perspective which may draw together some important but scattered observations about ecology and economy within a coherent overall framework of understanding. For example, we may note the following 'differences that make a difference' in ecology and ecosystems:

- Ecological order derives from limits and these limits are an important characteristic of viability or sustainability; the economic order recognizes no limitations of this kind – it believes that if it does not continue to grow, and instead cuts back and retreat, the economic order will be destroyed.
- The differences of production and consumption in the ecological and economic orders are such that while economic activity renders ecological activity more fragile, ecological activity adds robustness to ecosystems. In the throughput of an ecological order every 'consumer' transforms or recycles biological 'waste' into food. There is very little waste in an ecological system. A second loop recycles biological entropy into potential for self-reproduction.

To conclude: if the interface of ecology and economy reveals fundamental discontinuities of order, joined only through the special characteristics of recursive communication, then the notion of balance inherent in 'sustainable development' is a falsely constructed expectation. We can provocatively ask if the alternative agenda put forward by environmental NGOs provides a better recognition of possible discontinuities than the agenda of the various United Nations organizations established to support sustainable development?

CIRCLING THE SQUARE: THE CASE FOR DOWNSIZING THE ECONOMY

Instead of the continuity that is usually assumed or is pretended to exist in the relationship between ecology and economy, we have been examining the inherent discontinuity that exists between them. The urgent challenge for an ongoing industrial society is to find some new *modus vivendi* between the two. This looms as one of the major challenges of the twenty-first century. When these spheres operate as they do in such completely different modes, rhythms, and time horizons, it is not clear how a modern industrial society can synchronize its frenetic, escalating existence with natural and biological cycles.

As mentioned already, the pre-industrial world had its legendary 'seedtime and harvest' to designate the agricultural economy's 'natural' cycle – its annual *rites de passage*, that offered the prospect of an economy more closely tied to or integrated with its ecology. These seasonal rhythms and its natural-resource endowments were supportive of and woven into the traditional forms of socio-economic integration referred to earlier, such as reciprocity and redistribution. While we may yearn for some vanished past, we cannot return to it if we wish to remain committed to some form of industrial society. Although a new relationship between ecology and economy is required, we can hardly at the moment frame the questions properly, let alone set down a successful formula for mutual coexistence.

As we begin to come to grips with this issue, we are at least compelled into some form of 'damage control', so as to forestall further deterioration of plant and animal species, forests, the ozone layer, and so on. The new social models we have discussed in the previous section will have to be developed within the context of the existing economic framework within which industrial economies operate. The problem is akin to rebuilding the foundation of our house while continuing to live in it; or, more drastically, rehulling a boat while it is foundering on the high seas.

The outstanding commitment or set of objectives that come to us through Keynesian economics, is to full employment, moderate price stability, and moderate economic growth. In the light of the actual performance of the global economy in the past decade and a half, some might be led to believe that with the process of sputtering expansion and of 'jobless growth', the economy has taken a sharp turn in the road. From time to time, we have had shrinking economies in countries such as Canada, more of course by default than by deliberation. We have directed the increasingly constrained resources of economic policy to a rearguard effort to bolster our economic performance, with sporadic and modest success. Yet we keep exponential economic growth before us as our increasingly nostalgic target.

However, in light of the challenge to global ecosystems, it may be time to face the other way and look at some variant of the 'downsizing' of the entire global industrial apparatus – particularly on the eve of the anticipated Chinese industrial boom to be fuelled by the burning of soft coal. We may have come to the threshold of tolerance of the global ecosystem to sustain in the twenty-first century the pattern of industrial commitment and ecological depredation of the past two centuries.

But the difficulties of abandoning the familiar course and embarking on a radically new one are almost as daunting as the ecological threat that we wish to avoid. Downsizing the economy is not simply a matter of all of us making do with less. The blunt fact is that we have no experience in the systematic reorganization of an industrial economy geared to producing less in a controlled and coordinated fashion. Such a step, if it is not well considered, may put the entire industrial apparatus as well as the social institutions we have developed at risk. We can do little more here than list some of the issues at stake.

The discipline of economics, with its mandate to 'optimize' or to 'maximize' should in principle be reversible, so as to encompass the objective of downsizing the economy in an orderly and efficient fashion. For example, the factor 'mix' (of land, labour, and capital) can be readjusted so as to produce an optimum in a new set of circumstances where one of these factors is restricted. After the mix is altered in favour of, say, selective conservation, with perhaps an orderly decline in total production as well, we would be doing 'less with less'; but in such a way as to obtain the maximum benefit from this diminished productive process – in other words, the optimal shrinking path. We could also make provision for economic casualties and other accompanying costs of retrenchment.

What is more difficult to deal with is the incentive structure for the main players, such as the private firm or the large corporation. If, for example, through reduced 'quotas' of production there were reduced profits or indeed losses due to high fixed overhead costs, there would be little incentive for the private sector to make new investments in plant or equipment or even to refurbish what has depreciated.

At the aggregate level, a sharp decline in private investment may exert a series of accelerating downward pressures on the economy. The cumulative effects of declining incomes and declining employment may initiate cascades of economic and social dislocation which it may be difficult to contain. The question is whether these will become haphazard, random events, or whether this process can be mapped out and guided properly with adequate techniques for damage control and compensation for the victims. The specifics of such an economic plan and its financing will have to be left to a later discussion. Significant discrimination between industries which exact a greater burden on our ecological system will have to be made. Likewise, geographic regions will have differential impacts and environmental pressures, and may have to be treated differently.

It should be stressed that the 'downsizing' we are advocating is a response to the pathological trends in the present system of global ecological management. In the first instance, it is a strategy for giving the environment more breathing room to absorb our demands and maintain some of its own integrity. Ultimately we consider 'downsizing' as preceding the implementation of one of the numerous varieties of 'steady' or 'sustainable-state' models, which we do not have the space to review in this chapter.

But 'downsizing' is also a strategy that needs to be combined with the removal of the current pattern of global financial subsidies for inherently unenvironmental practices. The most flagrant example of this is the energy industry, which is riddled with inequitable subsidies for fossil fuels and nuclear power that block the introduction of environmentally friendly technologies. These technologies are further subsidized as export technologies, and are rapidly being adopted by developing countries whose previous cultural practices were often more sustainable than the new technologies on offer. Other related unecological subsidies include subsidies for agricultural monocultures, transportation, and legislative bonuses for bad practice (such as immunity from prosecution for liability).

As we have also noted, the management of fisheries resources is another example (which could be echoed in other resource industries) where overcapitalization has 'locked in' an exploitative, destructive set of extractive practices. It is at this level, where a macro-level policy process promotes micro-level market pathologies, that the most damage is done; and where multilateralism, for example, may have an important role to play.

But the challenge is far from being essentially an economic one. The religion of consumerism which now pervades our civil society has brought us a form of social peace and multicultural harmony, just as long as tomorrow and next week carry the promise of more purchases, more gadgets, and more consumer durables. A shrinking economy will undermine this central pillar of social consensus. What new social values can conceivably stand in its place?

Social peace has also been bought in the post-war period by the division of the ever-growing 'larger pie' amongst a growing portion of the less affluent members of society. A shrinking economy will necessarily mean as well, a shrinking welfare state. It will raise the even thornier question of whether we will persist in the goal of greater income redistribution in these circumstances. The revival of belligerent class consciousness may well result from the new framework where the majority (but not all) incomes are frozen or shrinking.

The questions that appear at the outset to be 'economic' in these circumstances, turn out quickly to be political, social, and in the end moral. Among the most onerous of these is the redefinition of our obligations to the less developed countries. This closely interlaces with widely ranging environmental issues related to their process of development.

CONCLUSIONS

Our conclusion is in the form of a warning, which has been raised in this chapter most directly and poignantly in the example of the collapse of the Canadian East Coast fish stocks. We have come to wonder if the syndrome exposed by that case – that is, the pathological fixation on a single number or set of numbers as a signalling mechanism of the health or illness of mutually interacting complex systems – will be perpetrated on a global scale by a move towards 'sustainable development'. There is a widespread hope among managers and environmentalists that our increasing ecological sophistication will prevent such recurrences, and will force us to pay more attention to the danger signals emanating from Nature.

However, our fear is that the East Coast case is emblematic of a darker truth: that there was always a great deal of sophisticated information and warnings available; but if the underlying communications system is epistemologically flawed, the fixation syndrome will eventually be forced to treat these warnings again as 'noise', albeit at a new level of global sophistication.

The alternative route is that we devise better ways and means by which to 'charge the reactions of environmental effects' (in Luhmann's words) to ourselves. In this approach our social and political systems will gain rationality to the extent that we reintroduce the differences between the economy and the ecology into our political and social systems, and are guided by how we learn to evaluate these patterns of difference. This is quite the opposite from assuming some kind of seamless identity between the two, and attempting to 'adjust' the characteristics of the larger ecology to sustaining the 'needs' of the smaller economy.

Although we are arguing against 'sustainable development', we are not arguing *for* a reversion to a prior strategy – either unsustainable growth or a pre-industrial utopia. We are interested in a healthy industrial (or post-industrial) system which is managed by a rich multiplicity of signals, and not by managerial single-mindedness masquerading as 'sustainability'. To reconnect to those signals, we have argued that it is the economy that should be downsized, and not the ecology. This downsizing will provide much needed space not only for the re-entry (and the reinforcement) of signals from the ecological system, but for the reconsideration of signals from a variety of social concerns and values that have been overshadowed in the glare of an all pervasive 'single vision'.

Otherwise we will continue to fall victim to signal failures of our own creation.

NOTES

1. In February 1992, we published, under the auspices of Science for Peace, Canada, 'Nature's Veto: UNCED and the Debate Over the

Earth'. That document was designed to be a contribution to the upcoming Rio Summit later that year. We have decided not to revisit that paper directly here, but to extend and expand upon some of its themes, in light of what has happened (or not happened) in the interim. We would like to thank Robert Cox and his colleagues for giving us the encouragement and opportunity to write this chapter.

2. For a more extensive summary of the emerging situation, see Tolba *et al.*, 1992.

3. This image derives from Gregory Bateson 1972, 'Ecology and Flexibility in Urban Civilization', in *Steps to an Ecology of Mind*, p. 498.

4. See for further details, Robert C. Paehlke 1989.

5. See E.P. Thompson 1978.

6. See Chris Manes 1990.

7. See Richard C. Lewontin 1991.

8. All ecological systems display constant patterns of reiteration produced by their operational closure, which at the same time also offset control of throughput via the phenomena of boundary formation. As Varela remarks: 'In a unit with operational closure, what appears as *coherent or distinguishable* behavior ... has a peculiar nature indeed. On the one hand, it appears as a single property of the unit itself; on the other hand, when we attempt to examine the origin of such a property through its own properties, we find that there is nothing but an indefinite iteration of the same; its starts nowhere and it ends nowhere. The coherence is distributed through an ever repeating circle that is infinite in its circulation, yet finite, since we can see its effect or its results as a unit's property' (Varela, 1984, p. 316).

9. As Varela notes, the circularities that occur within the autonomous process of *autopoiesis* were traditionally termed vicious circles. But he assures us: 'There is, of course, no more intrinsic mystery to [the loopiness of] autonomy than there is to control' (Varela 1984, p. 311). A loop is completed between inside and outside whereby two levels are collapsed, intercrossed, and entangled. While we, as observers, may want to hold this entanglement of loops in separate levels, they become inseparable in the process of molecular self-production. Many variations of specific configurations can be played on this basic theme of tangled loops, and thus give rise to self-production of a host of different cells. Varela argues that the basic phenomenon of *autopoiesis* is always the same: operational closure of elements in separate levels intercrossed at a boundary to constitute a unity. Autonomy arises at the point of their intercrossing. Perception of this self-referring phenomenon is another issue.

10. Both Maturana and Varela acknowledge the inspiration of Bateson but were mainly responsible for Bateson's reformulating his own 'recursive epistemology' in the last few years of his life (Harries-Jones, 1995, pp. 168–191).

11. They explain that if the unity of any biological system lies in those fields of relation expressing a form of closure, then the boundary of any subsystem within it must also replicate this form. Thus social subsystems must be of the same form, but simultaneously different from

their surroundings. The only field of relations that adequately expresses both unity and difference in this manner, they argue, is one of communication, not matter, not energy. The physical self-production of organisms through mutual specification of chemical transformations sustained through physical closure of boundaries, must also have communicative components and processes in conjunction with these physical components. A field of enquiry which begins with the recursive properties of 'self-reproduction' must then come to grips with the more elusive communicative recursion of 'self-reference'.

12. Luhmann uses the concept of resonance to designate the interplay of human systems and their ecological surround. For Luhmann there are two resonances that have to be taken into account. The one designates ecological interconnection between society as a whole on its boundary with ecosystems. The other is the resonance that exists at the boundary within various function systems, or institutions, where communication about environment actually takes place. Luhmann argues that environmental disturbances produce too little resonance on the 'external side' of the boundary of human society as a whole while the situations at the 'internal side' of boundaries of society where communication actually takes place, produces too much resonance within society.

13. During the next seven years (1978–85) the euphoria that had been engendered by the declaration of the exclusive economic zone was reinforced by the steady growth of the stock, by continually improving catches, and by the belief that the [20 per cent mortality rate] objective was, indeed, being met. In those circumstances, scientists, lulled by false data signals and, to some extent, overconfident of the validity of their predictions, failed to recognize the statistical inadequacies in their bulk biomass model and failed to acknowledge properly and recognize the high risk involved with the state-of-stock advice based on relatively short and unreliable data series . . . and the open and increasing skepticism of [low-tech] inshore fishermen . . .' (Harris, 1990, pp. 2,3 quoted in Finlayson 1994, p. 31).

14. Lande, Engen and Saether propose that once species population is assessed, harvesting requires some form of banking mechanism 'to smooth fluctuating harvests'. May points out that their suggestion also requires 'sole owner' regulation and there are practical problems in implementing any policy of 'sole ownership' which enables setting discount rates at zero, especially on a global scale. And when 'economic motives impel towards extinguishing the resource, things are correspondingly more difficult'. Indeed they are! The two articles suggest a categorical divorce from economistic forecasting of resource management, and the urgent need for adopting alternative forms of control. Yet, as both groups of authors show, their solutions require social and political policies that cannot be enforced.

REFERENCES

Bateson, Gregory 1972, *Steps to an Ecology of Mind*, New York: Ballantine Books.
Bateson, Gregory 1991, in Rodney E. Donaldson (ed.), *A Sacred Unity: Further Steps to an Ecology of Mind*, New York: HarperCollins Publishers.
Dobuzinskis, Laurent 1987, *The Self-Organizing Polity: an Epistemological Analysis of Political Life*, Boulder, Colo.: Westview Press.
Finlayson, Alan C. 1994, *Fishing For Truth: A Sociological Analysis of Northern Cod Stock Assessments 1977–1990*, St John's, Newfoundland: ISER, Memorial University of Newfoundland.
Giddens, Anthony 1991, *The Consequences of Modernity*, Stanford, Calif.: Stanford University Press.
Harries-Jones, Peter 1995, *A Recursive Vision: Ecological Understanding and Gregory Bateson*, Toronto: University of Toronto Press.
Harris, Leslie 1990, *Independent Review of the State of the Northern Cod Stock*, Ottawa, Ontario: Department of Fisheries and Oceans.
Lande, Russell, Steinar Engen and Bernt-Erik Saether 1994, 'Optimal Harvesting, Economic Discounting and Extinction Risk in Fluctuating Populations', *Nature*, 372, 3, November, pp. 88–9.
Lewontin, Richard C. 1991, *Biology as Ideology: The Doctrine of DNA*, Concord, Ontario: Anansi Press.
Luhmann, Niklas 1986, *Ecological Communication*, Chicago, Ill.: The University of Chicago Press.
Manchester Guardian Weekly, 15 April 1995, p. 8.
Manes, Chris 1990, *Green Rage: Radical Environmentalism and the Unmaking of Civilization*, Boston: Little Brown.
Maturana, Humberto and Varela, Francisco, J. 1980, *Autopoiesis and Cognition*, Boston, Mass.: Boston Studies in Philosophical Science, vol. 42, in association with D. Reidel.
May, Robert M. 1994, 'The Economics of Extinction', *Nature*, 372, 3, November, pp. 42–3.
Morin, Edgar. 1977, 1980, *La Methode*, vol. 1: *La Nature de la Nature*; vol. 2: *La vie de la vie*, Paris: Seuil.
Naess, Arne and David Rothenberg (trans. and ed.) 1989, *Ecology, Community, and Lifestyle*, Cambridge (UK): Cambridge University Press.
Odum, Eugene P. 1989, *Ecology and Our Engangered Life-Support Systems*, Sunderland, Mass.: Sinauer Associates.
Paehlke, Robert C. 1989, *Environmentalism and the Future of Progressive Politics*, New Haven and London: Yale University Press.
Polanyi, Karl 1957, *The Great Transformation*, Boston, Mass: Beacon Press.
Postel, Sandra 1994, 'Carrying Capacity: Earth's Bottom Line', in Lester R. Brown (ed.), *State of the World in 1994*, New York: Norton, pp. 3–21.
Rapport, David J. and James E. Turner 1977, 'Economic Models in Ecology', *Science*, vol. 195, (28 January), pp. 367–73.
Rodman, John 1995, 'Four Forms of Ecological Consciousness Considered', in Alan Drengson and Yuichi Inoue, *The Deep Ecology Movement: an Introductory Anthology*, Berkeley, Cal.: North Atlantic Books, pp. 242–56.

Sachs, Wolfgang (ed.) 1993, *Global Ecology: A New Arena of Political Conflict*, London & New Jersey: Zed Books; Halifax, N.S.: Fernwood Publishers.

Thompson, E.P. 1978, *The Poverty of Theory and Other Essays*, New York and London: The Monthly Review Press.

Tolba, Mostafa K. *et al.*, 1992, *The World Environment 1972–92*, London: Chapman and Hall for UNEP.

Varela, Francisco, J. 1984, 'The Creative Circle', in Paul Watzlawick (ed.), *The Invented Reality: How do We Know What We Believe We Know? (Contributions to Constructivism)*, New York: Norton, pp. 309–23.

6 Environmental Rights, Multilateralism, Morality and the Ecology

Tariq Osman Hyder[1]

As the theme of the United Nations University symposium was 'Future Multilateralism: Tasks and Political Foundations' I would like to begin by offering my vision of what exactly we are aiming at, or should be aiming at, and what we all should be working for – multilateralism in the future and the fate of the inhabitants of this planet. I would submit that the essential goal and task before us is to strive for the recognition of a minimum standard of equity for each inhabitant. In a global civic sense this would encompass a system of universally recognized obligations, rights and entitlements.

I am concious of the fact that there is a school of thought that holds that extending the ambit of human rights to social, economic and environmental rights is counterproductive as it dilutes the effective struggle to achieve minimum human rights in general. Nevertheless I do strongly believe that this is not correct and that what we have to aim for is recognition that a basic environmental right exists for each inhabitant of this planet, at one level within the society or nation-state of which he or she is first part and then an individual environmental right in the inter-state or global plane. Of course in the classical legal sense there is only a right if it is enforceable. However, the first step in the process comes with recognition of a right. This is how the concept of 'human rights' has developed, by broadening the scope of recognition rather than relying on measures of enforcement. The recognition of a right, enforceable or not, gives it a moral weight.

Until now multilateralism has mainly been concerned with the inter-state system: the obligations of states towards each other, their rights and their entitlements. Of course, the United Nations system and ancillary structures have tried to put together declarations and agreements which would gain global recognition for a

136

minimum standard of state behaviour and the human rights of citizens within the state system with suggested safeguards for minorities, the disadvantaged and the weak, such as ethnic minorities, women, children, the elderly and the physically and mentally handicapped.

However, all these attempts when it comes to the individual have naturally recognized that in each case this represents a civic contract between the individual citizen and the state in which he or she resides. The basic rationale has been that without a territorial definition for protection, no system of obligations, rights and entitlements can exist.

Of course, there have been exceptions. War, hostilities and armed action were originally regarded as manifestations of the extension of state policy by other means when normal diplomatic intercourse had failed. With World War II a moral rationale was introduced and legitimized by the Nuremberg trials concerned with the charge of crimes against humanity. The genocide convention expanded the sphere of potential international concern and possible action against violators. United Nations actions in Korea, Somalia, Burundi, Rwanda, Iraq, Cambodia and Bosnia, whatever their degree of success, have moved the United Nations, and therefore the multilateral system, from a traditional reliance on peace keeping to peace making. (Of course we have to recognize that while the Nuremberg trials were based on a moral rationale, they were framed in legal terms which have often been criticized for being overstated since they were the product of the victors over the vanquished.)

An important implicit objective of multilateralism, since the League of Nations, has been to bring about a minimum standard of equity between each nation state. In this the one-country-one-vote system has, despite its detractors, produced an acceptance at one important level of this principle of equity in the multilateral system. There are those who label the United Nations and its organs a 'talk shop' where nothing really gets done. However, in this respect it is this medium which has become the message. In the United Nations system, the one-country-one-vote system gives a certain minimum right and entitlement to each country and with it a certain minimum dignity on the world scene. Countries with power and influence have to enter the debating procedure to gain broad recognition for their programs and objectives.

It may be asked if the objective of equity constituted or constitutes a real objective of the major powers to put together the modern multilateral system. Certainly it constitutes an objective of the developing countries, and to some extent has been accepted by all countries as part of the multilateral process despite the realities of *realpolitik*.

Of course, the Security Council with its five permanent member-veto system and with the sole power for mandatory demands, reflects the fact that in the real world, real power lies with the strongest. This reality is the evidence that the old multilateralism has not succeeded in taking us far towards an acceptable standard of global equity between nations and therefore shows our failure to progress as much as we should have towards equity between citizens. At the same time this heightens the need to give thought to ancillary approaches towards individual equity amongst the citizens of our world, towards a recognition of a global civil society through individual recognition and effort. It must also be added that the developing countries have much to improve within their own boundaries in various aspects of political and human rights. Most are trying to do so.

I would like to briefly examine the evolutionary structure in human societies of the rise and acceptance of systems of obligations, rights and entitlements. From the beginning of mankind the evolution of social units beginning with the family have depended upon how civic obligations, rights and entitlements have developed. In the family unit, basic norms of obligations evolved, first towards each other's mate and then the even more binding obligation towards children. Where there was a basic obligation, a corresponding nascent right also developed. The right would take centuries to become in any sense of the term a 'legal right' but till that time a moral recognition in society in general towards what constituted an obligation and what constituted a right led over time to the evocation, enunciation, recognition and codification of these personal rights, obligations and entitlements.

The process began with the family unit, and then went on to the clan and tribal unit, as the basic structure of civic obligations and nascent rights and entitlements progressed upwards with the development of human societies. As nation states evolved so did personal law and criminal law. The balance between what was owed to the ruler, be it a person, a group of individuals or a government, the obligations of the ruler towards his or her subjects and the rights of the subjects remained over centuries, and one view would say in some cases until now, in favour of those who ruled over those who were ruled. This course of development in civic society paralleled to some degree the evolution of obligations and rights within the basic family unit. The legal rights of women and children have taken longer to be recognized than those of the *paterfamilias* or putative *paterfamilias*.

The evolution of obligations, rights and entitlements in the multilateral system has only been similar to some extent in terms of scope to what has taken place within the rise of human societies and the nation state. There is a recognition of equity within the interstate multilateral system as set forth in the one-country-one-vote rule in the United Nations General Assembly and indeed in the entire United Nations system. But as far as the individual nation state is concerned within the multilateral system, when it comes to political rights or economic rights – or rather political power or economic power – they are not at the same level and there is no equity. International law to some extent has been the consequence of the evolution, the objectives, and doctrines of the most powerful states, tempered by the rise of the multilateral United Nations system.

Therefore, while at one level we must view the future of multilateralism as an effort to search for equity between nation states, at another level we must proceed in parallel in a quest for equity between individuals world wide. While in all societies there are differences due to class and wealth, in the aggregate the world-wide rights, obligations and entitlements of the individual citizen within each state are limited and defined by the political and economic power of that state.

To give a few examples let us look to what happens to UN peace keepers killed on duty. While the normal rule of life insurance companies everywhere is that the amount paid out depends upon the premium charged, and despite the fact that the United Nations could well take out a universal life insurance policy on each UN peace keeper, in fact if one of them unfortunately is killed on duty, the amount paid to the next of kin depends on the economic level of the country from where he comes.

Under the Warsaw Convention for air travellers a basic universal liability was accepted by all carriers for all passengers. This was subsequently modified for all passengers flying to and from North America irrespective of their nationality. Attempts are now being made to modify carrier liability further so that again it would depend on the country of origin of the passenger irrespective of the fact that the same travel fees would apply for everyone.

The standard practice in the international legal system has been that if one state desires to try an individual residing in another state, it should seek the extradition of that individual by so requesting the other state which must give its consent. However, in one important country, the United States of America, the courts have ruled that it would be legal for the law enforcement officials of that country unilaterally to go after and bring back a wanted individual from another country.

For individuals born in the South, for the foreseeable future there is very little hope, unfortunately, that they will attain any level of political or economic equity. That is why I believe that global environmental or ecological considerations provide a relatively new but important fulcrum for the quest for global individual equity. Countries and individuals are not ready to share to any significant degree the elements that make them influential and powerful, mainly their economic wealth and military power potential. However, a strong moral case can be made that each individual on this earth has an intrinsic entitlement and environmental right to an equitable share of the global commons, the atmosphere and the oceans, to air and to water, and that on the part of all there is an obligation to recognize and to give effect to these rights and obligations. This is an argument that can be made without reference to the degree of countervailing power available to the Southern countries in the field of the environment.

This is why I believe that the interface between multilateralism and the ecology provides us with a new dimension towards global individual equity and towards the recognition on one plane of a degree of equitable dignity for each individual. In order to see how far we have come and how far we have to go let us now examine the different perspectives of the North and South on ecology.

The Rio process provided the forum for developing and developed countries to attempt to define on their own terms what exactly 'sustainable development' meant to them. The developed countries which were already economically well off put their emphasis on the environment and its protection. The developing countries which were and are still struggling to meet basic human needs, put development first.

The developed countries differentiate environmental problems between 'global' and 'local' impacts. By global they mean environmental impacts which already have effects world wide or are likely to have such effects in the near future. These effects are in the main caused by excessive consumption, particularly in the developed countries, and include stratospheric ozone depletion and rapid climate change from global warming due to the atmospheric build up of carbon dioxide and other greenhouse gases. By local impacts they refer to the local environmental issues that are of primary concern to the developing countries and result principally from the burdens of poverty. The effects of poverty on the environment include water and soil pollution, desertification, aridity and air pollution. Historically, these problems have been left for developing countries to solve as best they can with their own limited resources, supplemented by the limited inflows of Official Development Assistance (ODA).

But the link between environment and development was recognized at the beginning of the UNCED process. The starting point was UN General Assembly Resolution 44/28 of 22 December 1989. In its preamble to this resolution the General Assembly noted, *inter alia*, that it was:

> Gravely concerned that the major cause of the continuing deterioration of the global environment is the unsustainable pattern of production and consumption, particularly in industrialized countries. Stressing that poverty and environmental degradation are closely inter-related and that environmental protection in developing countries must, in this context, be viewed as an integral part of the development process and cannot be considered in isolation from it.

In the operative part of that resolution, the General Assembly, among other things:

> Affirms further that the promotion of economic growth in developing countries is essential to address problems of environmental degradation. Affirms the importance of a supportive international economic climate conducive to sustained economic growth and development in all countries for the protection and sound management of the environment.
>
> Notes that the largest part of the current emission of pollutants into the environment, including toxic and hazardous wastes, originates in developed countries, and therefore recognizes that those countries have the main responsibility for combating such pollution.

The UN resolution also indicated that the Earth Summit should include among its objectives:

> Ways and means of providing new and additional financial resources, particularly to developing countries, for environmentally sound development programs and projects in accordance with national development objectives, priorities and plans and to consider ways of effectively monitoring the provision of such new and additional financial resources.

The developing countries felt that the resolution and the process it had set in motion adequately reflected the responsibilities of the present situation with respect to global environmental degradation. The responsibilities for developed countries thus included not only curbing their own profligate patterns of consumption and production but also providing the new and additional financial and technological resources that developing countries would need to combat a situation not of their own making. As Haas, Keohane and Levy have pointed out in their book *Institutions for the Earth* there are 'leaders' and 'laggards' in the global environmental process.[2]

As the global environment negotiations unfolded, however, it became obvious that the developed countries, having acquiesced to Resolution 44/228, no longer felt bound by either its language or its intent. In every negotiating forum, they sought to give primacy to environmental protection at the cost of the universal right to development. The words 'new and additional financial resources' proved unacceptable to some developed countries: few developed countries were ready to enter into an immediate and specific commitment in this regard. There were exceptions to this general trend: the Nordic countries and Japan proposed specific timetables for increased development assistance flows and offered to commit more funding for the environment.

Yet, despite their acceptance of the language of Resolution 44/228, the developed countries would not accept responsibility for their historical contribution to the build-up of carbon dioxide in the atmosphere or agree to divide the global responsibility in proportion to past emissions. They proclaimed that reiterating such issues would amount to 'finger pointing' and such unnecessary accusations would make it difficult for them to sell any resulting convention or declaration to their citizens and to their treasuries. The developed countries accused the developing countries of using the environment as a 'club' with which to beat additional financial resources from the recession-strapped economies of the North.

The repetition of these narrow positions by the developed countries led to a sombre, pessimistic, and introspective mood in many developing-country delegations towards the end of the process. It appeared to many that the developed countries had accepted Resolution 44/228 only to draw the developing countries into the negotiating process. Once engaged in the process, the developing countries would have to continue until a compromise was reached. It seemed that the developed countries assumed that their superior economic strength would win out over the core interests of the developing countries.

The developed countries saw the global warming scenario essentially as a zero sum game in which their own high *per capita* emission levels and consumption and quality of life would suffer if the developing countries were allowed unlimited economic growth. To forestall this eventuality, the developed countries' position throughout the climate negotiations was that the developing countries must also acknowledge their responsibility to combat global pollution and adverse global environmental change. As a step in this process, the developing countries would be required to prepare reports on their national sources and sinks of greenhouse gases. These reports would be monitored and reviewed and the developed countries would use these reports as a criterion not only for giving additional assistance, but presumably also for assessing and reprogramming the current levels of economic assistance. This linkage seemed particularly disturbing to developing countries which, in general, believe that existing assistance flows are already inadequate. They note that, due to unfair trade practices, there is currently a net negative flow of resources from developing to developed countries. Hence, many developing-country delegations worried about whether the whole process would have gained them anything of value, or if, on balance, they would be net losers.

However, the net results of the UNCED process represented a positive step forward. While the Biodiversity Convention and Agenda 21 have their own importance, to my mind the most concrete results of the Rio process were:

a) The Rio Declaration.
b) The Climate Change Convention.
c) The resultant establishment of a permanent Global Environment Facility (GEF).

The Rio Declaration, which I will return to later on in this chapter, constitutes an important step forward in the development of 'soft law' on the inter-relationship between environment and development and therefore for an equitable balance between 'rights' and 'obligations', on an interstate and individual level.

The Climate Change Convention committed the developed country parties in Article 4(3) to provide new and additional financial resources to meet the agreed full cost incurred by developing country parties in their reporting requirements under Article 12(1). Of more significance in this the most crucial article of the Convention (Article 4[3]), the developed countries committed themselves to provide such financial resources, including those for the transfer of technology, as would be needed by the developing country parties to meet the 'agreed full incremental costs' of any implementing measures they take to fulfill their obligations under the Convention. This paragraph also specifies that the implementation of these commitments shall take into account the need for adequacy and predictability in the flow of funds.

By contrast, the extent to which developing country parties were bound to implement their commitments under the Convention was specifically conditioned in Article 4(7) on two very important provisos. First, the developing countries will be required to implement their commitments under the Convention only to the extent that the developed country parties effectively implement and fulfill their own commitments related to financial resources and transfer of technology. Second, the developing countries will condition the implementation of their commitments on the notion that economic and social development and poverty eradication are their first and overriding priorities. Hence it became clear that progress towards the objective of the Convention depends on the provision of adequate funds and technology to the developing countries and on the recognition that their developmental objectives cannot be subordinated to purely environmental goals.

For its part the Global Environment Facility represents an egalitarian step forward *between* the one-country-one-vote United Nations system and the more usual international financial institutions' system where a country's influence is measured by its financial contributions. Secondly, the Global Environment Facility provides in essence the only new additionality for new funding for the environment and though limited it is of high quality because it is grant assistance.

We now turn to examining what has transpired since Rio on the North-South front when it comes to the ecology. The most important shift has been due to the increasing globalization of the world economy. Economic issues are surplanting political issues to a large extent and this is also true between multilateralism and the ecology.

Before and during the Rio process the developing countries of the South were concentrating on the demand for 'new and additional resources' and for 'technology transfers on assured and concessionary terms'. It has now become increasingly clear that ODA inflows are being supplanted by private investment flows although they retain much importance. In the same way globalization has led to increased North-South technology transfers driven by factors of pure economic self-interest. Through liberalization most developing countries have opened up and barriers to trade have fallen with the GATT/WTO accords.

One of the key issues during Rio was the question of NGO participation in the process. Subsequent developments in the Human Rights Summit, the UN Conference on Population and Development, the World Summit for Social Development and the Fourth World Conference on Women in Beijing, have shown that this too is now an accepted and settled subject. Therefore, the old North-South issues of finances, technology transfers and NGOs have been overtaken by newer concerns.

The key recognition now is that environmental development will increase with growth. It is not an either or situation. Within this ambit there are now relatively newer North-South issues. Trade constitutes the most important economic issue. Next is the issue of the global commons: how to deal with biodiversity, the atmosphere and the oceans. These issues all relate to equity: how to share the burdens and benefits.

The degree of polarization and divisiveness has abated somewhat. The OECD countries and the G-77 on the issue of the environment and ecology are no longer monolithic blocs as they were to some extent during the Rio process. In environmental and trade negotiations groups of countries are finding issues of common concern across the North-South divide.

For instance when it comes to *per capita* entitlement of the global commons, the position of Brazil is different in some degree from that of India and China. Russia does not stand with the OECD. On some issues there is a difference between the Western Europeans and the North Americans. Japan on the issue of technology transfers has a different position from that of many other developed countries. During the negotiations on the Basel Convention a few significant developing countries opposed the ban on toxic waste export to Southern countries by 1998. One large developing country felt that its commercial interests were being adversely affected. Another country which is just about to join the OECD was probably thinking of its requirement to export waste.

With the growth of regional economic organizations such as NAFTA, ASEAN, SAARC and ECO, regional coalitions are being formed. With the end of the Soviet Union, the Second World is no more, with its former constituent parts either leaning towards the First World or part of the Third World.

In North-South forums while the struggle for equity by reforming the international monetary system and the world's armament or disarmament system will continue, it is in the environment and development field where substantive negotiations will continue to take place particularly in the Climate Change Convention which so directly affects not only the world's environment but the development paths of both the North and South. Developed countries understand that their emissions are directly related to sustaining their economic potential. Developed countries want the developing countries, particularly the larger developing countries, to limit their emissions. However, as these countries have a *per capita* emission rate which is only a small percentage of the emission rates of developed countries, they naturally feel that the developed countries should pay the cost of the additional resources required for cleaner technologies and sources of energy. However, at least the North and South in this important Convention agree to a degree of shared responsibility for the future although there is still a great difference of views on their mutual rights and obligations.

We now have a situation on the global North-South front that on the one hand there are and will continue to be increasing coalitions across the North-South divide on a variety of environmental and developmental issues. At the same time, through avenues such as the Climate Change Convention and the Global Environment Facility, the beginnings of a new North-South partnership of cooperation is in its initial stages of evolution. On the other hand, since the major issues of priorities and responsibilities have still to be resolved, I feel that it is still in the interests of the South, of the Group of 77, to unify their positions and negotiating strategy as much as possible.

In this respect I believe that it is in the interests of the South to give the Rio Declaration the pivotal position that it deserves as a foundation for their objectives. The South has not taken advantage of this declaration sufficiently till now. By the same token, the developed countries which are also parties to that declaration, with a few declared reservations on the part of a small number of countries, tend to ignore the Rio Declaration because it provides such an equitable balance between environment and development, the North and South and the individual rights, obligations and entitlements not only of nation states but also of individuals world wide. The Rio Declaration constitutes the environmental charter for our age.

I would like to briefly explain why this is the case. In its preamble the Declaration lays down the objective of establishing a new and equitable global partnership through the creation of new levels of cooperation among states, key sectors of societies and people. It calls for new international agreements which respect the interests of all and protect the integrity of the global environmental and developmental system.

- Principle 1 puts human beings at the centre of concerns for sustainable development and lays down their entitlement to a healthy and productive life in harmony with nature.
- Principle 2 gives each country the sovereign right to exploit its own resources pursuant to its own environmental and developmental policies with the responsibility that it should do so without damaging the environment beyond its own boundaries.
- Principle 3 was the most difficult to negotiate and affirms for the first time in the United Nations the right to development. During the negotiations some developed countries' negotiators made the point that if developing countries with their large populations had the right to reach the same level of development as the developed countries, then the resources of the world would be exhausted.
- Principle 4 affirms that environmental protection constitutes an integral part of the development process.
- Principle 5 highlights the importance of eradicating poverty.
- Principle 6 calls for special attention for the LDCs.
- Principle 7 calls for global partnership to restore the earth's ecosystem. In view of the different contributions to global environmental degradation, states have common but differentiated responsibilities.

The developed countries acknowledge the responsibility that they bear in the international pursuit of sustainable development in view of the pressures their societies place on the global environment and of the technologies and financial resources they command.

- Principle 10 relates environmental issues to participation by all concerned citizens who have also the right to be fully informed and to have access to judicial and administrative proceedings and remedies.
- Principle 11 calls for effective environmental legislation while recognizing that different standards may be necessary for countries in different stages of development.
- Principle 12 expresses the importance of an open international economic system that would lead to economic growth and sustainable development. It explicitly prohibits trade policy measures for environmental purposes from being used as a means of arbitrary or unjustifiable discrimination or as disguised restrictions on international trade. This is also most relevant today when developing countries feel that the environment is being used as a means to reduce their comparative advantages in many areas of international trade.
- Principle 13 addresses the need for national laws for liability and compensation for the victims of pollution and environmental damage.
- Principle 14 calls for cooperation to discourage or prevent the relocation and transfer to other states of activities and substances that cause environmental degradation and are harmful to human health.
- Principle 15 accepts the precautionary principle.
- Principle 16 accepts the 'polluter pays' principle.
- Principle 17 calls for environmental impact-assessment statements.
- Principle 18 requires interstate notification of natural disasters or other emergencies likely to cause harmful environmental effects.
- Principle 19 requires timely notification for trans-boundary adverse environmental effects.
- Principles 20 and 21 give women and youth the position they deserve.
- Principle 22 does the same for indigenous people.
- Principle 23 calls for the protection of the environment and natural resources of people under oppression, domination and occupation.
- Principle 24 speaks out against warfare and for the protection of the environment in times of conflict. An attempt to condemn

nuclear weapons in this declaration was opposed by a power, the United States of America, which reasoned that the use of nuclear weapons could be legitimate under national and international law.

- Principle 25 declared that peace, development and environmental protection are interdependent and indivisible.
- Principle 26 calls on all states peacefully to resolve their environmental disputes and by appropriate means in accordance with the charter of the United Nations.
- The declaration ends by calling on states and to people cooperate in good faith and in a spirit of partnership in the fulfillment of the principles embodied in the Rio Declaration and in the future development of international law in the field of sustainable development.

It must be admitted that the developing countries have not sufficiently used the Rio Declaration to advance their objectives in a variety of environmental, developmental and trade negotiations. Moreover, there is a general reticence on the part of the developed countries to further the development of international law in the field of sustainable development, which would require giving increasing importance to the 'soft law' of the Rio Declaration thereby in time turning it eventually into new and important elements of international law.

I would like to conclude by emphasizing again that if we are to move to a more successful multilateral system, we must work for equity amongst nations at one level, and equity amongst individuals world wide at another level. Environment and the ecology provide a very important opportunity for advances on both levels. There is growing awareness about the environment amongst people everywhere. This needs to be harnessed within countries for the recognition of equitable environmental entitlements within each country, between countries, and between all individuals everywhere so that one more element of their natural dignity can be assured.

We may be moving towards a world united in some respects by globalization where economic issues are often surplanting political issues. However, without an equitable balance, without the recognition of developmental and environmental rights as very important elements of human rights, we will not be able to reach a better and more stable world. The classical free market system calls for free movement of capital, goods, services and labour. However, increasingly the movement of people and labour is being restricted. We also have to analyse how far the rise of irrational and extremist movements are due to perceived or misperceived notions of inequity and lack of recognition for individual dignity.

Within the broad canvas of a future and better multilateral system, I believe that the increasing recognition that each individual possesses an intrinsic environmental right provides a moral dimension through which the ecology in its interaction with multilateralism can help move us closer to our objective.

NOTES

1. The author's views expressed in this chapter are his own and not necessarily those of his government.
2. Peter M. Haas, Robert O. Keohane, and Marc A. Levy (eds.), *Institutions for the Earth: Sources of Effective International Protection* (Cambridge: The MIT Press, 1993).

PART III

Human Rights and Participation

7 The Quest for Human Rights in an Era of Globalization

Richard Falk

THE SURPRISING EMERGENCE OF HUMAN RIGHTS IN THE LAST HALF CENTURY

A Westphalian conception of world order would appear resistant to the emergence of human rights, the latter being understood primarily as claims against governments to uphold certain standards of behaviour in the treatment of their citizens.[1] The fundamental binding idea of the *modern* juridical framework based on territorial sovereignty is that governments are not subject to standards or procedures of external accountability in the treatment of their own citizens or others under their control without an official expression of prior consent.[2] And this jural thinking reflects the underlying Hobbesian view of an anarchic international society in which community and civic ties are absent, and morality and legality have little role to play.[3] This understanding of statist logic underpins 'realist' schools of thought about international politics, with their stress on 'national interests' as the only reliable guide for policymakers and leaders and their critical rejection of any higher morality in international life as a courtship with dangerous utopian illusions.[4]

Thus it seems natural to inquire as to why governments have *voluntarily* subverted an earlier unconditional sovereignty by participating in the creation by stages of an elaborate normative architecture that began to be explicitly constructed in 1948 with the formulation of the Universal Declaration of Human Rights – which has turned out to be one of the most seminal documents ever enunciated through the operations of the traditional intergovernmental dynamics of the 'old multilateralism'.[5] The same sort of inquiry could be made with reference to the imposition of international criminal liability in the immediate aftermath of World War II; of course, to the extent that the Nuremberg innovation was limited to the leaders of the defeated countries, the subversive impact seemed containable in its wider challenge to sovereign prerogatives. The tension in this setting was between the impulse to avoid having the war crimes trials scorned as 'victors' justice' and the threat posed to statism in the future by the idea of a generalized criminal accountability.[6] Interestingly, in direct contrast to human rights, the superpowers both refrained from accusing their rival of violations of the Nuremberg Principles, although there were several situations during the Cold War years in which such accusations would have been definitely plausible. The difference in treatment can probably be best explained by recognizing that governments could handle human rights claims, discounting them as hostile propaganda, whereas the war-crimes accusations would directly engage the reputations and legitimacy of the highest leaders, rendering diplomatic contact problematic, and in the case of the West, play into the hands of extremist political opposition at home.[7]

It seems evident at the outset that no such subversive intention was being consciously promoted by formulating in more specific terms the generalized Charter mandate expressed in the Preamble and article 1 to promote human rights. The drafters of the Universal Declaration were not heavyweight diplomats, but idealists briefly called in from the cold to take on a task that was viewed cynically or indifferently at the time by top leaders, a matter of trivial relevance to the conduct of government or diplomacy, whether human rights were conceived of as a matter of commitments to shape internal governance (directed at the self) or to influence foreign policy (an instrument directed at the other). The advent of international human rights started off as mainly a public relations undertaking in a post-World War II atmosphere dominated by the United States, an interpretation, strongly supported by the declaratory character of the foundational document, signalling the absence of any American enforcement intent.[8] Additionally, some of the governments that proclaimed their endorsement of the Universal Declaration were even at the time administering public order systems that were tightly controlled and systematically oppressive. That is, there existed in 1948 a manifest contradiction between the norms being endorsed and prevailing patterns of behaviour. Why, then, would such political leaders expose themselves to claims based on their failure to adhere to the norms that had been officially and previously endorsed within the legitimizing framework of the United

Nations? The participating governments and their leaders undoubt-edly perceived these early moves to internationalize human rights in many different ways, but hardly anyone viewed such initiatives as a significant potential threat to the unobstructed exercise of sovereign rights.

And yet a certain historical setting seems the best explanation of why the human rights project was launched within the UN frame-work so soon after the Organization was founded, and despite the onset of East/West tensions. The general atmosphere of public opinion in the West, as shaped by the United States, emphasized the failure of the liberal democracies to heed Nazi internal repress-iveness in the years of build-up to World War II, and it was widely regarded as important to posit an international humanitarian re-sponsibility in relation to the re-emergence of totalitarian abuses in the future. Further, the Communist countries were already battling the West for the ideological high ground with respect to issues of societal well-being, and thus regarded diplomacy relating to human rights as an opportunity to challenge the Western emphasis on individual civil and political rights by championing and invoking the socialist emphasis on economic and social rights of a collective nature.[9] In contrast, Communist governments were prepared to give lip service to the constitutionalism associated with civil and politi-cal rights. Their consistent view was that sovereignty, as an opera-tional reality, insulated such societies from any type of meaningful accountability to external authority. There existed the added as-surance that the absence of an active civil society in the socialist bloc meant that these norms could not be meaningfully invoked internally as a challenge to governmental dominance. Thus, hu-man rights, at most, were regarded primarily by political elites as providing an arena for the exchange of propaganda charges on the plane of international relations. They were not perceived initially as posing a subversive threat to the supremacy of the state in rela-tion to persons situated within territorial boundaries.[10]

Thus the initial impetus in support of human rights on a global level was facilitated by this dual recognition that the normative standards being adopted were either redundant or unenforceable. The liberal democracies were particularly intent on achieving re-dundancy because of their worries about the potential activism of their respective citizenries. Authoritarian countries seemed surpris-ingly willing to subscribe to normative standards wildly inconsist-ent with their internal operating codes presumably because of their dual sense that there was no prospect for either implementation from without or pressure from within. For liberal democracies the endorsement of human rights, in general, represented values associated with their convictions about the dignity of the individual, including even the less seriously embraced economic and social rights reflecting a then-prevalent ethos of welfare capitalism. For authoritarian states, engaged in the active abuse of their citizens as a whole, an endorsement of human rights may have served such governments as a convenient disguise in the wider world of states where their legitimacy was under varying degrees of attack. Norms of human rights also functioned, in part, as moral claims in the ideological rivalry for the hearts and minds of peoples throughout the non-Western world that was at the centre of the cold war.[11]

In the early decades of this process of internationalizing the protection of human rights, the Westphalian view of statism held sway, and was reinforced by geopolitical structures and priorities, including the awkwardness of large overseas colonial empires. Further, the gradual ascendancy of the realist world view even in the United States, possibly the last partial idealist holdout among influential countries, minimized the impact of human rights on diplomacy. For instance, the West was far more concerned with maintaining strategic solidarity against the Soviet bloc (and with the protection of foreign investment and a market-oriented climate) than it was with whether its allies abandoned authoritarian rule. Indeed, the United States often lent its overt support and occasionally resorted to interventionary means to stabilize the rule of anti-human rights regimes so long as their orientation was anti-Marxist.[12] And for Soviet bloc countries a combination of Soviet interventionary supervision and the suppression of domestic dissent effectively nullified any human rights impact on the style and substance of rule.[13] What did happen, then, during this initial 20-year period was the laying of foundations for a potential human rights culture, but the conditions for its actualization in terms of improved political and material conditions for the peoples of the world were almost totally absent, and not generally foreseen. As a result there was little academic interest in human rights during this period, and what did exist, tended to be descriptive and moralistic. Indeed, in these early years, what with the persistence of colonialism and the tendency of many authoritarian governments to affirm their commitment to human rights, an aura of hypocrisy surrounded the subject.

THE RISE OF IMPLEMENTING PRESSURES

Various developments at different levels of social order gave human rights an increasing, if inconsistent and uneven, place in power calculations that were shaping the outcome of political struggles occurring in various parts of the world. First and foremost was the anti-colonial movement which challenged, in many settings throughout Asia and Africa, the most prevalent form of oppressive rule, intensified by its alien character that subordinated the nationalist impulses of many non-Western peoples. The United Nations General Assembly, and later the non-aligned movement, gradually came to endorse these anti-colonial struggles, and this gave an enormous push to the substance of human rights as a world order achievement even if not explicitly formulated as a matter of human rights. Indeed, several crucial UN resolutions built a bridge between the dynamics of decolonization and the emergence of human rights as a serious dimension of world politics (GA Res. 1514, 1540). The bridge was completed when common article 1 of the two human rights covenants, opened for signature in 1966, did what the Universal Declaration failed to do, namely anchored the specificity of human rights claims in the fundamental rights of all peoples to self-determination.

But there were other factors at work, as well, that moved generally in the same direction. From the start of the human rights movement there were strong supporters of the idea of applying external pressure on others to uphold human rights standards situated within the bureaucracies of leading Western states. Their presence did ensure a kind of forward momentum for efforts to strengthen and elaborate an applicable human rights framework, and their influence was particularly great in relation to nascent European institutions and within the United Nations. That is, although realist perspectives tended to dominate the pinnacles of state power, there was a significant, partially 'subversive' presence within the sinews of government itself that adhered to neo-Wilsonian or idealist views and believed that some sort of global community based on law and morality was both possible and necessary.[14]

The cumulative influence of human rights as legal norms did give the notion of external accountability an increasing credibility, at least in Western Europe, especially subsequent to the creation and operation of the Strasbourg human rights mechanisms that took the radical step of allowing citizens in the participating countries to challenge alleged infringements on human rights in external administrative and judicial arenas.[15]

Secondly, the anti-colonial movement, and later the anti-apartheid campaign, created robust transnational political support for the human rights norm of self-determination, which although absent from the Universal Declaration, became the foundational basis for other human rights, and the bridge between political and civil rights and economic and social rights. The right of self-determination was later elevated to the eminence of being posited in a common article 1 in both human rights covenants, providing the bridge between economic, social, and cultural rights and political and civil rights. Here, for the first time, historical currents of change associated with anti-colonial nationalism, reinforced by a mixture of geopolitical support (Soviet attitude) and ambivalence (US attitude), gave political backing to the most fundamental of all human rights claims, namely, the right of all peoples to determine the shape of the governance structure at the level of the state and to be free from alien and oppressive rule, at least in the form of colonial administration.

As newly independent countries in Africa and Asia gained access to the United Nations, and influenced the recommendations of the General Assembly, important normative backing was given in a series of resolutions to anti-colonialism and the anti-apartheid campaign directed against South Africa. The US government, leader of the free world, had often to bite its geopolitical tongue, in order to avoid allowing the Soviet Union to stand alone as the great power champion of 'Third World' causes, but by no means consistently. The United States role in Indochina and its virtually unconditional support for Israel over the years discloses a willingness to subordinate human rights concerns to its strategic priorities. Nevertheless what made an aspect of the human rights agenda politically potent was the anti-colonial result of a convergence between self-determination norms and very powerful, prevailing anti-colonial and anti-racist patterns of nationalism. Furthermore, the geopolitical setting led both superpowers, although asymmetrically and inconsistently, to give their support to such patterns. In the West, as well, there were domestic constituencies that were in favour of self-determination and anti-racist values that added their political weight to international factors. These latter pressures generally arose from elements in the population of Western constitutional democracies that didn't share the geopolitical analysis or outlook of the policy makers, but were, in contrast, guided by normative conceptions of social and political justice or accentuated ethnic or ethnic solidarity with those being denied fundamental human rights.

Additionally, improving prospects for the implementation of human rights standards and the growing salience of human rights issues can be attributed to the transnationalization of specific civic initiatives directed at these goals. The role of Amnesty International was especially significant in the 1960s and 1970s, with a host of other groups becoming active later on. This unanticipated civic source of agency in relation to human rights lifted the subject matter out of the hands of propagandists, and demonstrated the leverage that can be exerted by citizens' groups relying upon the responsible use of information. Of course, countries that were rigidly authoritarian were the least responsive to such pressures; but many states, especially those linked to the Western alliance, were sensitive about attacks upon their legitimacy, fearing aid cutbacks and a weakening of support.

Even Communist countries were not oblivious to such impartial exposures of severe human rights failures, either because their legitimacy ultimately depended upon being accepted on the international level or because their interest in expanded trade and investment would be furthered by a clean bill of health in relation to human rights. The reliability of the information and the overall integrity of these transnational civil efforts also induced the liberal democracies themselves to take human rights more seriously in their dealings with others. Yet, at best, this responsiveness was partial and selective, being consistently subordinated to geopolitical factors.

The main contention being made here is that this transnational political agency gave to human rights advocacy a political potency, in the domain of implementation, and caused a subversive effect on state/society relations that far exceeded what might have been expected if developments had been truly subject to the discipline of the Westphalian or statist outlook.

At the same time there is a danger of romanticizing and exaggerating these developments. The main human rights NGOs were very much outgrowths of Western liberal internationalism, and looked mainly outward to identify abuses in Communist and 'Third World' countries. In part, this reflected a civilizational, as well as partisan and ideologized orientations. It was expressed in the form of a very selective emphasis by human rights organizations on the abuse of dissenters and political opposition or on the denial of

Western-style political liberties.[16] Human rights activism originating in the West ignored almost totally the social, economic, and cultural content of the agreed substantive norms despite their presence in widely invoked and ratified international instruments. In other words, human rights progress, while definitely subversive of statist pretensions in certain key respects, still remained generally compatible with the maintenance of existing geopolitical structures of authority and wealth in the world, and as such exerted only a marginal influence. Authoritarian practices even by states of secondary significance are normally effectively rendered immune to external human rights pressures, whether these emanate from states, the United Nations system, or transnational social forces.[17]

The confused status of human rights in international life is suggested by the treatment of the rights of indigenous peoples. To begin with, until indigenous peoples themselves adopted militant tactics to depict grievances, their distinctive vulnerability and normative demands were totally neglected, and if not forgotten altogether, were misunderstood, as was the case in the original human rights instruments. To the extent that the position of indigenous peoples was taken into any specific account, it was in forms that actually embodied antagonistic approaches arising out of paternalistic assumptions.[18] But as a consequence of effective civic activism by indigenous peoples a generally receptive niche was created within the UN system in the shape of the Informal Working Group on Indigenous Populations. The Working Group has met annually in Geneva during recent years for a few weeks in each summer, producing an activist transnational network, and has clarified the human rights demands of indigenous peoples that had been previously ignored (or worse) by states, international institutions, and even by leading NGOs. Whether these symbolic steps of getting on the agenda and influencing the normative architecture will yield impressive and consistent substantive results is doubtful, given the obstacles.

At the very least, however, the dynamics of transnational activism have been indispensable to achieve a clarification of the genuine normative demands of indigenous peoples.[19] As with other human rights struggles, substantive success will depend on mobilizing supportive social forces of sufficient influence, a difficult challenge for indigenous peoples who must combine their wider participation on national, regional, and global levels with battles waged in local, often remote settings, where their opponents represent strong vested economic interests and which may involve challenging elaborate development projects with large infusions of capital.

The movement to uphold the basic rights of indigenous peoples has enjoyed enough success over the last two decades to challenge simplistic notions of capitalist and modernist primacy. At the same time, the limits of this success help us appreciate the relative strength of these dominant forces that are structuring the contemporary world order. As a result the very survival of indigenous peoples around the world remains in acute jeopardy.

THE ADDED COMPLICATION OF GLOBALIZATION

Most thinking about the implementation of human rights remains preoccupied with obstacles at the level of the state. The problems of penetrating the authoritarian state while avoiding the interventionary diplomacy of the colonial era are especially troublesome. The old multilateralism, reinforced by transnational social forces, or the new multilateralism, has made human rights concerns of considerable political significance in a series of specific settings. But there are some countervailing tendencies that constrain in many circumstances the further development of human rights in the near future, especially those of an economic and social character. These constraints can be best understood in relation to ideological climate, an altered balance of social forces, and the structural impact of the regionalization and globalization of capital and trade relations.

Ideological Climate

The collapse of the Soviet Union, the discrediting of socialism and the insistence on minimizing state investment and welfare roles contribute to a current policy consensus among elites often usefully identified as 'neo-liberalism'. In this atmosphere, support for economic and social rights, as specified in the main international law instruments on the subject (including The Right to Development), is virtually non-existent, although still enjoying nominal or rhetorical support.[20] Addressing the basic needs of the poor is entrusted, essentially, although not completely or evenly, to the operations of the market and the spill-over benefits of economic growth, privatization and increasing investment. Normative claims that insist on immediate and obligatory action by the state to overcome the social distress caused by poverty and joblessness are subordinated to a posture of deference to market forces and to a variety of economic restructuring priorities, most notably deficit reduction. This deference is reinforced by the absence of viable alternative orientations toward economic policy.

It should be acknowledged that a series of Asian countries' sustained economic growth, combined with a reasonably balanced distribution of material benefits to much of the population, has effectively achieved the substance of economic and social rights. A separate mechanism is not needed to achieve such rights if the dynamics of economic growth result in the material well-being of an increasing proportion of a given society.

Altered Balance of Social Forces

This circumstance of ideological adversity is accentuated by the decline of organized labour in most countries, giving business and finance-oriented viewpoints greater influence and control over mainstream party politics and in relation to governmental bureaucracies. This decline in the influence of labour partly arises from the same factors that have fashioned the neo-liberal consensus, but partly also from shifts in the nature of work in societies where manufacturing and industry is being superseded by services, and tangibles by intangibles. As a result, the industrial/manufacturing core of organized labour is becoming ever more peripheral to the social and economic order.[21] In effect, the role of the state is being reformulated in Europe and North America to minimize its role with respect to the social agenda of society, especially in the countries of the affluent North. For rapidly developing countries in the South the opposite tendencies are evident, with a more modern society expecting a larger role for government in providing a safety net for its citizens: in effect, a levelling down in the North, but a levelling up in the South with varying effects on reshaping the role of the state in relation to the realization of economic and social rights.

The Discipline of Regional and Global Capital

Perhaps most important of all is the pressure on all governments to avoid burdening economic activity in such a way that competitive pressures reduce market opportunities and performance.[22] The structural character of this pressure is evident in the strong recent tendency of social democratic political leadership around the world to shift their emphasis deliberately from people-oriented to market-oriented approaches to governmental policy. Even Sweden in a period of Social Democratic Party leadership has been abandoning, by stages, 'the Swedish model', that earlier had been a source of pride. The leverage of the private sector is made greater by the transnational mobility of capital, which through threats of flight has the effect of exerting downward pressure on domestic tax rates, wages, and business regulation. Throughout the world this same set of influences seems operative, and works against efforts to promote the well-being of the most economically and socially disadvantaged. In this sense, globalization structurally inhibits the protection of economic and social rights in such a way as to be relatively immune, at present, from the new multilateralism, which to the extent that it addresses these issues still tends to emphasize civil and political rights.[23] In some of the South and East Asian countries the situation is somewhat inverted, with economic and social rights being a more acceptable agenda priority for activist groups than civil and political rights and more in accord with the performance record of government. To the extent that this latter class of countries is developing at a very rapid rate of growth there are spreading social benefits that include all strata of society, although at rates and effects that vary from country to country.

There is an emergent tension between the promotion of economic and social rights at the level of the state and disciplinary impact of global market factors. It poses difficult questions as to whether governments locked into wider competitive frameworks retain the effective discretion to ensure that their own citizens can satisfy basic human needs of an economic and social character.[24] At present, the countries of the North are 'downsizing' in relation to the provision of public goods to their populations, and opposition political parties even of social democratic persuasion are not challenging such orientations. Regional frameworks could provide, in some settings, a partial solution. The notion of 'a social Europe' entails a commitment to reconcile economic factors with the claims of peoples with respect to the full gamut of rights. Whether such a regional approach is viable over time is questionable, as the unevenness of regions in a globalized world economy will sustain the downward pressures on public goods, including the provision of basic needs to the poor.

In other words, globalization, as shaped by a neo-liberal ideology, appeals to the earlier project of the humane or compassionate state, and confines the effective role of the new multilateralism, at least for the foreseeable future, to the civil and political domain. An aspect of this pessimistic assessment arises from the dual relationship of neo-liberalism to mobility: increasing transnational mobility of capital combined with increasing territoriality of labour, creating vulnerability of workers in high-wage countries, thus reinforcing their hostility and a special resistance to most categories of transnational economic migration.[25]

ANTICIPATING A STATIST BACKLASH

The emergence of global civil society in the form of multi-layered networks of variously aligned transnational forces has so far resulted in an ambiguous response from the old multilateralism, especially that associated with the United Nations system.[26] The UN has remained very much of a statist instrument and, beyond that, operates within limits set by a few dominant or hegemonic states, especially in relation to the peace and security activities of its principal organs. Nevertheless, the organization has opened up spaces that have allowed access of impressive proportions to the new multilateralism of transnational social forces. Reference has already been made to the Informal Working Group on Indigenous Populations, but perhaps even more significant, has been the participation of transnational social elements in the main UN global conferences on significant policy issues, starting with the Stockholm Conference on the Human Environment in 1972 and continuing in an upward spiral of influence until the Beijing Conference on Women and Development in 1995. To be sure, the mode of participation was indirect, by way of counter-conference formats, but the consciousness-raising impact of the conferences, by way of media treatment, and the shape of the final documents were definitely influenced by the efforts of the new multilateralists.

In reaction to these developments, states were losing their degree of ascendancy in a manner quite at variance with their loss of autonomy in relation to the global economy. With respect to globalization, the policy elite tended to be drawn from globalist circles, but in relation to transnational social forces, by and large, the interaction was characteristically an encounter across ideological, class, gender and ethnic lines. So long as the Cold War was at the centre of geopolitics, transnational activism was perceived, and even celebrated, as evidence of 'freedom' in the West as contrasted with rigid state controls in the East, and was treated by the East as 'a free propaganda good' as the target of activist groups were generally the governments of leading states in the West. But now such activism is perceived by the policy elite more objectively and consensually, and its anti-statist nature, and support for human rights and the environment are clearly exposed. In this period of increasing downsizing of commitment of government to the statist organs of the UN and of economic restructuring that involves reduced government spending for social purposes, there is building a more determined, although largely silent, opposition to any kind of subsidization of the new multilateralism, as well as an appreciation that the UN spaces in which these tendencies became most manifest were being effectively, and often antagonistically, appropriated by anti-statist perspectives. If this assessment is generally true, then one would expect the UN system in this period to contract these spaces, making them less available, squeezing the budget supporting the work on indigenous peoples and avoiding sponsorship of consciousness-raising conferences that serve as mobilization sites for the new multilateralism.

If this statist backlash ensues, then the resilience and resourcefulness of transnational social forces will be put to the test. Can new arenas of interaction be identified and participation financed? Can the use of the internet generate new types of transnational electronic empowerment that fills part of the vacuum? Can tactics be devised that draw battlelines in symbolically evocative ways? Greenpeace has had capacity throughout its entire period of existence and varieties of Green politics displayed such a political flair in its early years, especially in the Federal Republic of Germany.

ON THE COMPLICATING RELEVANCE OF CULTURE AND CIVILIZATION

Suggestions have been prominently made to the effect that the inner normative core of human experience possesses universal validity and is embodied either in 'a human rights culture' or in the legal content of international human rights.[27] Such a position claims to locate human rights as norms and claims beyond 'the clash of civilizations'. Within the historical circumstances arising out of an ideological climate dominated by neo-liberal perspectives and reinforced by pressures toward competitiveness and fiscal downsizing at corporate and governmental levels, there is certainly an attractiveness about reintroducing values into the political arena by way of human rights possessing an equivalent universal normative currency. Indeed the failure to reunite secularism with a seriously applicable moral agenda appears to have generated a dangerous social vacuum that encourages and strengthens various destructive forces such as drugs, crime, religious and ethnic extremism, youth suicide, death rock; as well as regressive backlash movements that seek to reimpose traditional constraints. Of course, neo-liberalism continues to contend that market-driven politics and secularism are leading to a peaceful world of prosperity and moderation, in effect, the best of all possible worlds. What is actually emerging, however, is a consumerist cult that lacks any inner dynamic of moral responsibility toward those who are excluded or impoverished. This challenge has deepened since the end of the Cold War due to the collapse of the socialist 'other,' the related weakening of the labour movement which provided the main vehicle for promoting social goals in capitalist countries and the emergence of non-Western civilizational voices.

However, it has turned out to be difficult to promote human rights as an alternative to socialism.[28] For one thing, the market-driven logic rejects that portion of human rights protection that is directed toward the satisfaction of individual or group basic needs. For another, the West has used its advocacy of human rights as a way of challenging the behaviour of non-Western societies, arousing the suspicion that human rights are, in function, a post-colonial rationale for interventionary diplomacy and the reassertion of Western civilizational superiority. This Western advocacy is further discounted as hypocritical because of its refusal to be applied self-critically to the failures and ongoing suffering within affluent Western societies. Along similar lines, the moral claims of human rights, as codified, are resisted, because of their Western origins and their purportedly unbalanced emphasis on the rights of the individual without a corresponding concern with the well-being of the community; in this regard, the human rights culture, so-called, is being perceived, especially by political Islam, as part of the civilizational decadence of the West, emerging out of a background that included colonial exploitation, racism and interventionary diplomacy, and a foreground of ultra-permissiveness and irreverence, as embodied in Western popular culture, dress codes, and sexual practices. Against such a background, the civilizational and religious traditions of Asia, and elsewhere, it is argued, provide more integral and persuasive moral guidance than can be found in the guidelines for action contained in human rights traditions as applied in the contemporary West. Encouraged by the recent success stories of Asian economic policies, there is a conviction in Asia and elsewhere that a better non-Western path to prosperity and stability exists than is provided by going the Western constitutional way;[29] and more relevantly, that these non-Western alternative views on the place of religion and morality will be effectively destroyed by globalization unless actively resisted, and this includes resistance to a wholesale opting for human rights as inscribed in the main instruments of international law.

Finally, the globally active agents of the new multilateralism in the human rights domain have consistently behaved as if human rights meant only political and civil rights, thereby making it easier to view these transnational initiatives as quasi-conspiratorial extensions of the ideological outlook of globalization from above.[30] Such a perception is reinforced because civilizationally and societally human suffering in the non-Western world is associated primarily with massive poverty, giving an instinctive priority to such claims as are associated with 'the right to development', and economic and social rights as compared to the defence of the liberal agenda of civil and political rights.[31] At the same time the United States as the prototypic bearer of human rights of the Western style is reasonably seen as indifferent to homelessness and racism, and as the focus of a moral cesspool of sexual depravity, drug use, and crime – hardly a model to be emulated by a society seeking a better future. Under these conditions the temptation is to retreat from universalism to multiculturalism, reinforced by a kind of revived statism that is detached from any widespread normative commitment to democracy.[32]

Part of the resistance to human rights in the non-Western world, especially by oppressive governments, needs itself to be demystified. This kind of reaction will only be effective if it mainly represents a response that emerges from within a country, or at least within a given civilizational constellation. It is important to expose manipulative efforts by repressive elites to avoid even minimal external pressures based on notions of accountability embodied in international law instruments. China and Indonesia have been particularly notorious in this respect. Their true motives are revealed by their insistence on unconditional sovereign rights, opposing the establishment of external accountability even if based on a regional framework of action, and a refusal to respect peaceful voices of opposition.

Can these temptations to repudiate the grounding in international law for human rights be successfully resisted? Can the human rights enterprise, norms and procedures be sufficiently emancipated from their ambiguous Western antecedents and contemporary mechanism of geopolitics? Does a basis remain, after cultural and civilizational perspectives and differences have been taken into account, to find meta-civilizational support for a human rights culture that is linked to the projects to strengthen global civil society and to build cosmopolitan or transnational democracy?[33] Can the opportunistic rejection of human rights be effectively distinguished from genuine and necessary critical scrutiny within all civilizational spaces? Such questions help to suggest an agenda for the new multilateralism if it is to meet the challenges being posed.

MEETING THE CHALLENGE: POSITIVE PERSPECTIVES

Globalization is undermining the normative achievements of the old multilateralism in a variety of ways, especially through its tendency to impose the discipline of global and regional capital upon states. Fortunately, other historical forces are working in different and opposite directions, including the emergence of transnational social forces that are animated by a human-centered vision of change and stability. Out of this complex interplay, taking account of dramatic degrees of unevenness in economic, political, social and cultural circumstances, the struggles for human rights in this era are taking their distinctive shape.

The immediate challenge with respect to human rights is associated with whether the new, bottom-up multilateralism can sustain its momentum in the face of two sets of deteriorating circumstances: the closing off of niches within intergovernmental arenas, especially the United Nations, and the claims of intra-civilizational autonomy in relation to norms and procedures of an allegedly extra-civilizational character that are stigmatized as 'Western' or as a Trojan Horse validating post-colonial intervention by the West. Both of these difficulties are linked to globalization, as prior sections have argued.

In this final section attention is given to ways forward that remain mindful of such obstacles.

Inter-civilizational Dialogue

In this period it is of utmost importance to disentangle antagonistic ideological stereotypes – various forms of Orientalism, including its opposite, 'Occidentalism' – from support for state/society relations conducive to the realization of human rights comprehensively conceived.[34] The possibility of dialogue presupposes civic space that permits more transnational mutual understanding, which is particularly important in relations between Islam and the West, but also between China and the West.[35]

Because of the hegemonic past and present of the West, it is initially important for the dialogue to move primarily South to North, Islam to the West.[36] There are hegemonic features of globalization, including a secular consumerism, that create serious structural difficulties for countries seeking to maintain their non-Western, non-secular identities; also, the insistence that the community counts, that individuals have duties as well as rights, and that a Universal Declaration of Human Responsibilities could be helpful in creating a greater willingness by non-Western human rights activists to oppose authoritarian cruelties within their own civilizational space.

Economic and Social Rights

One way to overcome non-Western reactions to calls for inter-civilizational dialogue is to treat economic and social rights as deserving of as much support in specific settings as civil and political rights. Anti-debt coalitions and the efforts of the Third World Network contain projects in which Western human rights initiatives could join forces with activists and their organizations in the South. Efforts to regulate multinational corporations and transnational banking would also enable conditions to exist in which respect for economic and social rights could be improved, and shared transnational, North-South concerns could lead to coalitions of effort and commitment.

Such a dynamic may occur spontaneously. The dramatic and powerful French strikes of December 1995 can be interpreted from various angles, but one factor was resistance to the sorts of budgetary discipline required by Maastricht objectives and perhaps more broadly, a disease within the French populace in relation to the perceived drift toward supranationalism, and its impact on political identity and the character of the French nation. This resistance may be disclosing an emergent radicalism in the West that as a core element will re-conceive of human rights by a primary reference to economic and social rights, especially if political parties, elections and representative institutions in these Western societies continue to seem less and less responsive to the range of actual human concerns. In one respect, this possible new politics will seek to preserve the nation-state character of France in the face of efforts by business and finance to reconstitute identity by relation to market opportunity.

Ethos of Nonviolent Politics

The future of the new multilateralism in relation to the promotion of human rights will depend on whether credible political movements can arise to displace existing patterns of leadership. For various reasons, including the degree to which globalization rests upon an ethos of violence, any effective countervailing normative orientation will need to rest its appeal and effectiveness upon non-violent political orientations. The various democratic transformations of the 1980s encourage the belief that non-violent mobilization of political energies can effectively challenge a variety of repressive political arrangements. The outcomes in the Philippines, Eastern Europe, the Soviet Union, South Africa and Israel/Palestine are inspirational, even if the new political realities are disappointing. Even the various failed democratizing attempts in China, Burma, Nepal and Thailand are suggestive of the extent to which revolutionary politics in this era are essentially seeking, by non-violent means, to put a human rights culture in place of authoritative and exploitative political systems.[37]

The new multilateralism, in this sense, will not succeed over time, unless it explicitly and avowedly repudiates the war system as it operates within the framework of the old multilateralism. In this respect, the human rights imperative is a radical one at this stage, as continued accommodation with mainstream political and cultural violence will increasingly contradict the possibilities of sustaining individual and group conditions of human decency.

Shifting Patterns of Accountability

There are at least two possible constructive directions of effort, given the likelihood that intergovernmental initiatives will be stymied: regional and subregional frameworks and citizens' initiatives.[38] The current appeal of regional and sub-regional frameworks is their potential capacity to reconcile resistance to extra-civilizational pressures with intra-civilizational commitments to the construction of decent human societies, although the dispersion of peoples means that civilizational space is not identical with geographical space. This complicates the whole emphasis on the inter-civilizational reality, but in a manner that can be addressed by way of tolerance and respect within the territorial space of the various 'others'.

In addition, informal frameworks of accountability could gain increased relevance in the years ahead, focusing attention on transnational patterns that produce human abuses which the old multilateralism prefers to overlook, such as the use of secret banking facilities to hide public funds stolen and appropriated from societies or the encroachments of government and business on the lands and rights of indigenous peoples.

This format was pioneered by Bertrand Russell in a tribunal formed to investigate allegations of American war crimes in Vietnam during the 1960s, and has evolved in many settings since then. The Permanent Peoples Tribunal, with its base in Rome, has done notable work for more than two decades, in a series of instances ranging from the plight of Amazonia to the abusive impacts of the Bretton Woods institutions, to the interventionary diplomacy of both superpowers during the Cold War in such countries as Afghanistan and Nicaragua. These initiatives, undertaken without authorization by states or international institutions, have documented those injustices that the guardians of globalization prefer to ignore. Since the media follows, in most instances, the guidelines of these guardians it has been generally difficult to obtain serious attention for the results of these inquiries even when carefully documenting hitherto unacknowledged infringements on human rights. Whether the new modalities of the Internet will provide such initiatives with more effective ways to gain influence for their activities beyond their local place of occurrence, is yet to be established.

Internalization of 'Universal' Norms

The Western origins and orientation of human rights may be a burden in a period of greater civilizational assertiveness, but to some extent non-Western civilizations have their own equivalent or parallel standards of approved conduct that have been shaped through time, including in interaction with the West. In this respect a global socialization process has internalized in all civilizations a resonance to many basic human rights claims, although there are contested zones where contradictory claims are being made, and where there are important differences as to language, substance and relation to the past.

Within this framework the universal and the particular can both find authentic, yet often controversial, expression beneath the overarching rubric of human rights. Just as money or language function both generically and in relation to particularities of time and place, so is the same true for human rights.

Whether these several factors can enable the new multilateralism to grow stronger under current conditions, and thereby help human rights to adapt successfully to the rigors of globalization and civilizational resurgence is highly questionable at this point. What seems evident is that such an adaptation will require radical innovations on the part of initiatives identified here as globalization-from-below. If successful such initiatives could transform the future of world order in beneficial ways, but if not there is likely to be a great deal of disillusionment and mutual recrimination associated with human rights as a dimension of international political life.

NOTES

1. Human rights are also associated with protection against cruel and oppressive practices. Non-citizens located within a territory are also protected.
2. Internal accountability evolved unevenly, yet cumulatively, in the modern Western transition from royal absolutism to constitutionalism, a process that can be traced back to the Magna Carta, with antecedents in ancient Athens and Rome.
3. For a less rigid view of this dichotomy between domestic and inter-

national society, yet still situated firmly in the realist, anti-utopian tradition, see Hedley Bull, *The Anarchical Society* (New York: Columbia University Press, 1977).

4. For the classic formulation see Machiavelli, *The Prince*; for a contemporary perspective see Hans Morgenthau and Kenneth Thompson, *Politics Among Nations; The Struggle for Power and Peace*, Sixth Edition (New York: Knopf, 1985). For influential critical assessments of the distorting impact of moralism and legalism on international relations thinking see the main writings of E.H. Carr, George Kennan, Henry Kissinger and Reinhold Neibuhr; also Robert Cox for an extension of critical realist thinking to encompass the political economy, 'Social Forces, States, and World Orders; Beyond International Relations Theory', in Robert Keohane (ed), *Neo-Realism and Its Critics* (New York: Columbia University Press, 1986) pp. 204-54.

5. The evolutionary strengthening of domestic constitutionalism over the course of several centuries and in vastly different national circumstances were inevitably the result of concessions to societal pressures, and were in this respect essentially involuntary; undoubtedly, the most notable expression of these leaps forward in constitutional protection of individuals within domestic political space occurred in connection with the American and French revolutions. Later extensions of protection to individuals arose out of the labour movement as a defensive reaction to the hardships imposed on workers by the early phases of the Industrial Revolution. This pattern of implementation from below within domestic space anticipates the main argument of this chapter about the role of transnational social forces in accounting for the unexpected potency of the movement to give international legal status to human right claims and standards.

6. Although the main purpose of these trials was to avoid repeating mistakes made after World War I when the entire German nation was made to bear responsibility for the last war, there were other goals, as well. One such goal was to document the Nazi terror, especially the Holocaust: not only to educate international society about the depravity of Nazi Germany, but also to take seriously, if belatedly, the human suffering inflicted on the victims.

7. The subversive dimension of the war crimes issue has re-emerged in a vivid way in connection with the endgame diplomacy of the Bosnian War; the Dayton Peace Accord of 1995 took the extraordinary step of disqualifying anyone from a position of political leadership in the reconstituted Bosnia if he or she has been formally indicted for war crimes by the tribunal in The Hague; this was understood as applicable, at the very least, to the Bosnian Serb leaders, Karadic and Mladic. The same double movement is evident in the push within the United Nations to go forward with proposals for the establishment of a permanent International Criminal Court and resistance to such a formalization of individual criminal accountability. As of now, further stages in such a process are being carried on within the limits set by a geopolitical compromise to the effect that the authority of such a tribunal would only be engaged if the Security Council so decides.

Such a procedure brings the veto into play ensuring for the permanent members that neither their leaders, nor those of close allies, could be prosecuted as war criminals. In effect, even if such a court comes into existence it would in all probability steer clear of any process of general applicability, and confine its operation to criminal patterns that occur on the margins of international society.

8. But such an original intention did not determine the destiny of the human rights discourse. Unintended consequences and unanticipated agents of influence exerted various pressures upon human rights as merely declaratory. Thus, the discourse as initiated evolved as a process, becoming an instrument of geopolitical conflict and taking in a more juridical character when the norms of the Universal Declaration were reformulated in the form of international treaties: the International Covenant on Economic, Social, and Cultural Rights; and the International Covenant on Civil and Political Rights.

9. As human rights evolved in subsequent years, being carried forward by unanticipated currents of pressure, this division between categories of rights hardened, producing a clear encounter between the two leading orientations toward human rights which took the form of breaking the content of the Universal Declaration into distinct covenants. The US governmental attitude was pivotal, treating civil and political rights as already embodied in practice, making any internationalization of the obligations to uphold a matter of redundancy, while viewing economic and social claims as at best hortatory, and undeserving of legal protection. As support for the welfare state declined in recent years, coming into increasing conflict with the operation of the market and private sector, these human rights claims were dismissed as unworthy, partly because of their socialist implications.

10. In the United States, any attempted internationalization of human rights has been rigorously resisted at every turn by the right wing, essentially because it seemed to give 'enemies' a means by which to challenge the aspect of domestic social practice, which was doubly objectionable to these critics because it infringed on both sovereignty and federalism.

11. These differences in outlook and behaviour are well depicted in Harold D. Lasswell and Myres S. McDougal, 'Diverse Systems of Public Order,' in McDougal (ed), *Studies in World Public Order* (New Haven, CT: Yale University Press, 1960); see also the Falk chapter in *Human Rights and State Sovereignty* (New York: Holmes and Meier, 1981).

12. For a highly critical view of American policies in relation to human rights see Noam Chomsky and Edward S. Hermann, *The Political Economy of Human Rights* (Boston: South End Press, two vols, 1979); also Richard J. Barnet, *Intervention and Revolution*; for a spirited normative defence of this American approach see Jeane Kirkpatrick, or an orientation toward human rights that reflected anti-Communist ideology and led to the adoption of the Reagan Doctrine of assisting anti-Communist insurgencies by alleged reference to human rights considerations. See, for example, Jeane J. Kirkpatrick and Allan Gerson, 'The Reagan Doctrine, Human Rights, and International Law', in *Right*

v. Might: International Law on the Use of Force, Second edition (New York, Council on Foreign Relations, 1991).

13. The most blatant Soviet interventions in Eastern Europe were Hungary (1956) and Czechoslovakia (1968), but threats of Soviet intervention encouraged Communist regimes to tighten up their authoritarian control and, overall minimized the space available for implementing human rights of a civil and political character.

14. This idealist influence was more effective because it corresponded with political myths and traditions in America that retain vitality for a large portion of the citizenry, and can be invoked by political leaders at times to reassert the moral leadership and influence of the United States in world affairs, reclaiming a heritage as 'a Lockeanisation in a Hobbesian world.'

15. Cf. David Held on the deeper significance of this step in *Political Theory and the Modern State* (Stanford, CA: Stanford University Press, 1984), pp. 232–4.

16. A strong instance of ideologically tilted ratings for human rights performance were to be found in the annual Freedom House reports, which represented an alignment between official Western views of human rights and a fairly conservative sector of civil society.

17. Bloc barriers were important insulators during the Cold War, whereas indifference toward political outcomes of struggles in most Third World countries or Western hostility to Islamic militancy, even if democratically supported (as in the Algerian elections), protected most oppressive states from external pressures, given current global conditions.

18. This was certainly the case with respect to ILO Convention No. 107 (1956), text available in Burns H. Weston, Richard A. Falk, Anthony D'Amato (eds), *Basic Documents in International Law and World Order* (St Paul, MN: West Publishing, 1990), pp. 335–40.

19. As evidence of success by indigenous peoples in promoting their normative preferences and correcting the earlier misunderstandings see ILO Convention No. 169 (1989), text available in Weston, Falk, D'Amato, eds., *Documents*, pp. 489–97. For an even stronger expression of indigenous viewpoints see United Nations Draft Declaration of the Rights of Indigenous Peoples, which is currently being reviewed by the human rights bureaucracy prior to presentation to the General Assembly for final approval. See tentative text and resolution 1995/32 of UN Commission on Human Rights, *International Legal Materials* XXXIV: pp. 535–55 (March 1995). It is likely that the outcome of this process will be inconclusive as states seem likely to resist any move that legally confirm claims of self-determination by indigenous peoples, fearing state shattering implications.

20. On the right to development see Roland Rich, 'The Right to Development: A Right of Peoples?' in James Crawford (ed.), *The Rights of Peoples* (Oxford: Clarendon Press, 1988), pp. 39–54.

21. Such an assessment is provisional and selective. There is some evidence in the mid and late 1990s of a revival of labour militancy, especially where unions are firmly embedded in the public sector and basic utilities, as in France, Italy, and Spain.

22. But see the skeptical view of these pressures in Paul Krugman's book, *Peddling Prosperity: Economic Sense and Nonsense in the Age of Diminishing Expectations* (New York: W.W. Norton, 1995), pp. 245–92.

23. Even on the domestic scene in the United States, the anti-welfare climate of opinion is strong enough to immobilize welfare advocacy constituencies: see Tamar Lewin, 'Liberal Advocates Seem Speechless', *International Herald Tribune*, 25–26 November 1995.

24. For underlying philosophical specification see: John Rawls, 'The Law of Peoples', in Stephen Shute and Susan Hurley (eds), *On Human Rights: The Oxford Amnesty Lectures 1993* (New York: Basic Books), pp. 41–82. Rawls' views are set forth as purely a matter of state/society relations. His approach acknowledges that orientations other than liberal can satisfy the requirements of decency embodied in 'The Law of Peoples', but he fails altogether to consider whether governments have this option given external links and constraints associated with the way markets are organized.

25. For a variety of reasons xenophobia and hostility to immigration is on the rise, including efforts to shift responsibility for job loss and declining real wages to immigrants, legal and illegal. One of the striking features of globalization is that despite its rhetoric of 'freedom', the impact on the majority of persons is likely to be a decline in relative and absolute economic security. Such an impact is often discussed as an aspect of the polarizing effects of globalization, but it is also a consequence of liberating capital from the constraints of territorial space, while tying most workers more closely than ever, as well as tightening up indirect modes of mobility by way of immigration, refugee flows and asylum policies. For an imaginative and persuasive treatment of these themes see Susan Jonas, 'U.S. "National Security" vs. Regional Welfare as the Basis for Immigration Policy: Reflections from the Case of Central American Immigrants and Refugees,' in Kay Castro (ed.), *Transnational Realities and Nation States: Trends in International Integration and Immigration Policy in the Americas* (Boulder, CO: Lynne Rienner, 1996). A journalistic account reports that construction workers from Mexico's northern border can earn 15 times more by crossing to the United States and that enforcement efforts are increasing to reduce the number of illegal crossings. Sam Dillon, 'Enforcement Reduces Illegal Crossings from Mexico', *International Herald Tribune*, 25–26 November 1995. Another aspect of this pattern of economic legitimation and territorial protection in the North and criminalization and intervention in the South is evident in relation to such diverse issues as anti-terrorism, the drug war, and the non-proliferation regime as contrasted with arms sales.

26. The response at the regional level of multilateralism is uneven, but definitely part of the wider story. In Europe where the preconditions for a rudimentary form of regional democracy were present, at least until the end of the Cold War, the claims of the new multilateralism were accommodated by revolutionary means in the human rights area, creating formal institutions that were capable of responding directly to civic grievances, enabled to provide both accountability external to

the state, but also extra-statal procedures of direct recourse. Such possibilities were reinforced, as well, by the existence of the European Parliament. Regional developments outside of Europe, aside from initiatives intended to promote economic cooperation, have been minimal.

27. The former assertion is posited as the main position of Richard Rorty in his Amnesty Oxford lecture, crediting Gregory Rabassa with the phrase. See Rorty, 'Human Rights Rationality, and Sentimentality', in Shute and Hurley, note 18, pp. 111–34. The universalist argument is also made in Christopher C. Joyner and John C. Dettling, 'Bridging the Cultural Chasm: Cultural Relativism and the Future of International Law', *California Western International Law Journal* 20: (1989–90) pp. 275–314.

28. Difficult issues of agency and the causal impact of normative ideas are raised by such an assertion that cannot be addressed here. Suffice it to say, socialism owed its effectiveness, as Marx brilliantly perceived, to the prospect of mobilized, potentially revolutionary, industrial labour sectors of society. A limit on this effectiveness, which Marx much less clearly realized, was the weakness of transnational class solidarity as compared to nationalist bonds of solidarity. Human rights as a normative discourse became effective as a result of the convergence of geopolitical factors (ideological confrontation restricted by nuclear stalemate) and the rise of transnational civil initiatives. What is happening at the present is a softening of both these sets of empowering pressures, creating an impression of drift with respect to the political relevance of the human rights concept.

29. Many of these arguments are advanced in a significant way by Ahmet Davutoglu, *Civilizational Transformation and the Muslim World* (Kuala Lumpur, Malaysia: Mahir Publications, 1994); see his assertion, p. 24: 'This monopolistic tendency by the hegemonic powers to marginalize other cultures is also an aspect of the globalization of international economics . . . Western civilization in its attempts to globalize and impose its hegemonic paradigm, has effectively marginalized other cultures. If this process is not arrested, we may see the inevitable evaporation of other cultures and civilizations'.

30. For an essay relying on the terminology 'globalization-from-above' and 'globalization-from-below' see the Falk essay in Jeremy Brecher, John Brown Childs and Jill Cutler (eds), *Global Visions: Beyond the New World Order* (Boston, MA: South End Press, 1993), pp. 39–50.

31. The perspectives of JUST (Just World Society) in Penang, Malaysia are indicative of this orientation. See the proceedings of the 1994 conference, 'Rethinking Human Rights' (Kuala Lumpur) and the 1995 Penang workshop, 'Images of Islam: Terrorizing the Truth'. See also the book by founder and director of JUST Chandra Muzaffar, *Human Rights and the New World Order*, Penang, Malaysia, Just World Trust, 1983.

32. The alleged global democratizing trend post-1989 is ambiguous even if South and East Asia are left aside; for most of the countries in Eastern Europe and the countries that have taken the place of the former Soviet Union and Yugoslavia the democratic commitment is

cosmetic at best and may even be reversed or compromised by electoral outcomes. In the Middle East, as well, authoritarian rule flourishes beneath many banners, and even a military takeover may be preferred by the West to the risk of respect for democratic processes that end up handing the reins of government over to religious extremists. Abdel Monein Said Ali, Director of the Al Ahram Center for Strategic Studies in Cairo, was quoted as follows on the prospect for future elections being less than fair: 'Democracy in Egypt is not deep-rooted. Belief is still in the state. If you want something done, it is the state who [sic] will do it'. John Lancaster, 'In Egyptian Elections, Democracy Also May Win or Lose', *International Herald Tribune*, 28 November 1995.

33. See generally, David Held, *Democracy and the Global Order* (Stanford, CA: Stanford University Press, 1995); Falk, *On Humane Governance: Toward a New Global Politics* (Cambridge, UK: Polity, 1995); David Held and Daniele Archibugi (eds), *Cosmopolitan Democracy* (Cambridge, UK: Polity, 1994).

34. Edward Said, *Orientalism* (New York: Pantheon, 1978); proceedings of the JUST conference 'Rethinking Human Rights' in Kuala Lumpur, Malaysia, December 1994; Abdullahi Ahmed An-Na'im (ed.), *Human Rights in Cross-Cultural Perspectives: A Quest for Consensus* (Philadelphia, PA: University of Pennsylvania Press, 1992).

35. For constructive assessments that encourage dialogue see John L. Esposito, *The Islamic Threat : Myth or Reality* (Oxford University Press, 1992); Fred Halliday, *Islam and the Myth of Confrontation* (London: I.B. Tauris, 1995).

36. There are special obstacles that arise when the historical memory of inter-civilizational relations is one of abuse on the part of the subordinated civilization. The relations of the West with Islam, Africa, and indigenous peoples disclose different facets of this background that casts a long shadow of suspicion across efforts at reconciliation. Acknowledgement and apology seem important steps to be taken by the dominant side, not to erase the memory, but to move it beyond a preoccupation with past grievance. One other approach, taken in relation to Islam, is to overcome existing modes of discrimination that are, in effect, relegating Islam to the status of civilizational subordination. For discussion see Falk, 'False Universalism and Geopolitics of Exclusion: The Case of Islam', paper presented at Princeton Conference on 'Universalizing from Particulars: Islamic Views of the Human and the UN Declaration of Human Rights in Comparative Perspective', 24–26 May 1996.

37. These encounters need to encompass the claims of indigenous peoples as well.

38. The current effort to establish an International Criminal Court is illustrative of the likely inability to achieve goals by way of the old multilateralism.

8 Globalization, Multilateralism and the Shrinking Democratic Space

Claude Ake

Democratic space has been shrinking under pressure from a combination of social forces notably globalization. By all indications, this trend is irreversible, but the prospect of mitigating it remains an open question. I want to explore this prospect in the context of the unique and deadly threat of globalization to politics in general and democratic politics in particular.

Democracy has had an embattled history, struggling to survive in an environment in which support was rarely ever more than lukewarm and invariably ambivalent, confused or opportunistic, and opposition was always powerful, resourceful and unrelenting. The French Revolution was the watershed in this struggle. It had reached back to the Athenian idea of democracy as popular power. The nascent European bourgeoisie which had welcomed the French Revolution for giving impetus to the liquidation of the economic and political institutions of feudalism were appalled by its radical egalitarianism especially its theory of popular sovereignty. Not surprisingly they rejected its democratic theory and replaced it with liberal democracy.

Liberal democracy has significant affinities to democracy but it is substantially different. Instead of the collectivity, it focuses on the individual. Liberal democracy substitutes government by the people with government by consent of the people. Instead of sovereignty of the people, it offers the sovereignty of law. It celebrates specificity rather than universality. Most importantly, liberal democracy repudiates the notion of popular power.

Democracy was therefore replaced by what is essentially the political correlate of industrial capitalism. The core values of liberal

179

democracy and the market are the same; formal freedom, equality, egotism and private property. The social presuppositions of liberal democracy are the ideal characteristics of market society.

As is to be expected, the development of liberal democracy has been driven by the development of capitalism. To underline this, the classical contractual liberalism of the social contract theorists, especially Locke and Hobbes, corresponds to the ideal conception of the market, the market of perfect competition. As capitalism took hold, developed into monopoly capital and went into what Faucoult would call the panoptic mode, liberal democracy in turn abandoned political participation in any meaningful sense, embraced competitive elitism, the protectionist theory of democracy and finally came down to multi-party elections with highly flexible notions of free and fair voting. Through all this, democracy has been defined and redefined in an endless process of appropriating democratic legitimacy for political values, interests and practices that are in no way democratic. At the same time, the process has yielded an anarchy of meanings of democracy and spread confusion to the detriment of the concept of democracy which now means both too much and too little.

The one redeeming feature in this embattled history of democracy is that for all the attacks, subversion, displacement and trivialization of democracy, there was an unstated consensus on its legitimacy. Indeed the travails of democracy arose precisely from an attempt to appropriate democratic legitimacy for concepts or practices of democracy that are less than democratic. So in a paradoxical sense, even the attempts to trivialize, undermine or redefine democracy invariably affirmed the ideal of democracy.

THE THREAT OF GLOBALIZATION

The process of globalization threatens democracy in a manner that is uniquely different and extremely dangerous. It does not redefine democracy in theory or practice or bend it to the service of specific interests. It does not seek appropriation of democratic legitimacy for something else and it does not trivialize democracy nor does it reject it. Globalization is simply rendering democracy and political participation irrelevant.

The most obvious source of this effect is the diminishing relevance of the nation-state for democracy is ideally articulated in the context of national organization of politics and power. The nation-state is also the traditional repository of sovereignty. With the transnational-ization of more and more things, especially economic activities, decisions which affect people's lives and shape public policies deci-sively are made in distant places, often anonymously by agents and forces which citizens can hardly understand much less control. Factors of production move relatively freely across national boundaries as do goods and services. There is an increasingly complex web of bilateral and multilateral agencies, intergovernmental organizations and international regimes for various areas of the international economy regulating different aspects of world commerce. Finance and financial markets have been truly globalized. So it is increas-ingly unclear how much voters are deciding at national and local elections. The political entity which ideally materializes popular sovereignty has less and less power while the amorphous space of transnational phenomena which is not amenable to democratic control has more power. There is a polarization of democratic participa-tion without power on the one side, and power, inaccessible to democratization, on the other.

Globalization is desocializing society, obliterating the conditions which make political consciousness and the political 'public' possible. Phenomenal advances in communications technology driven by global marketing and the information revolution which it has spawned is reconstituting consciousness as information, information delivered in ever-increasing profusion and speed. And yet having established itself as consciousness, this information bears hardly any social experience. To begin with, it is not only a product of technology, it *is* technology. Form and content, message and medium are inter-twined in what is really a subsumption, the subsumption of informa-tion into technology. In its technological materiality, information is not communication, but non-communication. It does not allow for reciprocity, especially antagonistic reciprocities which are dy-namic; it is what Jean Baudrillard calls 'speech without response'.

Since this information is only a record encrusted in technology and carries no social experience, it does not integrate socially – this is just the other side of its non-communication. Rather it iso-lates, partly because of the way in which it is delivered and con-sumed. The technology connects us as discrete units in an electronic coherency while isolating us socially for it is delivered through the privacy of modems, storage devices and computer screens, and once it is delivered and received it becomes just a record or an environment disconnected from social praxis.

Global processes have framed a syndrome of isolation and desocialization at the confluence of the singularities of the new communications technology, information and the public sphere. As we have seen, the technology delivers information to us in relative isolation and largely devoid of social experience. The information itself is isolating; then, both technology and information define a new public sphere which is mediated in complex ways that desocialize it. This is not the bourgeois public sphere of Habermas so conducive to democratic politics, for it is decidedly non-dialogical.[1] Our visibility to each other in this new public sphere is abstract as is the space itself, which has hardly any boundaries, and is too fluid and too amorphous to elicit a sense of sharing in a social entity or to nurture political projects and democratic activism.

In this context there can only be a politics of disempowerment for here is a context in which the critical role of political mobilization is made abstract and concentrated in the mass media, a context in which political will and political choice achieve concreteness only as opinion polls. The mass media constitute and instrumentalize contemporary politics in a manner that amounts to self-constitution. They promise politics and participation only to deny them by crystallizing into a formidable power, and a formidable obstacle to politics. They deny politics by creating a realm of necessity which demands submission rather than creating a realm of freedom which facilitates and enjoins creativity.

As for opinion polls and electronic referenda, they only mock political will and political choice. Opinion polls present political will and political choice as facts and statistics to the total destruction of their democratic significations. The essence and saliency of political will and political choice in democratic politics is that they are dynamic processes, the living experience of preferring and willing, expressing the will and actively negotiating consensus on matters of common concern. The opinion poll and the electronic referendum precisely subvert this political process by virtue of the fact that they are stillborn, passive, intransitive statistics which have nothing to do with social participation, aggregation or social exchange.

Difficulties for Democratic Struggles

The process of globalization is producing a global environment in which emancipatory struggles including democratization are unable to find focus or meaning. The Cold War was a harrowing experience which cannot be viewed nostalgically. But at least in that era everything was charged with political significance which was invariably about the possibilities of democracy. The great ideological divide was conspicuous and intrusive, pressing everything into the political arena and compelling everyone to make political judgments and constantly to assume political postures. We were always soldiering for a political cause with an ubiquitous presence full of historical importance. In the Cold War era, allies and opponents were easily identified and generally understood. There were specific power centres to focus on; there were grand ideologies which readily suggested how to interpret events and how to proceed, and there were ready-made allies to mobilize and tested modalities of struggle to utilize. Most significantly, even though both sides in the Cold War spoke different languages, bristled with hostility and believed that their differences were deep and irreconcilable, both camps were in fact a dialectical unity. For each camp had a vision of a world of progress, rationality and democracy, a vision to which it was passionately committed.

All that has changed. There is now no epic ideological struggle to politicize every difference and every social space. Since the substance of this politicization was progress, rationality and democracy, these concerns have largely lost their importance. Now, there is only one vision of a rational world society which has been supposedly realized at 'the end of history'. What remain are minor adjustments and final touches which call for no serious politics, only some administration and private initiatives. For those who see in the triumph of this world view the meeting of the real and ideal, there would be no point in lamenting the atrophy of politics. For them, the non-feasibility of democratic politics and democratic struggles poses no problem. On the contrary it merely attests to what has been achieved.

But the real is not yet the ideal and history is far from over. There are many who see a world of increasingly asymmetrical power relations in which their weaknesses are reproduced endlessly. These people are conscious of their marginality, their tenuous control over their lives, their lack of access to democratic participation and their exposure to abuse and oppression. Entire countries in the world feel this way; and a greater number of people within all nations, including the most developed, share these feelings, and are in need of politics and of emancipatory and democratic struggles. How to wage these struggles is the problem. As we have seen, because of globalization, there are hardly any power centres to attack: the oppressors are not easily identified. Political mobilization is very difficult because of the subsumption of the social into the market, the isolation of individuals owing to the primacy of information over communication, the general desocialization of life and the ever-increasing number of social activities (such as shopping, education, meetings, sports and cultural events) which technology now delivers to us in the privacy of our homes and offices.

The difficulties of democratic struggles are compounded by the porosity of the national space caused by transnational phenomena. How can people organize against oppressive power which is impersonal, invisible and fluid, power which is always flowing into spaces beyond our grasp and immune to the institutional checks on power in our locality. It is not just power that is fluid. We too are 'fluid', and also despatialized, for our interests are increasingly tangled with people and events far from us. Consequently our local or national space is increasingly unlikely to encompass the interest groups which are critical to us. The international or global space becomes ever more relevant instead. Unfortunately, the expansion and porosity of our space does not enhance our power by facilitating a larger, more powerful coalition, but gives us only a disorienting sense of spacelessness and little room for political action. Political mobilization, especially interest aggregation and interest articulation, is all but impossible in the fluidity and anonymity of this new political space. Even if mobilization were possible, how would the struggle be focused? At what power centres, and with what power resources?

Remedial Options

What is to be done about the shrinking, democratic space? Gilbert has suggested projects of resistance by citizens, a new democratic internationalism akin to the environmental movement or the peace movement.[2] Both Page and Connolly envisaged new political arrangements above the level of the state and below it to serve a new cosmopolitan democracy.[3] Held is rather more specific about the new cosmopolitan democracy. He posits arrangements by which transnational phenomena and concerns such as environmental problems and tariff regimes could be regulated by large representative international bodies such as the European Parliament and an 'international civil society'.[4] Burnheim suggests functional bodies which could be regional or global to govern specific spheres such as the environment or trade. The bodies could be chosen from those who clearly have an interest in the matter in question, by lot, or any statistical system that guarantees objectivity.[5]

There are serious problems with these options, arising from some misconceptions of the causes of the shrinking democratic space. It is instructive that these proposals run in the direction of setting up, at the regional or global level, some institutions for overseeing a sphere of transnational phenomena. There is the question of the democratic import of these institutions or arrangements but that is a different issue.

The critical problem is the sedimentation of power in blind amorphous transnational social forces that appear to have no centre and which, like market forces, have considerable autonomy from the individuals whose day-to-day decisions and activities produce them. The very nature of the social forces especially their anonymity, spatial diffusion, and the complex mediations of their impact virtually excludes the possibility of setting up institutions and political arrangements to control them. Globalization tends to break up territoriality and nationality for functional and interest groups and democratic arrangements have to be congruent with this reality. Segmented into such interest and functional categories, structures for democratic participation will be specific to the functional categories such as tariff regimes. If that happens what would have been achieved is only the democratization of interest and functional groups. This will be a trivialization of democracy since the real need for political participation arises in the context of the conflict of the claims of divergent interests. It will be like democratizing a labour union without giving consideration to the fact that democratization of the union has to go hand in hand with the democratization of the broader social field of forces in which the labour union confronts other interests, some of which are very powerful.

Indeed, what actually happens is even worse than this. Given the effects of globalization, it is not even likely that the democratization of the transnational functional group is achievable. With minor exceptions, for instance the sphere of the environment, those who will be the most conscious about transnational phenomena and their implications for their interests will be players such as large corporations which also wield the most powerful influence, and not ordinary people who invariably lack a global reach or a global perspective and are often not fully aware of how transnational phenomena affect them.

The functional regimes are useful, but they are not really an adequate solution to the question of democratization in the international sphere. Too much optimism has been drawn from the prevailing anarchy in the international sphere and the lack of power structures to block new democratic initiatives. For instance, Dryzek argues that the decentralized and anarchic international system which renders it dangerous 'means too, that this system possesses no central authority analogous to the state, such that a host of impediments to democracy do not exist here'.[6]

In fact a host of formidable impediments exists, for there is no democracy in anarchy, or in an amorphous social space without a self-conscious community. There may well be opportunities for decision making through consensus, for instance the UN Conference on the Law of the Sea, but Dryzek also recognizes that 'such examples hardly constitute transnational participatory democracy in action'.[7]

The multilateralism of specific regimes is less useful still for defending participatory space in the national scene. It does not and cannot really counteract the social atomization of the new information technology which isolates individuals and attacks sociability by making it increasingly easier for individuals to carry out a wide range of cultural and economic activities alone by means of computers. Besides, the new technology also impairs political consciousness by rendering the 'bourgeois public space' redundant and by dissociating social meaning from social communication which is reduced to 'bits' of information inscribed in technology.

That is only one aspect of the basic irrelevance of multilateralism to the defence of democratic participation on the national scene. The other is that globalization, the transnationalization of things, tendentially transfers important decision-making powers from the national to the transnational sphere. As the national state and its managers cede more and more power to transnational forces, the reason for democratic participation disappears, for the point of such participation is to share in the exercise and the control of power. Unfortunately, it is difficult to see any way of reversing or mitigating this transfer of power from the state sphere.

There is a significant objection to this assertion. In a special feature on democracy and technology, the *Economist* (London, 17 June 1995) argues that democratic politics is largely about communication and that the new technology of communication such as the Internet, which allows anyone with a computer and a modem to address millions of people, has opened new possibilities for democracy.[8] More people can have more access to more information for better decisions; representatives can be more in touch with their constituencies; issues can easily be put to a very wide audience through e-mail; and policy decisions can be taken through electronic voting which enables some element of direct democracy (as Alvin and Heidi Toffler argue in their book *War and Anti-War: Survival at the Dawn of the 21st Century*).[9]

There are difficulties with this. Apart from the dangers of arithmetical majoritarianism which include an insensitivity to minority interests, these political arrangements oversimplify issues, impair interest aggregation and consensus building, reinforce social atomization and conflate political participation with opinion polls. As already mentioned, the opinion poll is ultimately stillborn and intransitive and bears little relation to the participative process of debating, aggregating interests and negotiating strategies and consensus, even defining corporate identities and constructing collective projects amidst social contradictions. Finally there is also the problem of the erosion of power from the local space which is left with largely trivial decisions. If that is granted, political participation is not greatly helped by elements of electronic direct democracy.

MULTILATERALISM, TERRITORIALITY AND DEMOCRACY

A critical limitation of defending democracy through functional regimes such as WTO and NAFTA is the failure to reckon with the spatial aspects of democracy. For democracy to make sense, there should be identifiable power centres in a territorial entity coterminous with a community which is conscious of itself as a corporate, self-governing entity. There can be no democracy in amorphous space through which power is infinitely diffused. Whatever arrangements are made to recontextualize and defend democracy must emulate the nation-state in terms of a discrete spatial and social entity and a specific power centre.

The obvious candidate is regionalism, which acknowledges the need to transcend the nation-state while recognizing that the need has not been met. It is useful to distinguish the older regional arrangements associated with hegemonic stability such as SEATO and CENTO which have little integration, from the 'new regionalism'.

These new regional arrangements are not externally imposed but internally engendered; they are usually concerned with integration since they are also political projects of transnational governance, for example, the EU, the OAU, the OAS and ASEAN.

The regionalist multilateralism which is relevant to democratic space is so by virtue of being a political project, by being concerned with transnational governance. That is the crux of the difference between regional bodies such as NAFTA, ECOWAS, and WTO which are concerned with economic cooperation, free markets or a functional regime such as tariffs, and bodies such as the OAU which may have these objectives but are also specifically political projects of transnational governance. The difference may be one of degree. A regional body may change from one to the other. For instance ASEAN was originally a security arrangement against the threat of communism especially from Laos, Vietnam and Kampuchea, but it is now turning into an organization for economic cooperation; its members signed a free trade agreement in January 1993. SADCC, on the other hand, started with the political objective of uniting to reduce dependence on the apartheid regime of South Africa. With apartheid gone, it is more interested in the idea of a common market.

Political regionalism such as the EU expresses an important reality. One aspect of this reality is that while the nation-state may be less relevant, political consciousness ideally requires a territorial focus of political identity, and self-rule requires a discrete social entity with an identifiable power centre. It is partly because of this that globalization is spawning regional arrangements rather than discouraging them.

The functional multilateralism of regimes such as the WTO and the Bretton Woods institutions has little or no potential for democratic space even though it may be participatory. These amount to interest groups dominated by a few powerful actors. This is all the more so because many of those whose interests they affect have limited awareness of their impact on their lives and cannot easily find any leverage for participation. The more political multilateralism of the EU, by contrast, has the potential for a federal structure with a weaker centre and stronger units, prospects of a new common political identity (European identity), an international civil society and direct election of representatives to the federal centre.

However, the limitations are all too obvious. The federal centre is likely to be perceived as remote, obscure and inaccessible to popular control. There may be diffidence about the value of individual participation in a large complex entity. It is easy for the new power centre to be a conservative alliance of national governments, a bulwark against change and accountability. Civil society is under-developed. Most importantly, by its very nature, globalization renders boundaries, including the regional boundaries, porous to external forces beyond the control of the regional authority, while allowing the erosion of the power of the regional authority into amorphous global space.

Democracy and Multilateralism in Less Industrialized Countries

It is useful to make a distinction between the wealthy industrial-ized and the poorer less industrialized countries, for the impact of globalization is highly varied. While it homogenizes and brings things into proximity, it also creates hierarchies and differentiates between things, universalizing some, particularizing others, marginalizing and exterminating yet others. This is largely because it expresses the global march and conquest of capitalism. As the process proceeds, the poorest regions of the world are getting more marginal and their competitive strength is diminishing. Indeed their economic and technological distance is so great that poor countries seem effectively delinked. Whether this is a short- or medium-term phenom-enon which will change in the very long run remains to be seen. For now, the reality is separation and growing inequality.

The problems of securing democratic space seem somewhat differ-ent in this context. To begin with, since the development of capi-talism is still rudimentary in poor countries, they suffer less from the technocratic capitalist culture. There is not yet a collapse into consumer identity and the market has not subsumed the social. Since the information revolution has not fully arrived, they suffer less from the desocialization process of the new information tech-nology which is isolating individuals more and more and leaving them only electronic connectivity. They are still very much face-to-face societies where politics is not in the least problematic.

That does not mean that in these parts of the contemporary world, democracy is not encountering any problems. The problems are merely different. Having largely accepted the cult of wealth and seeing the wealthy countries as the image of their future, the poor countries are very submissive and a triumphant capitalism is less tolerant of the sensitivites of the weak and of home-grown solu-tions. One result of this is the enormous power of the Bretton

Woods institutions over the economies of poor countries which are increasingly obliged to endure the rigors of draconian structural adjustment programs. Not the least of the problems of these SAPs is that they express and reinforce the democratization of society and they epitomize the worst aspects of exogenous development, namely power without responsibility or accountability.

Democracy in the poorer countries has suffered from the invigorated materialism of a triumphant capitalism. Despite political conditionality and the presumed commitment of the donor countries to democracy, there is a prejudice in favour of putting development before democratization. Along with this, there is a tolerance of authoritarian regimes which perform well economically. For instance, some African dictators such as Ibrahim Babangida of Nigeria and Jerry Rawlings of Ghana were able to trade democratization for structural adjustment. In poor as well as rich countries democratization of the economy, that is, the market rather than the state, is what matters. It is extremely difficult for the poor to change these tendencies, which reflect the consensus of the powerful donor community. The multilateralism of the donor community in support of development, whether in the form of initiatives by the G-7 nations or the Global Coalition for Africa or the Bretton Woods institutions, reproduces these tendencies which are no asset to democracy.

Multilateralism has been limited in poor regions even though it is an obvious weapon of the weak. Resources have been lacking as has been confidence, partly from seeing their future as being more like the 'other'. The complexities of social pluralism have not helped much; neither has the colonial legacy which oriented poor countries and even regions within countries to the metropole rather than towards one another. During the Cold War all forms of hegemonic multilateralism were imposed, but they were so crudely driven by the interests of the super-powers that they tended to discredit the very idea of multilateralism.

The few multilateral institutions which emerged in the poor regions have not done much for democracy. More often than not, the associating countries were ruled by regimes of doubtful democratic credentials. To the extent that their agendas transcended the self-interest of the leaders of government, they were nationalist rather than democratic agendas. The regional organizations associated with hegemonic stability were more conservative still. Popular nationalist regimes were less reliable Cold War allies than alienated authoritarian regimes with adequate coercive resources.

Yet something has changed, and the prospects of democratic openings through multilateralism are marginally better. At the end of the Cold War a triumphant West is consummating its hegemony; it is making the final push towards the universalization of the market (or the market solution) and liberal democracy. These twin values constitute the mission of the post-Cold War era.

Even though there is more emphasis on the market, the current triumphalism also proclaims the inevitable universalization of liberal democracy and there is an attempt to promote it through political conditionality. Despite considerable ambivalence and lack of evenhandedness in its application, political conditionality has given some impetus to democratization especially in Africa. It has raised the cost of authoritarianism and emboldened those struggling for democracy. It has created an international environment which is more conducive to democratization. For instance in Malawi, Western pressure was decisive in forcing President Banda to hold the referendum on the adoption of a multi-party system and the national elections which removed him from power. In the Central African Republic, President Kolingba who had been defeated in the election of 22 August 1993 only agreed to accept the result when France, on which his regime was highly dependent, halted all bilateral cooperation. Political conditionality contributed to multi-partism and elections in many African countries including Ghana, Ivory Coast, Benin, Kenya, Togo, Cameroon and Zambia.

But while support by Western governments can be useful, it is often lukewarm, ambivalent, and self-defeating. After the Cold War, the Western countries are more inward looking, in a safer world environment. Governments are less inclined to make democratic interventions in obscure and distant countries knowing that a successful intervention will not bring them a great deal of credit at home while a misbegotten intervention could do considerable harm.

The support of Western governments for democratization in poor countries owes a great deal to civil society, particularly the intervention of pro-democracy organizations such as Human Rights Watch, Amnesty International, academic communities, churches, foundations, minority rights groups, area studies associations, the media, labour unions, and so on. Pro-democracy elements in Western civil society are forming networks and alliances with pro-democracy groups in the democratizing countries. An excellent example is the cooperation between the Nigerian civil rights organization, the Campaign for Democracy (CDC) and the Civil Liberties Organization (CLO) with Africa Watch and the New York Committee of Lawyers and the National Democratic Institute (NDI). Even more remarkable is the cooperation between the minority rights and environmental movement, the Movement for Survival of Ogoni People (MOSOP), with the writers' organization PEN, Human Rights Watch, and Greenpeace. These developments have placed democratic struggles in a more supportive international environment and marshalled forces which have increased the price of oppression in poor countries. A promising associational multilateralism is emerging.

It is not all promising, however. These multilateral networks come alive in the presence of highly visible and dramatic abuses so their vitality tends to be *ad hoc*. They address the exceptional, the *cause célèbre*. But democracy demands a routine in which the exercise of freedom to self-governance and immunity from oppression and arbitrary power become normal. The new associational multilateralism suffers from lack of reciprocity: the civic organizations in one region give, those in the other receive, in what is often a patron-client relationship which is inherently undemocratic. Finally, associational multilateralism does not come to grips with the dangers to democracy inherent in globalization. Indeed it presupposes the existence of a region which has not been substantially transformed by capitalist modernity.

CONCLUSION

Perhaps after all we should be lamenting the demise of democracy instead of celebrating its triumph. In its long embattled history, democracy is facing its deadliest peril yet in the contemporary world. Globalization is rendering democracy irrelevant through processes that are essentially irreversible. The demise of democracy can be mitigated through regional arrangements of transnational governance or associational multilateralism; but not very much.

NOTES

1. Jürgen Habermas, *The Structural Transformation of the Public Sphere: An Inquiry into a Category of Bourgeois Society* (Cambridge: Polity Press,

1989) and 'Further Reflections on the Public Sphere', in Craig Calhoun (ed.) *Habermas and the Public Sphere* (Cambridge: MIT Press, 1992).
2. Alan Gilbert, *Democratic Individuality* (Cambridge: Cambridge University Press, 1990).
3. Benjamin I. Page, *The Rational Public: Fifty Years of Trends in American Policy Preferences* (Chicago: University of Chicago Press, 1992). William E. Connolly, 'Democracy and Territoriality', *Millennium* 20 (1991): pp. 463–84.
4. David Held, *Political Theory Today* (Stanford: Stanford University Press, 1991); David Held, *Democracy and the Global Order* (Stanford: Stanford University Press, 1995).
5. John Burnheim, *Is Democracy Possible?* (Cambridge: Polity Press, 1985).
6. John S. Dryzek, 'Democracy Versus the International Political Economy', Paper for the International Political Science Association. Berlin, 21–25 August 1994.
7. Ibid.
8. *The Economist* 335 (17 June 1995).
9. Alvin and Heidi Toffler, *Creating a New Civilization: The Politics of the Third Wave* (Washington: Progress and Freedom Foundation, 1994).

REFERENCES

Ake, C. 1992, 'Devaluing Democracy', *Journal of Democracy*. vol. 3, no. 3, pp. 32–6.
Ake, C. 1991, 'Rethinking Democracy in Africa', *Journal of Democracy*, vol. 2 no. 1, pp. 32–44.
Almond, Garbriel A. and Verba, S. 1963, *The Civic Culture: Political Attitudes and Democracy in Five Nations*, Princeton, NJ: Princeton University Press.
Almond, Gabriel. and Verba, S. (eds) 1980, *The Civic Culture Revisited: An Analytical Study*, Boston: Little, Brown & Co.
Archer, M.S. 1990, 'Foreword', in M. Albrow and E. King (eds), *Globalization, Knowledge and Society*, London: Sage Publications.
Aristotle, *The Politics*, Harmondsworth: Penguin, 1981.
Arnason, J.P. 1990, 'Nationalism, globalization and modernity', *Theory, Culture and Society*, 7(2–3).
Baudrillard J. 1980, 'The Implosion of Meaning in the Media and the Implosion of the Social in the Masses', in K. Woodward (ed.), *The Myths of Information Technology and Post Industrial Culture*, Madison: Coda.
Beetham, D. 1981, 'Beyond liberal democracy', *Socialist Register*, 1981, pp. 190–206.
Berelson, B. 1952, 'Democratic Theory and Public Opinion', *Public Opinion Quarterly*, 16 (Autumn), pp. 313–30.
Berelson, B., Lazarfield, P.F. and McPhee, W. 1954, *Voting*, Chicago: University of Chicago Press.
Boyne, R. 1990, 'Culture and The World-system', in M. Featherstone (ed.), *Global Culture: Nationalism, Globalization and Modernity*, London: Sage.

Brittan, Samuel, 1975, 'The Economic Contradictions of Democracy', *British Journal of Political* Science, 51, pp. 129–59.

Burnheim, John 1985, *Is Democracy Possible?: The Alternative to Electoral Politics*, Cambridge: Polity Press.

Cohen, J. and Rogers, J. 1983, *On Democracy*, New York: Penguin.

Connolly, William E. 1991, Democracy and Territoriality, *Millennium: Journal of International Studies* 20 (3), pp. 463–84.

Dahl, R.A. 1956, *A Preface to Democratic Theory*, Chicago: University of Chicago Press.

Dahl, R.A. 1961, *Who Governs? Democracy and Power in an American City*, New Haven, Conn.: Yale University Press.

Dahl, R.A. 1971, *Polyarchy: Participation and Opposition*, New Haven: Yale University Press.

Dahl, R.A. 1979, 'Procedural Democracy', in P. Laslett and J. Fishkin (eds), *Philosophy, Politics and Society*, Fifth Series, New Haven: Yale University Press, pp. 97–133.

Di Palma, Giuseppe 1990, *To Craft Democracies: An Essay on Democratic Transitions*, Berkeley: University of California Press.

Dryzek, John S. 1990, *Discursive Democracy: Politics, Policy, and Political Science*, Cambridge: Cambridge University Press.

Dryzek, John S. and Jeffrey Berejikian 1993, 'Reconstructive Democratic Theory', *American Political Science Review*, 87, pp. 48–60.

Dryzek, John S. 1994, 'Democracy Versus the International Political Economy', Paper for the International Political Science Association, Berlin, 21–25 August.

Economist 1991, 'Global Village, Traveling Peasants', *The Economist* 321 (7737) 14 December (18).

Enzensberger, H. 1970, 'Constituents of a Theory of the Media', *New Left Review*, 64, pp. 13–36.

Friedman, J. 1990, 'Being, in the world: globalization and localization', *Theory, Culture and Society*, 7, pp. 2–3.

Fukayama, F. 1992, *The End of History and the Last Man*, New York: Free Press.

Ghai, D. 1992, *Structural Adjustment, Global and Social Democracy*, Geneva: UNRISD.

Giddens, A. 1991. *Modernity and Self-Identity: Self and Society in the Late Modern Age*, Stanford, CA: Stanford University Press.

Habermas Jürgen 1992, 'Further Reflections on the Public Sphere', in Craig Calhoun (ed.), *Habermas and the Public Sphere*, Cambridge: MIT Press.

Habermas Jürgen 1989, 'The Structural Transformation of the Public Sphere', *An Inquiry into a Category of Bourgeois Society*, Cambridge: Polity Press.

Habermas, Jürgen 1976, *Legitimation Crisis*, London: Heinemann.

Held, David 1987, *Models of Democracy*, Cambridge: Polity Press.

Held, David 1992, 'Democracy: From City-states to a Cosmopolitan Order?' *Political Studies*, 40 (special issue), pp. 10–39.

Hettne, Björn and Inotai Andras 1994, *The New Regionalism: Implications for Global Development and International Security*, Helsinki: UNU/WIDER.

Khilnani, Sunil 1991, 'Democracy and Modern Political Community: Limits and Possibilities', *Economy and Society*, 20, pp. 196–204.

Knox, T.M. (trans. and ed.), *Hegel's Philosophy of Right*, Oxford: Oxford University Press, 1967.

Lindblom, Charles E. 1977, *Politics and Markets: The World's Political Economic Systems*, New York: Basic Books.

Locke, J. 1963, *Two Treatises of Government*. Cambridge: Cambridge University Press.

Mazrui, A.A. 1990, *Cultural Forces in World Politics*, London: James Currey.

Meyer, J.W. 1980, 'The world polity and the authority of the nation-state', in A. Bergesen (ed.), *Studies of the Modern World System*, New York: Academic Press.

Miller, David 1992, 'Deliberative Democracy and Social Choice', *Political Studies*, 40 (special issue), 54–67.

Mittelman, J. 1995, 'The Challenge of Globalization: Surviving at the Margins', *Third World Quarterly*, 15, pp. 427–47.

Offe, C. 1984, *Contradictions of the Welfare State*, London: Hutchinson.

Robertson, R. 1992, *Globalization: Social Theory and Global Culture*, New York: Sage Publications.

Schumpeter, J. 1976, *Capitalism, Socialism and Democracy*, London: Allen and Unwin.

Smith, A.D. 1990, 'Toward a global culture?' *Theory, Culture & Society*, 7(pp. 2–3).

Truman, D.B. 1951, *The Governmental Process: Political Interests and Public Opinion*, New York: Knopf.

Wolff, J. 1991, 'The global and the specific: reconciling conflicting theories of culture', in A.D. King (ed.), *Culture, Globalization and the World-System: Contemporary Conditions for the Representation of Identity*, London: Macmillan.

9 High-speed Growth, Crisis and Opportunity in East Asia

Walden Bello

In response to the stagnation enveloping the German economy, Hans Olaf-Henkel, head of the Federation of German Industry, said in April 1996 that efforts to maintain the 'workplace consensus' that underpinned Germany's 'social market' economy would leave employers 'with no choice but to do what they did in the last few years. We will vote with our feet, and go abroad'.[1]

Olaf-Henkel was clearly referring to Asia. Interestingly enough, Germany's Chancellor, Helmut Kohl, had just voted with his feet and visited Bangkok, where he was a key figure in the institutionalization of the Asia Europe Leaders' Meeting (ASEM), a superbody of 15 European and ten Asian heads of state designed to intensify trading and investment ties between Europe and Asia. ASEM, in turn, could not be understood without taking into consideration the formation of the Asia Pacific Economic Cooperation (APEC), a trans-Pacific economic association uniting the United States and six other non-Asian countries to 12 Asian economies around the vision of achieving 'borderless trade' by the year 2020.

The Asia-Pacific region, in other words, is seen in Western government and business circles as the new El Dorado, as the land of unceasing economic growth that will serve as the driver of the world economy in the twenty-first century. With the seemingly limitless expansion of middle-class markets that it promises, the Asia Pacific is often portrayed as some sort of fountain of youth that will restore the dynamism of American and European capital, which can no longer be sustained in their home economies.

The image of prosperity, however, masks a process of growth marked by high ecological costs, a widening gap between agriculture and industry, and increasing inequality in income distribution. Moreover, a head-on conflict is developing between the Asian and non-Asian government and economic elites for the domination of this vast market. Rapid growth is, in turn, leading not to peace among countries but to growing tensions, if not to outright conflicts in a region which has become the world's fastest growing market for conventional arms. Growth has also been accompanied by growing antagonisms within countries where rapid economic growth has taken place largely within authoritarian or restricted political systems. Farming populations who have been marginalized by the growth process join the urban masses created by it to demand more democratic systems of rule.

The first decades of the twenty-first century, in short, could just as likely see the unravelling as the continuation of the Asia-Pacific bonanza.

STATE-ASSISTED CAPITALISM AND HIGH-SPEED GROWTH

Rather than a single factor, a variety or concatenation of developments explain the emergence of a dynamic growth process in Asia, including the impact of aid and military expenditure owing to the Cold War, the creation of mass buying power via land reform in Korea and Taiwan, an economic strategy in which export of labour intensive manufactures played a key role, and, in the case of Southeast Asia since the late 1980s, the massive inflow of Japanese investment capital owing to the massive rise in the value of the yen that made manufacturing in Japan no longer competitive. This is not the place to discuss the relative contributions of these conditions. There is, however, one thing that cannot be underestimated, and that is the leading role of the state in the development process. Despite efforts to stress the leading role of the market by such institutions as the World Bank,[2] the prominence of the state is undeniable.

In the case of Korea and Taiwan, the most successful of the 'first generation NICs', high speed growth was associated with an economic strategy with the following features:

- strategic economic planning managed by government, exemplified in some countries by 5 to 10 year plans;
- government targeting of specific industries for development and generous subsidization of private enterprises to support the targeted industries;

- building strategic economic depth by moving in a planned fashion from the development of consumer goods industries to intermediate goods and capital goods enterprises;
- reserving the domestic market for local entrepreneurs by maintaining tight restrictions on imports and foreign investments;
- adopting a mercantilist trade strategy consisting of limiting the entry of foreign imports into the domestic market while aggressively winning and dominating export markets, resulting in a growing trade surplus; and
- in the case of Korea, though not in Taiwan, bold, Keynesian-style manipulation of macroeconomic mechanisms such as deficit spending, loose credit policies, massive foreign borrowing to lay the infrastructure of a capital goods sector; and
- systematic undervaluation of the currency relative to hard currencies and the employment of different subsidy schemes for exporters in order to keep exports competitive in world markets.

Protection of the domestic market, aggressive mercantilism in export markets, and pervasive state intervention in the total economy – these are key elements in the Northeast Asian recipe for 'NIChood'. True, market mechanisms operated, but, especially in Korea, they were deliberately distorted in the short term to build up strategic economic depth. For instance, Korean technocrats deliberately violated the classical free-market principle of consumer sovereignty – 'Give the consumer the best product at the lowest price' – for the larger strategic goal of strengthening national economic sovereignty. Thus, if the price of Korean-made computers in the domestic market was three to four times that in export markets, this was in order to allow local conglomerates and monopolies to recoup the losses they incurred in battling the formidable Japanese in export markets. To borrow economist Alice Amsden's classic statement, 'not only has Korea not gotten relative prices right, it has got them deliberately wrong'.[3]

But what about the Southeast Asian 'stars' of the last decade, specifically Thailand, Malaysia and Indonesia? Are their high rates of growth not due to their adoption of liberal, market-oriented policies? True, in Indonesia, Malaysia and Thailand, the state may have played a less aggressive role than in Korea, but activist state policy, in the form of protectionism, mercantilism and regulation, has nevertheless been central in the drive to industrialize. For instance, Thailand began to register the 8–10 per cent growth rates that dazzled the world in the late 1980s, when it was moving to a second stage of 'import substitution', or using trade policy to create the space for the emergence of an intermediate goods sector.

In the case of Malaysia, while it is true that some privatization and deregulation favouring private interests took place in the late 1980s, it would be a mistake to overestimate the impact of these policies or to see them as the wave of the future. Indeed, the most successful Malaysian enterprise of the last decade was a state-directed joint venture between a state firm and a foreign automobile multinational, Mitsubishi, which produced the so-called Malaysian car, the Proton Saga. The Saga now controls two-thirds of the market and turns a profit. Yet its development exemplified all the so-called 'sins' of state intervention that neoclassical economists have warned about: discriminatory tax treatment of competitors, strategic industrial targeting or a systematic plan to manipulate market incentives to create a local car industry, and forced local sourcing of components to encourage the growth of local supplier industries.[4]

As for Indonesia, some reform along market-oriented lines has taken place, but the state continues to be a very important actor in the economy. Hardly any of the big state enterprises have passed to the private sector. State enterprises contribute about 30 per cent of the nation's GDP and close to 40 per cent of non-agricultural GDP. Government production accounts for 50 per cent of the GDP of the mining sector, 24 per cent of manufacturing GDP, 65 per cent of banking and finance, and 50 per cent of transport and communications.[5] Indeed, there has been a resurgence in recent years of statist policy aimed at using trade policy, subsidies, and other mechanisms to create a heavy industry nucleus around which to centre the economy, including the development of an integrated steel complex, a shipbuilding complex and an aircraft industry.

Indeed, one can, without too much distortion, say that Southeast Asian growth over the last decade may be said to be an offspring of 'state-assisted capitalism' and Japanese investment, about which more will be said later. Suffice it to say at this juncture that while the activist state in East Asia has been central to the phenomenon of 'high speed growth', it is now seen as a threat to those Northern interests exposed to global competition from Asian capital as well as a massive obstacle to those trying to enter the Asian market to share in the fruits of the so-called Asian miracle. While the World Bank continues to extol the supposed virtues of market-led growth in the region, the US Trade Representative's Office regularly denounces the Asian 'tigers' as closed and protected markets that also discriminate against American investors. Typical of these attacks was former Commerce Secretary Mickey Kantor's description of Korea as 'one of the toughest markets in the world' for American exporters, as well as a 'particularly difficult market in which to invest'.[6]

THE OTHER SIDE OF THE ASIAN MIRACLE

Worsening Income Distribution

State-assisted or 'NIC' capitalism has come under fire not only from Northern interests but also from the Asian progressives and environmentalists. The latter claim that while absolute incomes have certainly risen in most of the so-called 'newly industrializing countries', this trend has been accompanied by worsening income distribution in Korea, Taiwan, China, and Singapore. In Thailand, which has exhibited the highest average growth rate among developing countries over the last 30 years, income distribution has degenerated to Latin American levels: from 1975 to 1990, the income share of the richest 20 per cent of the population rose from 49.3 per cent to 57.3 per cent, while that of the poorest 20 per cent dropped from 6.1 to 4.1 per cent.[7] These trends not only raise questions about social justice but also indicate the social instability is built into the high-growth model.

Indeed, the wave of militant labour activities that has marked management-labour relations in Korea, Taiwan, the Philippines and Indonesia in recent years has been a response to a sense that it is the working class created by high-speed industrialization that has paid the costs of that growth but received so little of its benefits. In Korea, the conjunction of repression, regressive income distribution and military-style management has created an extremely class-conscious work force, some of whose actions against management border on the insurrectionary.[8]

The Crisis of Agriculture

Throughout Asia, the biggest gap in income distribution has developed between the city and the countryside. In Korea, average rural household income dropped from parity with average urban household income in 1975 to 85 per cent in 1989.[9] The drop was even more precipitous in Thailand, where the average income of an agricultural worker dropped from one sixth of that of workers in other sectors in the early 1960s to one twelfth by the early 1990s.[10] Not surprisingly, more than three quarters of those living below the poverty line were found in the countryside, making poverty, in the words of one economist, 'almost entirely a rural phenomenon'.[11]

The deterioration of the countryside was not a result of market forces but of policy. The Asian industrial miracle was built at the expense of agriculture. From Korea to Thailand, agriculture served as the source of capital for industry that was extracted through taxes or unequal terms of trade between agriculture and industry imposed by such mechanisms as direct or indirect controls to keep down the prices of agricultural goods.

With low returns from agricultural production, the countryside provided a great incentive for the migration to the urban areas of peasants that formed the work force for the new industries, a movement of people that, in less than 25 years, 1965–88, slashed the rural population of Korea by half, from 15.8 million to 7.8 million. In the case of Taiwan, rural depopulation was less a question of market forces than of policy, as agricultural technocrat and later president Lee Teng-Hui admitted: 'The government has intentionally held down peasants' income so as to transfer these people – who originally engaged in agriculture – into industries'.[12]

Low returns also discouraged investment in agriculture and agricultural technology, thus burdening the NICs with a high-cost agriculture over time. By the mid-1990s, Korean rice cost five to seven times more than the price of foreign rice,[13] and, with the strong pressure on the country to open up its rice market to subsidized rice from the USA, Korea confronted no less than the 'disintegration of the rice farming household', as one government report put it.[14] Indeed, agricultural technocrats in both Taiwan and Korea were talking about a future with a marginal role for agriculture and extreme dependence on food imports to feed the population under the guise of 'rationalizing' agricultural production.

Farmers, however, were determined to take a last stand, and the ratification of the Uruguay Round of the General Agreement on Tariffs and Trade (GATT) in 1994 and public discussion of the Asia Pacific Economic Cooperation (APEC), both of which sought radical liberalization of agricultural markets, provided them with form to publicize the case for their non-extinction to not unsympathetic domestic audiences.

The Savaging of the Environment

Like the crisis of agriculture, the savaging of the environment was one of the dominant features of NIC development throughout East Asia. In Taiwan, often considered 'Asia's dirtiest spot', the lower reaches of virtually all major rivers are biologically dead because of a combination of unregulated industrial and human waste dumping. Twenty per cent of the country's farmland, the government itself admits, is polluted by industrial waste water that is a legacy of the strategy of decentralized industrialization with zero zoning and pollution controls followed by the Kuomintang (KMT) government. As a result, 30 per cent of the rice grown on the island in the late 1980s was said to be contaminated with heavy metals beyond officially tolerated levels.[15]

Korea's environmental fate is very similar to Taiwan's. Seoul's air continues to have one of the highest concentrations of sulphur dioxide in the air, and two thirds of the rain that falls on the city contains enough acid to threaten human health. Much of the country's tap water is unsafe, with a heavy-metal content far above acceptable levels. Because of massive dumping of organic and industrial waste, including great quantities of carcinogenic substances like waste phenol, the country's two major rivers, the Han and the Nakdong, are said to be approaching biological death.[16]

Thailand telescopes in a particularly vicious way the ravages of the first stage of growth, the rapid depletion of natural resources, with those of the second, the ecological impact of high-speed industrialization. Owing to unrestricted logging, less than 20 per cent of the country remains under forest cover, down from more than 60 per cent in the 1950s. Meanwhile, the lower reaches of the Chao Phraya River that runs through Bangkok are close to being anaerobic or biologically dead owing partly to uncontrolled waste water disposal by factories, 27 000 of which – out of a national total of 50 000 – are concentrated in the national capital region.[17] A massive explosion caused by a chemical reaction in the thickly populated Klong Toey harbour area in March 1991 underlined the utter lack of regulation over toxic substances: years later, stillbirths, miscarriages, birth defects, skin diseases and other chemical-related illnesses marked the lives of many people exposed to chemical fallout.[18] Likewise, the mysterious deaths of about over a dozen workers employed in electronics companies in one of the country's prime industrial estates was attributed by many experts to contact with toxic substances at work.

The issue, according to environmentalists, is not that there are no laws regulating industrial production. Indeed, some of the environmental legislation in Asia is among the best in the world, on paper. Implementation is the problem, and implementation is guided by a belief pervasive in the bureaucracy and technocracy of the Asian countries that some measure of environmental degradation is a necessary cost of economic growth. As one environmental expert in Thailand claimed, the unstated understanding between the government and the corporations, whether they be Thai, Japanese, NIC, European or American, is that the latter 'will make zero investments in pollution control'.[19]

JAPAN'S *DE FACTO* TRADING AND INVESTMENT BLOC

Increasing inequality, agricultural crisis and environmental degradation are not the only features of the 'NIC' growth model that is worrisome to many Asian progressives. Also problematic in their view has been the ambivalent role played in the region by Japan. On the one hand, Japan's dynamic economic growth has certainly served as one of the main stimuli to the regional growth of the Asia Pacific since the 1960s. Japanese capital and Japanese technology played a critical role in the industrial transformation of Korea, Taiwan and Southeast Asia, but it was a process of growth that was also marked by the development of an unequal division of labour and technological dependency – in other words, a process of integration-cum-subordination. Interestingly enough, this critique of Japanese capital's role in East Asia voiced by Asian progressives is shared in its essentials by US government and corporate interests, though for markedly different reasons.

Japanese Capital and the Development of Northeast Asia

When Japanese firms sought to escape the rising cost of domestic labour in the 1960s, their first choice of location was their former colonies, Taiwan and Korea. As these two economies sought to emulate Japan's export success, Japanese trading companies handled international trade for Taiwanese and Korean firms, with an estimated 50 to 70 per cent of Taiwan's exports passing through them.[20] And as Korean and Taiwanese industrialization took off in the 1970s, Japan provided a significant portion of the machinery and components utilized by Korean and Taiwanese enterprises to turn out toys, bicycles, radios, television sets and PC monitors for export. Japan was more tight-fisted when it came to technology transfers, but especially as the Japanese technology became more sophisticated and in many areas surpassed American technology, the Koreans and the Taiwanese became dependent on licensing available Japanese technologies in finished form to achieve their export successes, particularly in consumer electronics, automobiles, and semiconductors. In the period 1962–80, Japan was the source of nearly 59 per cent of approved technology licences, while the United States accounted for only 23 per cent.[21] This severe dependence on Japan for components and technology resulted in the development of a trading system marked by 'a highly unbalanced set of relationships through which South Korea and the other newly industrializing economies imported heavily from Japan to support their industrial development, and exported heavily to the United States to cover these imports'.[22]

Contemporary Taiwan and Korea are often portrayed as actual or potential rivals of Japan, with increasingly integrated economies marked by a growing high-tech sector. But this is an exaggerated assessment of the state of these economies. In reality, they have not been able to graduate from being labour-intensive assembly sites for Japanese components using Japanese technology. Taiwan's ability to turn out millions of personal computers a year has earned it the reputation of being a high-tech manufacturing centre. The Taiwanese computer industry is, however, really only an assembly line for IBM-compatible PCs made with off-the-shelf components imported from Japan and the United States.

As for South Korea, its image as a high-tech producer is belied by a few sobering realities: the Hyundai Excel may be the country's best-known export, but its body styling is Italian in origin, its engine is designed by the Japanese firm Mitsubishi, and its transmission is both designed and manufactured by Mitsubishi.[23] Korean television sets may be battling Japanese products in the United States, but Japanese components account for 85 per cent of their value. South Korea may be the world's fifth largest exporter of personal computers, but only the computer cabinet is actually made in the country.[24]

In this connection, the vaunted ability of the Korean electronics firm Samsung to produce the advanced 16-megabit memory chip to compete with advanced Japanese chips stands out precisely because it is the exception to the rule; most of the other Korean firms have a dependent relationship with their Japanese counterparts.

Instead of transferring state-of-the art technologies, Japan transfers less advanced ones to integrate Korean and Taiwanese firms as subordinate elements within an Asia-Pacific-wide division of labour designed by Japanese firms to enhance corporate profitability. The Japanese firm Hitachi, for instance, licensed 1-megabit DRAM (dynamic random access memory) chip technology to the Korean firm Lucky-Goldstar to acquire a reliable supplier of less advanced chips for its consumer electronics products, enabling it to focus on developing the 4-megabit chip.[25]

The same strategy of lowering costs or reducing risk by more fully integrating NIC producers into regional or global production plans has led Japanese manufacturers to buy equity in established car industries in South Korea and Taiwan. Mitsubishi already has a 15 per cent stake in Hyundai Motors, and it has integrated the Korean car maker into its system of international production by having it produce key parts of selected models. Practically all Taiwanese car makers now have significant Japanese equity investments, and they have been reoriented into a division of labour that, in the words of one Japanese analyst, 'is not an equal division of labour as seen in the European Community countries, but a vertical one within the automobile industry as a whole'.[26] In this 'inter-product division of labor', the Taiwanese firms specialize in 'low-priced compact cars, which have fewer parts and a higher percentage of labor in the entire process'.[27] Perhaps unwittingly using historically loaded terms, the writer concludes, 'China-Taiwan aims for co-existence and co-prosperity with Japan by producing the items that are not economically suitable for Japan [to produce]'.[28]

Japanese Capital and Southeast Asia

Southeast Asia joined the Northeast Asian NICs within a regional division of labour imposed by Japanese capital following the explosion of Japanese capital into the region provoked by the Plaza Accord of 1985. By sharply raising the value of the yen relative to the dollar, this agreement made production in Japan prohibitive in terms of labour costs, forcing the Japanese to move the more labour-intensive processes of their manufacturing operations to low-wage areas such as China and Southeast Asia.

In the period 1985–93, some $51 billion worth of Japanese investment swirled through the Asia Pacific in one of the most rapid and massive outflows of direct investment towards the developing world in recent history;[29] and it was one of the most profound in terms of impact, for at the end of the period much of the region had been, for all intents and purposes, integrated into the Japanese economy.

Undoubtedly, it is not only Japanese billions that have flowed to different points of East Asia in the past decade. Investments from Korea, Taiwan and Hong Kong have also been prominent, indeed in many countries outstripping the volume of Japanese investment. Such investments are, however, not usually strategically planned, being undertaken, for the most part, by small and medium-sized establishments with short-term perspectives. Japan's investment drive, however, has been promoted by the Japanese government and planned by corporate giants operating with global and regional perspectives.

One dimension of this integration is horizontal, that is, splitting up the production of different goods or the components of one product among different countries. In Matsushita's strategy, for instance, each country is assigned specific items to produce for export: colour TVs and electric irons in Malaysia, semiconductors in Singapore, and dry-cell batteries, floppy-disk drives, and electronic capacitors in the Philippines.[30] A more functional level of integration has been undertaken by car companies like Nissan, Toyota and Mitsubishi. In Toyota's scheme, Indonesia specializes in gasoline engines and stamped parts, Malaysia turns out steering links and electrical equipment, the Philippines produces transmissions, and Thailand manufactures diesel engines, stamped parts, and electrical goods.[31]

In addition to integration along lines of product specialization, a process of backward integration is tightening the links of the region to the core economy. In the first phase of this process, which began in the mid-1980s, Japanese automobile and consumer electronics firms relocated their plants to the region. This was followed by the out-migration of smaller Japanese companies that supply parts and components for the auto and electronics manufacturers. A third phase of backward integration may be about to begin, with the relocation of heavy and chemical industries that provide basic inputs to both the big manufacturers and their suppliers.[32]

Japan's current recession has hardly blunted this process; while investments in Europe and the US have slowed considerably, the movement of capital to the Asia Pacific continued at a brisk pace:

Japan's investment in the region rose from $5.9 billion in FY 1991 to $9.6 billion in FY 1994, while its investment in Europe fell from $9.3 billion to $6.2 billion, and its investment in the USA from $18.8 to $14.6 billion.[33] Moreover, in 1993, profits from Japan's operations in Asia exceeded those from the USA for the first time, an astonishing development when considered against the fact that as recently as 1980, only 2 per cent of Japan's corporate profits originated in Asia.[34]

Interestingly enough, then, Japan's recession accelerated the regionalization of the Japanese economy, as pressures built up on more firms to save on labour costs by moving their operations to China and Southeast Asia. This paradoxical phenomenon was captured by one commentary which asserted that '"the hollowing out" [of Japanese industry] is tantamount to an increased "interdependence" [with Asia]'.[35] It also appears that rather than following an internationalist investment strategy in the late 1980s and early 1990s, the Japanese government and Japanese corporations moved more decisively away from an international to a more Asia-focused investment strategy. Japanese investment in Asia as a proportion of total Japanese foreign investment rose from 12 per cent in 1990 to 23 per cent in 1994.[36]

The regional corporate thrust has been coordinated with Japan's burgeoning aid program. Close to 60 per cent of Japanese aid is now targeted at East and Southeast Asia. Programs such as the Asian Industries Development Plan and the ASEAN-Japan Development Fund are 'a joint public-private sector activity, which exploits the horizontal division of labour between Japan and Asia, and targets industrial, rather than resources or infrastructure development'.[37] This assessment is seconded by an American expert in Japanese aid, when he bluntly describes it as furthering Japan's attempt to strengthen 'control over an emerging Asian regional economy' by 'integrating the Asian economies under Japanese leadership'.[38]

Regionalization of the Japanese Economy

This process of corporate-driven horizontal and vertical integration has resulted in the creation not of a regional economy with plural centres but in the *regionalization of the Japanese economy*. The contrast between these two processes is captured by two contradictory descriptions of the impact of Japan on the region by two prominent diplomats, Saburo Okita and Hisahiko Okazaki. Okita has portrayed growth in Asia as akin to the flight of a flock of geese. In his view, Asian regional development is a 'process of consecutive take-offs with a built-in catch up process'.[39] With Japan as the lead goose,

> the nations of the region engineer successive take-offs and are soon moving to higher stages of development. It is akin to a V-formation, and the relationship among the countries in the formation is neither horizontal integration nor vertical integration as they are commonly known. Rather, it is a combination of both. And because the geese that take off later are able to benefit from the forerunners' experiences to shorten the time required to catch up, they gradually transform the formation from a V-formation to eventual horizontal integration.[40]

On the other hand, Okazaki, who is now regarded as one of the most prominent proponents of the Asian, as opposed to international, strategy for Japanese corporate capital, paints a different picture, and with surprising candour for a diplomat: 'Japan is creating an exclusive Japanese market in which Asia-Pacific nations are incorporated in the so-called *keirestsu* [financial/industrial] bloc system'.[41] The essential relationship between Japan and Southeast Asia, he contends, is one of trading 'captive imports, such as products from plants in which the Japanese have invested, in return for "captive exports", such as necessary equipment and materials'.[42]

This *de facto* trading bloc has been created without formal free trade agreements. As one report to the US Congress noted, discussion on whether a Japanese-dominated regional bloc would arise in response to NAFTA and the European Union 'is somewhat immaterial because a *de facto* trading bloc is already emerging. It is arising out of economic necessity, and, barring draconian barriers, will continue to grow regardless of whether or not free trade among the various economies develops'. It concluded, with undisguised envy: 'Japan's business executives do not need free trade to operate'.[43]

Indeed, the Japanese have managed to get trading arrangements among countries in the region to work to their advantage. This is certainly the case with NAFTA. As one Australian government report conceded:[44]

Japanese firms, such as automotive and motorcycle companies, have worked longer and harder at making ASEAN integration work than most other companies... [For instance], one Japanese motorcycle maker reported that an arrangement to ship components between its plants in Malaysia and Thailand had required years of patient work with government officials in each country.

Not surprisingly, Okazaki has pointed out that NAFTA is 'not worrisome' to the Japanese because it would lower tariffs for components manufactured and traded among the suppliers or subsidiaries of Japanese firms within ASEAN.[45]

There is, however, a basic instability built into this process of integration-cum-subordination, and this is the tendency of the Japanese economy to build up massive trade surpluses with the dependent economies. This is clearly the case with Taiwan and Korea, which registered deficits with Japan of $15 billion and $10 billion respectively, in 1992. And it is increasingly the case with the newer industrializing economies of Thailand, Malaysia, and China. China, the Southeast Asian countries and the Northeast Asian NICs currently have a combined trade deficit of more than $50 billion with Japan, even as they have a combined trade surplus of more than $60 billion with the United States.[46] This is basically a reflection of Japan's virtual monopoly of advanced technology, which allows it to add more value to its products relative to the low-tech manufactured products, processed agricultural goods, and raw materials that it imports from the dependent East Asian economies.

Not surprisingly, the massive Japanese presence has not been achieved without some cost to Japan's relations to Asians. Many Asians accuse the Japanese of having simply built up an integrated network of export platforms assembling Japanese components using Japanese technology, with no lasting structural benefits for the economy, without an 'industrial deepening' taking place. Japan does not hesitate to use its technological power to keep its dependent economies in line, according to many Asians. For instance, Japan now so completely dominates the making of the sophisticated machines that produce microchips that, as one Taiwanese specialist put it, 'If the Japanese refuse to sell the equipment, you're lost'.[47] The Korean government, a few years ago, accused the Japanese of informally banning the export of 200 ultra-modern high technologies to Korea until 1995 – by which time the Japanese firms would have exploited much of the market potential of these technologies.

Nonetheless, most Asian industrial elites see themselves as having a more strategic relationship with Japan than the United States. For one, as Okazaki has written, 'Few domestic entrepreneurs in Asian countries have had to develop in direct competition with Japan. The majority of these companies received capital and technology from Japan'.[48] In other words, though locked in a subordinate, dependent relationship, most Asian industrial elites derive more benefits than disadvantages from the system.

APEC AND THE AMERICAN ECONOMIC COUNTEROFFENSIVE

It is against this background of the emergence of a Japan-dominated trading and investment bloc that one must view the evolution of US economic policy towards the region, the most forceful recent expression of which is the push to make the Asia Pacific Economic Cooperation (APEC) a free trade area by the year 2020.

Washington cannot be accused of not being transparent in the reasons it backs such a development: it sees an APEC free trade bloc as a way to reassert a significant American presence in a part of the world that has slipped out of its economic orbit over the last three decades. Paula Stern, a key adviser to President Clinton, puts it this way: Intra-Asian trade now accounts for about 45 per cent of East Asia's total trade. This means East Asia is becoming less dependent on the USA as an export market and well on its way to becoming an integrated trade and investment area. When one combines this with the fact that according to Stern, investment regimes in Asian countries have 'made it more difficult to increase a US business presence on the ground', then the United States faces the prospect of steady marginalization from the region that will serve as the engine of the world economy far into the first decades of the twenty-first century.[49]

APEC would help reverse that trend. As Fred Bergsten, the American economist who headed up the now dismantled Eminent Persons' Group that masterminded the APEC 2020 free trade plan, told a US congressional committee, 'Given the fact that all of the countries in the region, outside North America in particular, have lots of trade barriers, very little would actually be required from the United States'.[50] Thus, 'trade liberalization or moving... to totally free trade in the region means enormous competitive gain to the United States'.[51]

Free trade, in the Washington game plan, is less a doctrinal belief than a strategy for regaining American competitiveness, for without the advantages that protected markets, subsidies, and various other mechanisms of support that the Japanese and other Asian governments extend to their producers, American transnationals can beat the competition. Thus, the strong thrust of American policy against the 'state-assisted capitalism' characteristic of the Japanese and other Asian economies. As former Undersecretary of State Joan Spero puts it: 'APEC... has a customer. APEC is not for governments; it is for business. Through APEC, we aim to get governments out of the way, opening the way for business to do business. It is our goal to make APEC the most user-friendly forum in the world'.[52]

APEC is the latest milestone of a tectonic shift from a 'universalistic' US foreign economic policy where trade and investment interests were subordinated to the grand strategy of containing Communism during the Cold War (and thus tolerant of many protectionist and restrictive investment practices of American allies in East Asia) to a particularistic one, that is, one obsessed with opening up markets to American goods and investments. APEC, indeed, is one of a number of mechanisms that are deployed in a complementary fashion to serve, not the ideological interest in creating an international free trade system in whose benefits all participants would share equally, but the specific interest of American corporations. As former Commerce Secretary Mickey Kantor put it, in his characteristically blunt, non-ideological fashion, before the US Congress: 'We have used 301, reinstituted super 301, [and] title 7...' – to open up markets around the globe.[53]

Aside from APEC, however, two other instruments are to be especially relied on: unilateral trade policy pressure and the General Agreement on Tariffs and Trade (GATT). Unilateral trade pressure has been the main instrument of American policy to 'liberalize' the Asia-Pacific since the early 1980s, with Washington's trade negotiators having threatened nearly all the East and Southeast Asian countries with threats to invoke the so-called 'Super 301' and 'Special 301' provisions of the US Trade Act of 1988, which mandate the American executive to take retaliatory measures against those accused of being unfair traders or of tolerating violations of the intellectual property rights of American corporations.

In 1995 and 1996 alone, the United States threatened 301 sanctions in highly publicized confrontations with Japan over auto parts imports, Korea over auto market opening, and China over intellectual piracy. In addition, most of the bigger Asian countries have experienced being placed in the various categories of violators in the order of severity of threatened sanctions: 'priority foreign country', 'priority watch list' and 'watch list'.

The other key mechanism used to pry open Asian markets and reassert a significant US trade and investment role was the Uruguay Round of the General Agreement on Tariffs and Trade (GATT). GATT, the negotiation and ratification of which was driven mainly by the United States, has committed the East Asian economies to end all quantitative trade restrictions and significantly reduce tariffs on imports in the next few years. Tariff reductions will work to the advantage of the US especially in agriculture, where American surpluses have mounted owing to a variety of government subsidies for production. Key in absorbing these surpluses are the now highly protected Asian agricultural markets. The United States Department of Agriculture (USDA) estimates that two thirds of the global increase anticipated for farm exports to the year 2000 will take place in the Asia Pacific, and it wants to make sure that by that time, this market will absorb some 60 per cent of American agricultural exports – up from the already large 40 per cent it accounts for currently.[54]

Especially relevant to the American design, however, are the GATT accords on 'Trade-Related Intellectual Property Rights' (TRIPs) and 'Trade-Related Investment Measures' (TRIMs). By tightening international regulations on patents, copyrights and trademarks, the first consolidates the pre-eminent US position in high technology by making the diffusion of technology dependent on restrictive royalty agreements and high royalty payments to American firms such as Microsoft and IBM. The TRIMs accord bans such measures as local content regulations, which require manufacturers to source a certain percentage of their components locally. Such measures have been used to build up automobile and other industries in Malaysia and Korea, for example, which have been regarded as threats to the global market dominance of American and other Northern transnationals. They have also drawn fire from the transnationals for interfering with trade among their subsidiaries, which are designed to manipulate stated prices of imports and exports low so as to reduce tariff impositions and thus keep down costs.

American officials have regarded APEC as a 'GATT-plus' arrangement that would accelerate trade liberalization beyond the Asian countries' commitments under GATT as well as serve as another institutional framework for the enforcement of intellectual property rights. It has not, however, been smooth sailing for the US agenda in APEC, owing to serious opposition to it among Asian governing and industrial elites. The APEC idea began as a suggestion from Japan's Ministry of Trade and Industry, which had in mind a loose forum for technical cooperation on economic issues along the lines of the Organization for Economic Cooperation and Development (OECD). The Australian government, obsessed with integrating into Asia to share in the region's economic dynamism, enthusiastically leaped at the idea, but in promoting it, gave it a new twist, that of becoming eventually a free trade area.

During the first three years since APEC's founding in Canberra in 1989, Washington's energies were elsewhere, in getting WTO negotiated and ratified. In 1993, however, partly as a fallback in the event WTO was not successfully negotiated, the USA took the leadership of the effort to transform APEC into a free trade area during the first APEC Summit in Seattle. The Asian governments were, however, able to prevent the formal declaration of a free trade area as a goal, with Malaysia's Mohamad Mahathir setting an example by boycotting the meeting. The Americans and Australians were unfazed, and at the second summit in Bogor, Indonesia, they prevailed upon the host, President Suharto, to support their blueprint of an Asia-Pacific free trade area by the year 2020. The Japanese lobbied behind the scenes to dissuade Suharto from going along but were unsuccessful.[55] The heads of state of the 18 APEC countries (including Chile, Mexico and Canada) signed the Bogor 2020 declaration, but the Malaysians and Thais were quick to append their formal positions that the vision statement was nonbinding and it certainly was not a treaty.

The scene of the next act in the APEC drama was Osaka in November 1995 – enemy territory in the view of the Americans. Throughout 1995, the Japanese tried, in their usual indirect and subtle way, to sabotage the 2020 vision. First, they argued that APEC had three legs – trade liberalization, trade facilitation, and economic cooperation. There was too much emphasis on trade liberalization, they said, and it was time to place the stress on trade facilitation measures, like harmonizing customs procedures throughout the region, and on economic cooperation in the form of aid to the less developed APEC member countries. Accelerated aid to the less developed APEC members was necessary, they argued, because trade liberalization in an uneven playing field would merely accentuate inequalities within the region. The Americans were not pleased, and they accused the Japanese of trying to convert APEC into an economic aid agency.

Next the Japanese tried to exempt agriculture from any liberalization plan, and here they were backed openly by South Korea, China, and Taiwan, and informally by Malaysia and Indonesia. Washington was enraged. Then at the actual summit itself, the Japanese view prevailed. A close reading of the Osaka document broadly affirmed the goal of regional trade liberalization, but it enshrined the principles that liberalization plans must be flexible, voluntary, unilaterally offered, and non-binding. The alternative position, favoured by the United States, Australia, and the other non-Asian countries, was that liberalization plans must be binding, negotiated comprehensively as part of a regional liberalization program, and contain a specific schedule for implementation.

In short, what happened at the muffled shoot-out at the 'Osaka Corral' was that the Japanese, with the support of most of the other Asian governments, were able to derail the 2020 free trade vision while paying lip service to free trade. Not surprisingly, the pro-free trade business magazine *Economist* said that the much-vaunted Osaka Action Agenda 'committed nobody to anything'.[56] It is unlikely, however, that Osaka was the last word in APEC's evolution. Indeed, it was merely one more skirmish in the deepening conflict between the USA and an increasingly assertive though informal Asian economic bloc whose members approximated those in Mohamad Mahathir's proposed regional economic alternative to the trans-Pacific APEC, the 'East Asia Economic Group' (EAEG). The latter, which was limited to East and Southeast Asian countries, drew the fire of Washington as creating 'a dividing line down the Pacific'.[57]

ASIA'S VOLATILE SECURITY SYSTEM

The deepening of economic conflicts in the Asia-Pacific region must be seen against the background of a regional peace and security situation that is far from stable. A few years ago, the conventional wisdom about the Asia Pacific was expressed by Tommy Koh, the former ambassador of Singapore, to the United States: 'The Asia-Pacific is a region of booming economies at peace with itself'.[58] In fact, as in many other areas of the globe, neither economic prosperity nor the end of the Cold War has brought the region closer to peace. Indeed, there is growing pessimism, exemplified in the 1995 Australian Defence White Paper's assertion that 'the relative peace in Asia may not last'.[59]

Washington's sending of two aircraft-carrier battle groups to the South China Sea in response to China's military exercises in the Taiwan Strait during the presidential campaign and elections in Taiwan in the middle of March 1996 brought home to many in Asia the fragility of the post-Cold War order. The event, which involved the largest armada assembled in Southeast Asian waters by the US Navy since the end of the Vietnam War, underlined how the unilateral exercise of American military force continues to be a central element of what passes for a system of security in the Asia-Pacific region. It also revealed the extent to which a new 'enemy', China, has come to fill the role of the Soviet Union as a rationale for the continuing massive American military presence in the region.

The American show of force in the Taiwan Strait cannot be understood without calling attention to the US Department of Defense posture statement entitled *US Security Strategy in the East Asia Pacific Region* that was issued over a year earlier, in February 1995. The central message of this detailed and comprehensive document was that the USA was reversing its five-year policy of drawing down its forces in the area and maintaining its troop level at 100 000 – a move that was hailed in many quarters as a measure that would promote regional peace and stability.

RESURGENT AMERICAN UNILATERALISM: A TRIUMPH OF THE PAST OVER THE FUTURE

On the contrary, the move was the triumph of the past over the future, of selfish national interest over the regional interest, of fear over courage and vision. The move was a throwback to the Cold War system of regional security, wherein the peace and security of Western-oriented elites rested on the threat of the exercise of US military force that was deployed in more than 350 major bases and facilities and legitimized by bilateral or trilateral mutual defence treaties with selected Asia-Pacific governments.

The Clinton administration's decision represented a step toward the closing of a window of opportunity that emerged with the ending of the Cold War for governments and people in the Asia Pacific to forge a new architecture for peace and security – one that would rest on multilateral mechanisms or institutions to resolve disputes, control arms, and eventually move the region towards disarmament. Furthermore, this reassertion of a system of security that might have been appropriate for another era is inadequate to address the particular mix of new and old conflicts and tensions characteristic of the post-Cold War era and is a prescription for crisis and instability in the medium to long term.

In justifying their reaffirmation of US military presence as the key mechanism of security in the region, American officials often say that the region is not ready for a multilateral system or that it is much too diverse for such an arrangement. The problem with this explanation is that it has the character of a self-fulfilling prophecy. The USA has been a leading force in killing or dampening major initiatives for multilateral security. And here we are not talking about proposals for collective security that have come from the former Soviet Union but initiatives launched by the United States' closest allies in the region.

Perhaps the most prominent casualty of American disapproval was Australian Foreign Minister Gareth Evans' October 1990 proposal to establish 'an all-embracing Conference on Security and Cooperation in Asia . . . built in some way on the . . . Helsinki CSCE model in Europe'.[60] Though Evans did not seek to disband the existing system of bilateral alliances between the United States and Australia, New Zealand, the Philippines, South Korea, Thailand and Japan, the Bush administration shot down his proposal, as it did an initiative from Canada to convoke a North Pacific Security Conference.

The United States has also tried to dampen enthusiasm for the ASEAN Regional Forum, which, for all its flaws, is a step in the right direction. When the Forum was founded in Bangkok in July 1994, then Secretary of State Warren Christopher was one of the few foreign ministers of participating governments absent from the meeting – no doubt a calculated move on the part of the USA to underline to the other countries the status it was according the organization. American officials have since often referred to the

Forum as simply a 'talk shop'. But perhaps the most telling recent put-down of ARF was former Defense Secretary William Perry's suggestion that a security dimension should be added to APEC, an economic grouping dominated by the US.[61]

President Clinton himself has expressed the official American view of the ARF and other multilateral security initiatives, saying that they 'are a way to supplement our alliances and forward military presence, not supplant them'.[62] And, one might add, they are even more acceptable if, unlike the ARF, where ASEAN has the initiative, they are strongly influenced by Washington.

Why is the United States so suspicious of multilateral security systems? Simply because after having for so long been used to moving troops and forces around at will, it is not about to subject the movements of its troops to multilateral controls. The complications that a successful multilateral organization could pose for American foreign and military policy in the region are cogently captured in a report by the US Congressional Research Service:[63]

> [A] problem would arise if East Asian governments used the ASEAN Regional Forum and other future regional security consultative organizations in attempts to restrain the United States from acting on certain security issues. The impasse between the United States and the NATO and CSCE countries over policy toward Bosnia-Herzegovina points up the potential for disagreements as Cold war-based mutual security interests decline. Four areas of US security policy in East Asia would appear to be subject to potential differences between the United States and some East Asian governments: US attempts to restrain Chinese missile and arms sales; US policy toward Taiwan, especially if Taiwan-China relations should worsen; US efforts to prevent North Korea from developing nuclear weapons; and US policy towards Japan's future regional and international military roles. The US Government and friendly East Asian governments might agree on some basic objectives on these issues, but they may disagree on the strategies and tactics to employ. Regional security consultative organizations could be focal points for the airing of such differences.

So, less than a decade after the collapse of the Berlin Wall, what we have in the Asia Pacific is a fallback on the US military presence as the principal mechanism for preserving the peace. But as in other things, the present is no simple reproduction of the past. For aside from the US military presence, the evolving system of regional security rests on two other key elements: balance of power diplomacy and arms races.

BALANCE-OF-POWER DIPLOMACY

Let us move on to the balance of power. With its CSCA proposal dismissed by the United States, Australia has been among the most active in trying to forge a balance-of-power regime in the Asia Pacific. The key aim of Australia's regional foreign policy is, to use Prime Minister Paul Keating's words, to 'ensure US strategic engagement', and a prime motivation of Australia's support for regional arrangements like APEC is that they provide a 'framework to help contain or manage competition between China, Japan, and the United States'.[64] Foreign Minister Gareth Evans describes the US military presence as the 'balancing wheel in the region', and conceptualizes Australian regional policy as placing the 'emphasis on traditional balance of power considerations', though with 'strong commitment' to multilateral dialogue.[65]

Australia finds itself in synch with its ASEAN neighbours, who have become equally assiduous practitioners of the balance of power, their declared aim being to check what they perceive as the strategic threats posed by Japan and China to Southeast Asia by keeping the United States in the Pacific. Thus, American bases had not yet shut down in 1992, when Singapore came forward to offer the US Air Force and the Seventh Fleet generous access and servicing arrangements. Currently, two US military units – the 497 FTS and COMLOG WESTPAC – are practically resident there. Access proposals followed in short order from Indonesia, Brunei, and Thailand. In this connection, let me refer to the February 1995 Pentagon Strategy Document. American deployments in Southeast Asia, it says,

> are dependent ... on a wide variety of access arrangements. We have formal access agreements, informal agreements for aircraft transits and ship visits, commercial arrangements for ship and/or aircraft repairs and maintenance, and occasional access arrangements with many countries for training and exercise purposes. These access arrangements have expanded in recent years, in part

due to regional fears that the closure of US bases in the Philippines would lead to our departure from the region, and in part is a result of gradually expanding bilateral defense relationships.[66]

One can argue, in fact, that for the ASEAN elites, the access arrangements are ideal, in that they avoid the nationalist backlash that can be ignited by fixed land bases, while providing essentially the same services for the massive floating base that is the American Seventh Fleet which used to be provided by fixed bases. Thus, we see ASEAN governments endorse the continuing US military presence as critical for regional security, as they did during the ARF meeting in Brunei, and in the same breath congratulate the United States for withdrawing its bases from the Philippines – a move that allegedly manifests Washington's respect for the ASEAN concept of ZOPFAN, that is Southeast Asia as a 'Zone of Peace, Freedom, and Neutrality'.[67] This is diplomatic hypocrisy at its worst – or best – since Indonesian Foreign Minister Ali Alatas, who commends Washington for respecting ZOPFAN, cannot be unaware of the fact that the new access and servicing arrangements with Southeast Asian countries, when combined with technological advances in communications and logistics, have placed the US military in a better position to project force than when it had Subic Naval Base and Clark Air Force Base!

ASEAN defence analysts, in fact, now explicitly talk about the 'multipolar balance of power' as being the centrepiece of ASEAN strategy, with the classical European balance of power emerging as a model. In the words of one analyst,

The principles of a *multipolar balance of power* seem to be gradually becoming the basis of international relations in the post-cold war era in which bigger countries tend to dominate smaller and weaker countries. Under the principles of a multipolar balance of power, a country which has become too strong will pose a threat to its neighbours and they will in turn undertake diplomatic and military cooperation to face the potential threat.

Under the system, a relatively big and influential country is needed to undertake diplomatic and military cooperation with smaller countries. This pattern existed in Europe a century ago or two where Britain played the role of a *balancer* against France and, subsequently, Germany. . . .[68]

Practising balance of power politics, continues the same writer, is 'not designed to create an arms race or widen the dispute'. Instead, the balance of power is 'designed to create real and sustainable peace and stability in the region, in which the regional countries are constantly interested'.[69]

The idea that the balance of power in the Asia-Pacific context will actually result in 'sustainable peace and stability' is, at the very least, dubious if one is guided by the historical record, especially that of the nineteenth-century European balance of power which is regarded as a model. Indeed, it is hard to understand why ASEAN defence strategists are so keen in reproducing nineteenth-century Europe in the Asia Pacific of the twenty-first century!

First of all, the so-called Concert of Europe encouraged not equilibrium but imbalance. Some countries tried to gain strategic superiority in order to feel secure, and others felt compelled to match their moves to 'restore equilibrium'. Not surprisingly, the classical European balance of power was accompanied by destabilizing arms races: between 1890 and 1914, military spending rose by 384 per cent in Germany, 284 per cent in Britain, 170 per cent in Italy, and 704 per cent in Russia.[70] With arms spending by some countries rising by 50 per cent or more in the last five years, East Asian nations are well on their way to matching, if not exceeding these rates.

Second, the classical balance of power may have largely kept the peace in the centre of the system for a century, but it was accompanied by the outbreak of smaller wars in the periphery. There were 67 wars between 1815 and 1914, most of them fought in the periphery, though there were three fought in the centre, on European soil. In this regard, the observation by one analyst that under balance-of-power regimes, smaller wars 'may be required for equilibrium' is not reassuring.[71]

But the fatal flaw in the classical European balance of power, as pointed out by Henry Kissinger – of all people! – in his book *Diplomacy*, was that the more and more intricate balancing mechanisms it required for maintenance over time led to its running out of the control of all the states involved, resulting in the Big Bang of 1914 and the even Bigger Bang of 1939.[72]

THE ARMS RACE

The idea that the balance of power in the East Asian context will actually result in 'sustainable peace and stability' becomes even more questionable if one looks at the third pillar of the informal system of security that now governs the region. This is the arms race, which is really one dimension of the balance of power.

The Asian arms market is now the second largest in the developing world. It accounted for 39 per cent of all arms transfer agreements in the period 1991–4, up from 26.3 per cent in 1987–90.[73] I would like to point out three of the more disturbing features of this development:

1. In the absence of viable multilateral security mechanisms to assure the peace, the vaunted prosperity of the East Asian region is leading not to less but to more potential instability. As a portion of GNP, defence spending may have gone down in most East Asian countries, but the high annual GNP growth rates have allowed it to continue growing at high or at least respectable rates in most countries except perhaps for the Philippines. Capital acquisition, moreover, is everywhere a priority. A few years ago, the conventional wisdom was distilled in Singaporean diplomat Tommy Koh's claim that 'The Asia-Pacific is a region of booming economies at peace with itself'.[74] Today, the truth seems to be closer to the 1995 Australian Defence White Paper's assertion that 'the relative peace in Asia may not last'.[75]

2. The biggest arms supplier in the region has been the United States. In the period 1991–4, the US accounted for 43 per cent of the value of all arms transfer agreements with the developing countries of the Asia-Pacific region, far outstripping Western Europe's 26 per cent share and Russia's 23 per cent.[76] Furthermore, the USA has also been associated with the most destabilizing deals: its sale of 150 F-16s to Taiwan, in clear violation of the terms of US-China normalization, helped torpedo what appeared to be an emerging *modus vivendi* – based largely on *de facto* investment and trade – between Taiwan and China in the late 1980s. It was also the American sale of F-16s to Singapore a few years ago that triggered the jet-fighter arms race in Southeast Asia, a development to which we shall return below.[77] Again, the rationale for the recent reassertion of American unilateralism as the key mechanism of peace and security has, in light of

this behaviour, the character of a self-fulfilling prophecy: through its arms sales policy, the United States has acted in a way that has contributed to regional instability; then it says that this instability makes its military presence necessary.

3. Finally, it must be emphasized that the arms races in the region are not simply a response to perceived threats from the big powers on the part of the smaller countries but also acts directed against one another on the part of the smaller countries. Looking at the race for ultra-modern jet fighters in Southeast Asia, for instance, Desmond Ball claims that 'Singapore's decision to purchase F-16s does seem to have acted as something of a stimulant for the subsequent Indonesian and Thai F-16 acquisitions, as well as fuelling Malaysia's interest in a strike fighter'.[78] Malaysia subsequently decided to buy 18 Russian Mig-29s along with eight F/A 18Ds. In fact, even the cash-strapped Philippine Air Force, which has been hankering for F-16s, may get its wish if the USA decides to divert to it at least 11 of the 28 F-16 fighters that were earlier earmarked for Pakistan but were not delivered owing to Pakistan's nuclear program.[79]

There is now in ASEAN not just a jet-fighter race but also a submarine race. The Thai Navy is desperately trying to acquire two diesel submarines because Indonesia already has two submarines, and Malaysia and Singapore have entered into agreements with foreign navies to train their submarine crews, which means that they have decided to buy submarines. Why submarines? Because as Thai Supreme Commander Watthana Wutthisiri notes, 'most of our natural resources are in the sea', and '[i]f we have no strong armed forces, we may regret it in the next five years when we are defeated in marine battles'.[80]

This competitive frame of mind is not surprising if one brings together two conditions: an area fraught with multiple unsettled territorial conflicts with the absence of a multilateral system for settling these disputes or at least to prevent them from exploding into open war. In addition to the better-known issues such as the six-country dispute over the Spratly Islands and Indonesia's continuing occupation of East Timor, we have in Southeast Asia alone the following:[81]

- the Malaysia/Philippine dispute over the ownership of Sabah;
- the dispute between Malaysia and Singapore over the ownership of the island of Pulau Batu Putih;

- the dispute between Indonesia and Malaysia over the islands of Sipadin, Sebatik, and Ligitan in the Celebes Sea;
- a boundary dispute between Indonesia and Vietnam over their offshore demarcation line on the continental shelf of the South China Sea;
- another offshore demarcation line dispute between Vietnam and Malaysia;
- still another a maritime boundary dispute between Vietnam and China;
- a potential dispute over Indonesia's Natuna Island, which is shown in recent Chinese maps to be within Chinese territory in the South China Sea;
- an economic zone dispute in the Gulf of Thailand between Cambodia and Thailand; and
- various disputes over fishing rights in the Gulf of Thailand between Thailand and Malaysia and in the Andaman Sea between Thailand and Burma, which have resulted in a number of explosive incidents, including one just three weeks ago where Malaysian patrol boats fired on and killed two Thai fishermen.

In short, when one goes beneath the rhetoric, the much vaunted ASEAN solidarity is very shaky indeed and can never be relied on as a substitute for a multilateral security system with clear-cut rules for peacefully resolving territorial disputes. One can be sure that with such a system becoming more and more difficult to erect, we will see the institutionalization within the region's militaries of strategic and tactical calculations such as those which underlie the Royal Thai Navy's determined push for a submarine. Allow me to quote a high-ranking admiral:[82]

Competition will continue to grow, especially competition to find resources in the sea – crude oil, ore, natural gas, fish. All countries want to use these resources to strengthen their economies, which could lead to disputes because of unsettled overlapping economic zones in the sea. Thailand, Malaysia, Vietnam, and India each have their own claims. If valuable resources are discovered, such as oil and gas, a dispute could arise. For instance, Cambodia thinks it owns gas which we are drilling for in the Gulf of Thailand. It wants another country to do drilling. Minor issues involving economic interests could lead to disputes. It would not have to be a big dispute. It could involve ships exchanging fire. The allies of the disputing countries would try to mediate and encourage a negotiated settlement. The scale of conflicts would be small. We have disputes with Malaysia over fishing in its territory. Fishing boats were seized and destroyed and some crews imprisoned. The same situation has occurred in Burma. An accumulation of these incidents could lead to the use of force some day. Any country wanting to use aggression against us would think again if it does not know the location of our submarines.

In any event, the Royal Thai Navy is reportedly interested in German submarines – the German 209 Class in particular – because, as one report notes, 'the Germans wrote the book on modern submarine warfare, and almost succeeded in strangling Britain into submission in both World War I and World War II'.[83]

Thus, ARF notwithstanding, the ASEAN governments have, for all practical purposes, fallen back on the old Roman dictum: *Si vis pacem, para bellum*. (If you desire peace, prepare for war.) Indeed, a contemporary expression of this mentality that now reigns among defence establishments in the region was provided by Malaysian Defence Minister Najib Razak, who said that the end of the Cold War has made the security environment in the region 'fluid and unpredictable', and advised governments to 'prepare for the worst scenario'.[84]

It is postures like this among the ASEAN elites that is rendering the ARF ineffective. For how can one talk about ARF being a serious multilateral endeavor if one automatically rules out of bounds for collective discussion intra-ASEAN territorial disputes and conflicts such as the Indonesian aggression agaisnt – the Indonesian military prefers to call it 'integration' of – East Timor? If the ASEAN elites complain about the United States not taking ARF seriously, they have partly themselves to blame.

THE JAPAN QUESTION

It is against this regional picture that we move to the question of Japan and the USA-Japan Security Treaty, which the Pentagon statement describes as the centrepiece of the US presence in the region. Several points must be made in this connection.

First of all, Japan's failure to stand strongly for a new multilateral order has been as damaging to East Asia's long-term security as Japan's failure to define itself clearly *vis-à-vis* the American trade offensive has been to East Asia's economic solidarity. Some analysts have hailed the recent defence advisory group report, the so-called Higuchi Report, as placing the creation for multilateral security mechanisms as the principal thrust of Japan's regional security policy in the next few decades. One may certainly applaud the report for its recognition of the importance of multilateralism and its support for the ARF. But one would have to admit that its discussion of multilateralism is laced with studied ambiguity while its reaffirmation of the centrality of the USA-Japan Security Treaty as the bedrock of regional security is loud and clear. It states, without seemingly sensing any contradiction, that

> [i]n order to further ensure the security of Japan and make multilateral security cooperation effective, close and broad cooperation with the United States is essential. The institutional framework for this is provided by the Japan-US Security Treaty. Henceforth the two nations should make efforts to make greater use of this framework and strengthen their cooperative relations so that they can act more positively in response to new security needs.
>
> In relation to the security environment in the Asia Pacific region, cooperation between Japan and the United States is an essential factor. In view of the continuing need to ensure that US commitment of [sic] this region is maintained as desired by many Asian nations, it is highly significant that Japan and the United States should renew their determination to maintain their security relations . . .
>
> From these international and regional viewpoints, the Japan-US Security Treaty will assume greater significance than ever before. In addition, it is necessary to reaffirm the significance of this treaty in the sense that it forms an essential framework for the active and constructive security policy Japan should pursue . . .[85]

The message here may not be crystal clear to Washington, which is always quick to come down on Japan for not expressing unconditional loyalty to 'the Alliance'; [86] it comes across loud and clear to the rest of Asia: Japan does not have the nerve to downgrade the USA-Japan security alliance and to decisively lead the region in forging a new multilateral system of peace and security. Typical of the timidity of Japanese officialdom is the following remark of a senior official of the Japan Defence Agency when queried about Japan's caution in pursuing multilateral initiatives: 'If

Japan vigorously works to promote multilateral security consultations or creates a framework for them, this would lead the United States to worry that Japan wants to disengage from relations with it'.[87]

The firestorm over the rape of a 12-year-old schoolgirl in Okinawa did not prevent the government of Prime Minister Tomiichi Murayama from sticking closely to established policy. Nor was it an obstacle to his successor Ryutaro Hashimoto's concluding an Acquisition and Cross Servicing Agreement (ACSA) with Washington that committed Japan to providing supplies and ammunition to American forces conducting military exercises in or near Japanese territory.

The second key point is that given two conditions – the centrality of the US military presence in Japan and the US government's worsening fiscal crisis – a large part of the costs of American strategy to maintain force levels in the Asia-Pacific region will fall on Japan in the form of demands for increased host-nation support. Between FY 1991 and FY 1995, the US defence budget fell from $303.5 billion to $263.8 billion, or a reduction of 13 per cent in nominal terms but of 20 per cent in real terms. At the same time, Japan's share of the burden of maintaining American troops has been on the rise. Currently, the total cost to Japan of maintaining the 45 000 American troops in Japan is in the order of $625.7 billion, while the cost to the United States runs to around 340 billion yen – which means that around 70 per cent of the total expenses needed to keep the US Armed Forces in Japan is now borne by Japan.[88]

Despite this already massive amount, American pressure to increase Japanese support has mounted. And Washington has essentially gotten what it wanted. Notwithstanding the firestorm over the Okinawa rape, the Diet subsequently passed the 'Host-Nation Support Pact' which commits Japan to increase its financial obligations to maintain the American troops up to the year 2001. Reportedly, Foreign Minister Yohei Kono and Japan Defence Agency Director General Seishiro Eto agreed to raise in FY 1996 by 4 billion yen.[89]

This leads to the third point, which is that in agreeing to bear a significant portion of the costs of the resurgent American military presence in Asia, Japan is, in effect, financing a military presence directed against itself. For the USA-Japan Treaty has always had several rationales. Even during the Cold War, the principal rationale of containing the Soviet Union was joined by the secondary rationale of preventing the independent rearmament of Japan. The situation after the end of the Cold War has raised what used to be the secondary rationale to a status at least equal to that of containing China or North Korea. One can, in fact, get a good debate going on whether the new American profile is meant principally to contain China or to restrain Japan from becoming a threat to both the USA and the region.

This is a growing understanding that is seldom formally acknowledged, though sometimes, like Japanese officials pontificating on Japan's role in World War II, key American officials slip. For instance, a few years ago, in an interview that incurred the displeasure of official Washington, Major General Henry Stackpole, then commander of Marine Forces in Japan, told the *Washington Post* that the main purpose of the US military presence in Japan is to prevent Tokyo from beefing up 'what is already a very, very potent military'. Already, he claimed, the Japanese have 'achieved the Greater Asia Co-Prosperity Sphere economically, without guns'. Since 'No one wants a rearmed, resurgent Japan ... we are the cap in the bottle, if you will'.[90]

This is an understanding that is now acknowledged increasingly openly by Japanese officials and analysts. For instance, Yoshiki Hidaka, chief researcher of New York's Hudson Institute, says quite forcefully in the *Voice* that the USA-Japan Security Treaty 'is based on a policy for preventing unilateral reinforcement of military power on the part of Japan and for preventing it from expanding its military influence in Southeast Asia or developing nuclear weaponry'.[91] In Hidaka's opinion, the Clinton administration's reversal of the Bush policy of drawing down forces in the Pacific was carried out 'with a view to protecting against military expansion on the part of Japan'.[92] Another security expert, Professor Terumasa Nakanishi of Kyoto University, asks the question: '[H]ow long can we tolerate an alliance which views oneself as a threat (while constantly facing the demand for increasing "contributions")'.[93]

The aftermath of the Okinawa incident has shown that the Japanese people are ahead of most bureaucrats and politicians in their perception of the strategic intent of the American bases. An opinion poll shows that only 5 per cent of the Japanese people believe that the bases are primarily for the benefit of that country,[94] which leads one to suspect that the American military presence may be tolerated in Japan mainly because it has been so focused in terms of land occupancy on Okinawa, which is in the periphery of the Japanese archipelago and whose people are treated as second-class citizens by most Japanese. Dispersing the bases throughout Japan as some have proposed is apparently no option because local resentment of bases in other parts of Japan is already high. Even then US Secretary of Defense William Perry acknowledged that other Japanese communities may be incapable and unwilling to support redeployments of American forces from Okinawa.[95]

This resentment has the potential of being translated into a political force. Under the old multi-seat system, the LDP always worked hard to assure the election of at least one pro-bases candidate in districts with American bases. However, according to Patrick Cronin and Michael Green, under the new single-seat system, 'this firebreak against local resentment of bases will vanish'.[96] Indeed, 'given the pressure on the higher levels of political leadership to build new constituencies, US bases will become attractive targets for the creation of new public works projects such as international airports and public housing'.[97]

All this shows that there is potentially a domestic base for a new security policy toward the region within Japan. What is sorely missing today are several other key ingredients. We have already touched on two of these: the lack of bold leadership and innovative vision. But the absence of another factor is equally critical: this is Japan's moral credibility within the region, which leads to the fourth point: Japan can potentially exercise strong leadership within the region in charting the direction away from the Cold War system. But the rest of Asia will not allow it to assume this role unless the Japanese people and political leadership assume responsibility without hesitation and without qualification for the crimes and atrocities perpetrated on Asian countries by an earlier generation of Japanese. Instead, what we have is a succession of high officials forced out of office because of their justifying or rationalizing Japan's colonial and World War II records.

Responsibility for the past, a paradigm of conflict resolution via multilateralism, and a program of significant arms reduction – these could be the elements of a potentially attractive and powerful Japanese strategy for a post-Cold War system that truly breaks with the past. Unfortunately, the Japanese are not up to the task . . . yet.

THE REVIVAL OF CONTAINMENT

Let us now turn to the relations of the United States with two regional actors, North Korea and China, which have been central in determining the Asia-Pacific security dynamic during the last few years.

Demonizing North Korea

When the cold war ended at the turn of the decade, pressures both from within the Asia-Pacific region and from the American public forced the administration of President George Bush to announce a 10 per cent reduction in American forces in the Pacific, in line with a projected global reduction of US military forces and a streamlining of the United States force structure. The absence of a clearly defined 'enemy', while welcome to most people, was worrying to Washington's military establishment, in particular the naval lobby that controls the US Pacific Command headquarters in Honolulu. To many of them, the Philippine Senate's refusal to give its advice and consent to a new treaty governing the presence of American military bases in the Philippines was an alarming development that could culminate in the rollback of American forces from the Western Pacific to Hawaii.

To a military establishment requiring a new rationale to justify its massive Pacific presence after the collapse of the Soviet enemy, North Korea was a godsend. Even before the Yongbyon reactor controversy broke, Washington was already dressing up North Korea as the 'greatest immediate danger to regional security', as the commander-in-chief of American forces in the Pacific put it in testimony to the US Congress in 1991.[98]

There is no doubt that North Korea has had a significant number of men under arms and has kept them at a high level of military preparedness, along with bellicose rhetoric against the USA and South Korea. But this behaviour was largely a carryover from the Cold War. Moreover, most serious defence specialists would probably agree with Andrew Mack's advice that in assessing North Korea's behaviour, one must consider that 'from Pyongyang's perspective, many American and South Korean actions and statements surely do seem threatening'.[99]

Indeed, Pyongyang may even have attempted to use the Yongbyong nuclear-power project partly as an effort to develop nuclear arms. But this response, while not excusable, certainly becomes understandable in the light of developments in the last few years. Put yourself in the shoes of the leadership in Pyongyang:

- You are told by the *New York Times* that the Korean peninsula has been identified by the Pentagon's first post-cold war defence guidance as the site of two out of seven scenarios of post-cold war conflict could be involved.[100]
- You are constantly identified as the main threat to regional peace at a time that you, in fact, have already effectively lost your traditional protectors, China and the Soviet Union, owing to the disappearance of socialist solidarity.
- Over 17 000 American troops stand on permanent combat alert on your southern border, their offensive skills constantly honed in annual war exercises carried out with South Korean forces.
- You read in the Pentagon posture statement that 'We [the US] are ... prepositioning military equipment in South Korea to increase our capability to respond to crisis. In light of the continuing conventional capability of North Korea, we have permanently halted a previously planned modest drawdown of our troops from South Korea, and are modernizing the American forces there was well as assisting the Republic of Korea in modernizing its forces'.[101]
- You are constantly treated to accounts in American and South Korean press about your economic troubles and how they are a prelude to your inevitable political collapse.

American actions, in short, have forced North Korea to assume some of the characteristics of a cornered animal, whereupon the US seizes precisely on some aspects of that behaviour in order to justify the concentration of even more force against it!

Indeed, what mainly strikes many Asian observers of the Korean drama in the last few years has not been North Korea's alleged aggressiveness but the way the American political and military establishment waved the alleged North Korean plan to produce weapons-grade plutonium at the nuclear plant at Yongbyon in order to force the Korean issue to the top of the region's security concerns and thus reassert Washington's control over the Asia-Pacific security agenda after its hold on this had been loosened by post-Cold War developments. In other words, the heightened demonization of Korea in the period 1991–4 was an indispensable mechanism to counter the pressure for troop reduction from a United States public weary of Cold War defence expenditures. It was also instrumental in interrupting the thawing of the Cold War that was occurring in the early 1990s between Seoul and Pyongyang, aborting Japan and

Australia's flirtation with multilateral systems for regional security, and dampening ASEAN's increasingly independent security initiatives.

Containment – that venerable strategic doctrine of the cold war – had not become irrelevant, the military establishment declared. As James Morley, a veteran Pentagon Asia hand, put it at a conference in Tokyo:

> The strategic picture has not changed from that of the cold war. Then we had an alliance of the status quo against a power that threatened the status quo. Today, there are still forces that threaten the same status quo, except now North Korea and China have stepped into the role that was formerly filled by the Soviet Union.[102]

China as 'the Enemy'

This brings us to China, which became the focus of demonization efforts, especially after North Korea agreed to forgo its plans to develop nuclear energy and accept a US-promoted international plan to supply it with nuclear reactors that were technologically very difficult to use to produce weapons-grade plutonium – a move that contradicted the Pentagon's campaign to paint North Korea as irrational and crazy. Moreover, it was simply difficult to convince Asian governments that a beleaguered regime with a collapsing economy was a credible regional threat. China, on the other hand, was big, economically successful, and many of its recent actions could be superficially interpreted as 'expansionist' in character.

Now, many aspects of Chinese political and military behaviour are certainly disconcerting and outrageous, especially the Tienanmen Square massacre. But one cannot allow what was undoubtedly criminal behaviour at Tienanmen on the part of the Chinese authorities to lead us to easy but erroneous conclusions about China's security policy. More precisely, the currently fashionable interpretation of Chinese behaviour as 'expansionist' by both Western and ASEAN defence analysts distorts a more complex reality that must be approached with more sophisticated analysis and policy instruments rather than a battle cry of meeting force with force and fire with fire.

First of all, if we look at the Spratly's dispute, which is adduced as *prima facie* evidence of Chinese expansionism, what we see is a process of setting borders by several claimants over an area whose possession has never before been determined. This is not a case of China crossing well-defined traditional borders in the manner of a

Hitler taking over Czechoslovakia or Poland or the USA taking over Mexican territory or the Philippines. What is problematic here is not, in fact, China's staking a claim to the area but its reluctance so far to settle the competing claims via methods of negotiation proposed by the other parties to the dispute. Calling China's behaviour expansionist in this context is far less justifiable than calling Indonesia's annexation of East Timor expansionist and imperialist.

Second, a key indicator of China's expansionist drive is said to be its program of massive militarization. Again, there is a gulf between the tag of expansionist and the reality. China's defence spending has been consistently on the rise since 1989. But this must be interpreted in the light of the fact that its spending steadily declined in the 1980s; the US Arms Control and Disarmament Agency, in fact, estimates that actual Chinese defence spending in 1989 was 25 per cent less than actual Chinese spending in 1979.[103] This was a time, it must be noted, when military spending by China's neighbours, notably Japan, South Korea and Taiwan, was rising at 4 to 5 per cent a year.[104] There is therefore a strong element of catch-up in Chinese defence spending behaviour.

China, it is true, has lately focused on acquiring sophisticated weapons systems. But the relatively antiquated Chinese force structure contrasts with the increasingly sophisticated force structures of its neighbours. China may have a 5000 jet fighter-and bomber-based air force, but these planes were what one American analyst describes as 'early 1960s Soviet derivatives that are often mechanically unreliable and therefore restricted in use'.[105] The Chinese Navy may have a large 100-plus submarine force, but the boats are very dated, with as many as one half no longer operational, and difficulty in communications reportedly keeps the boats close to shore.[106] Moreover, the Chinese army's command and control capabilities are weak, its force mobility is limited by the lack of transport helicopters, and the absence of a reliable air-refuelling system limits the range of Chinese aircraft.

In contrast, China's neighbours were able to equip themselves in the 1980s and early 1990s with advanced weapons systems, many of which were based on the West's and Japan's microelectronic revolution. Taiwan, always a worry to China, acquired F-16s and Mirage fighters, French and American advanced frigates, and new American-built air defence systems.[107]

Another constant worry of China, Japan, has first-rate C-31

capabilities. To fortify its capability for offensive operations to a distance of 1000 nautical miles from the Japanese coast, Japan, according to Desmond Ball,

> has a substantial and very modern naval force, including some 100 maritime combat aircraft, 64 major surface combatants... and 14 submarines. It is in the process of building several *Yukikaze*-class destroyers equipped with the *Aegis* system; it is modernizing its submarine fleet; it is planning to acquire tanker aircraft to extend the range of its air coverage; and it is considering the acquisition of 'defensive' aircraft carriers.[108]

Naturally, this has stirred the concerns of Chinese defence planners. But there are limits to China's ability to catch up. Even with the current pace of force modernization, says Australian analyst Paul Dibb, by 2010, 'China's power projection forces will be relatively small... in comparison to the forces available for defense in most of its powerful neighbors, namely Japan'.[109] Moreover, 'Japan's navy will remain in most respects... both qualitatively and quantitatively superior to that of China'.[110]

China's concern about the qualitative backwardness of its force structure appeared to have been heightened by the Gulf War in 1991–2, when American and other Western forces equipped with high-tech weaponry destroyed Saddam Hussein's army, which was very similar in force structure, weaponry and tactical doctrine to the Chinese Army. As Robert Sutter notes:[111]

> The ability of well trained Western forces armed with high-technology weaponry to conduct effective combined arms operations against Iraqi forces showed Beijing how far behind it actually was in dealing with modern warfare... It is clear as well that the forces deployed around China's eastern periphery (especially those of Japan, South Korea, and Taiwan) and to a lesser degree some forces in Southeast Asia (notably Singapore) have the kind of fire power, mobility, training, and experience that the allies used so successfully against Iraq.

The allegation of Chinese expansionism is coupled with an image of China as irresponsible, as a unscrupulous actor who will sell arms to anybody who can afford it to gain cash that can then be ploughed back to the military build-up. Again, between allegation and reality is a grand canyon. China's arms sales have, in fact, dropped significantly in recent years. Its arms deliveries to developing nations dropped from $9.6 billion in the period 1987–90 to $4.3 billion in 1991–4.[112] In contrast, the USA, which is now the world's largest arms dealer, accounted for arms deliveries to developing countries worth $28.2 billion in 1991–4, up from $20 billion in 1987–90.[113]

Who is destabilizing whom in Asia is clear from the figures: China's share of the Asian developing country arms market dropped from 7.1 per cent in 1987–90 to 3.2 per cent in 1991–4, while the United States share rose from 17.3 per cent to a whopping 43 per cent.[114] American sales included what was probably the most regionally destabilizing arms deal of the last decade: the sale of 150 F-16s to Taiwan by the Bush administration.

China's actions must, in other words, be examined in a historical and regional context, and when this is done, what emerges is a more complex behavioural pattern that cannot be fitted into the simple 'expansionist' label. Indeed, the behaviour approximates more to the balance-of-power model. Moreover, China's security policy must be analysed in the light of the clear priority the Chinese leadership has placed on economic modernization, where the United States and China's neighbours play a key role as markets and investors. The simplistic military expansionist model simply runs counter to the imperatives of export-market and foreign-investment driven economic growth.

China is, moreover, not averse to using multilateralism to manage competition conflict. At the United Nations Security Council, the Chinese have, for the most part, not obstructed initiatives considered critical for world security by the United States and other Western powers. China is eager to join the World Trade Organization and promises to live by its rules. China stole the show at the APEC Summit with its offer to reduce radically a whole range of tariffs as its so-called downpayment toward the goal of regional trade liberalization. China has participated in the ARF and acted in a conciliatory fashion, according to most observers.

For multilateralism to gain the serious adherence of countries like China, however, it has to be serious multilateralism, not multilateralism that is carried out as an 'adjunct' or 'auxiliary' of the unilateralist security policy of a regional superpower, as American officials choose to describe the ARF.[115]

China must be engaged in a serious multilateral enterprise to preserve the peace, but this effort will have to overcome the vested interests that have solidified to maintain the image of China as an irrational, expansionist power that can be brought into line only by the threat of force. These vested interests are: the US military, which will need the image of an expansionist China to support its continuing build-up in the region; Taiwan, for obvious reasons; and Indonesia, which needs a demonized China to distract attention from its hegemonistic project in East Timor and to justify its taking on the role as Southeast Asia's Big Brother protector.[116]

In the United States, the anti-China lobby is actually made up of two wings which cut across the civilian and military elite. The 'containment wing' seeks principally to advance its own institutional interests by playing up the China threat as well as prevent China from emerging as a virtual in the future via a strategy of 'cutting it off at the pass'. The other wing is a more ideological one, mainly represented by the right wing of the Republican Party, which was never reconciled to losing China in 1949 and sees no scope for positive change in USA-China relations except through the oustering of the Communist Party leadership.

Eclipsed by the policy of *de facto* alliance with China *vis-à-vis* the Soviet Union which was followed by the Republican administrations of Richard Nixon, Ronald Reagan, and George Bush, the old pro-Chiang Kai-Shek lobby has enjoyed a spectacular revival in recent years, being replenished with new voices following the Republican Party sweep of Congress in 1994. One of the members of the resurgent pro-Nationalist Chinese lobby is House Speaker Newt Gingrich, who publicly raised the idea that the United States should officially recognize Taiwan as an independent state – a position he says he no longer holds.

More alarming to Beijing, however, have been the following initiatives that have won approval either in the US Senate or the House of Representatives, though they still have to be enacted into law:[117]

- the supersession of the USA-PRC communiqué of 1982 restricting American arms sales to Taiwan by the US Congress' Taiwan Relations Act, whose provisions on arms transfers are less restrictive;
- a directive to the US executive to grant visas to *all* Taiwanese officials visiting the USA 'in a private capacity';
- the official recognition of Tibet as 'an occupied country' and the creation of the post of 'special envoy' to it; and

- the establishment of a Radio Free Asia to beam propaganda to China.

In the ongoing debate on the United States' strategic posture, the Clinton administration has been mainly in a reactive mode, swinging in typical Clinton fashion with the prevailing wing. On both security policy and economic policy, Clinton's moves toward China are difficult to characterize as a carrot-and-stick policy, as the administration claims, and come across more as a muddle of inconsistency, with predictable results. As Scott Kennedy and Michael O'Hanlon of the Brookings Institution have pointed out, 'Clinton's inconsistency and virtual silence has left a void that has been filled by single-issue interest groups, the far right and left on Capitol Hill, and other voices that are calling for a more confrontational approach toward China'.[118]

The Taiwan crisis of mid-March 1996 provided the opportunity to translate the increasingly dominant policy of confrontation into an operational strategy. It is this larger backdrop of strategic reorientation that allows us to make sense of what struck many as Washington's overreaction to the crisis: the sending of two carrier battle groups to the South China Sea, despite the almost unanimous consensus among defence analysts that China had neither the intention nor the capacity to invade Taiwan.

The truth is that the pro-confrontation lobby's two-carrier response was intended not only for the attention of Beijing but also for that of East and Southeast Asian governments and for the more dovish sections of the American establishment. There were, in fact, several messages:

- that China is a serious menace to regional stability which can only be dealt with by a powerful show of force;
- that 'engagement' of China, as proposed by Washington's doves, must be the subordinate element in a broader strategy of confrontation;
- that only 'forward deployed' military forces operating out of bases throughout the Western Pacific can be relied on to contain China, so 'Let's end this talk about rationalizing our bases structure and rely more on homeland-based expeditionary forces to deal with Asian problems';
- that aircraft carriers, with their splendid ability to project overwhelming power 'right onto the belly of the East Asian subcon-

tinent', remain the best weapons for maintaining the Asia-Pacific peace. 'So let's cut all talk of degrading the US Pacific Fleet from six carrier battle groups to four', as some defence analysts have suggested.

AMERICAN SECURITY AND THE TRADE CONNECTION

It is on the matter of China that we see most clearly a movement toward the synchronization of the United States' military unilateralism with its unilateralism in economic policy toward Asia. For the developments at the military and political level have been accompanied by dramatic American threats to impose unilateral trade sanctions on China, allegedly for allowing the violation of the intellectual property rights of American firms, and Washington's opposition to China's program for accession to the World Trade Organization (WTO), which has effectively blocked China's membership in this crucial multilateral organization.

The synchronization of economic and military policies in the case of China is not an aberration; it is likely to be a foretaste of things to come, as the economic conflicts deepen between the USA and Japan and the East and Southeast Asian NICs. For some time now, a game of pretend has been going on in the region, with most governments being players. The game rested on overt consensus by all parties that the stated US military strategy of providing a defence umbrella to the region was insulated from its aggressive unilateralist trade strategy of blasting open Asian markets by invoking the threat of the '301' provisions of the American Trade Act of 1988, which require the US executive to take retaliatory action against those considered as 'unfair traders'. This overt consensus contrasted with the deep fears of nearly everyone that American military strategy in the region would at some point synchronize with its trade strategy.

The game of pretend is up. In 1995, two events in particular signalled the likelihood of a closer integration of American military and trade strategies. During the meeting of the Asia Pacific Economic Cooperation (APEC) in November 1995, then US Secretary of Defense William Perry suggested that APEC, which the United States has tried to turn into a multilateral mechanism for opening up Asian markets, ought to have a security dimension as well. Earlier, Joseph Nye, then Under Secretary of Defense, made a speech in Tokyo that suggested that the US would 'probably with-draw our security presence' from the Asia Pacific if the countries in the area were to proceed to form the East Asia Economic Cau-cus proposed by Malaysian Prime Minister Mohamed Mahathir on the grounds that the latter would 'exclude the US from the region economically'.

In our view, however, if Asian markets do not open up signifi-cantly to American goods, a more likely response from Washing-ton would not be to reduce or withdraw its military umbrella in order to open up markets. Indeed, when intra-Asian trade as a proportion of total East Asian trade rises above its current 52 per cent, signifying not only a greater integration of the region as both a market and production base but also a lessening of the import-ance of US-Asian trade, the United States will be tempted to rely more and more on its military power to keep itself attached to Asia or face being cut off from a market that everybody agrees will be the locomotive of the world economy in the twentieth century.

To the sceptical, one must point out that there is, after all, an American naval tradition of using force or the threat of force to open up East Asian markets. The American military engagement with East Asia began after all, with Commodore Oliver Perry and his 'Black Ships' entering Tokyo Bay to demand that the Shogunate open up Japan to Western trade, or else. In this regard, isolation-ism in the United States has always been with respect to Europe, never to Asia – and the idea that the US would withdraw from the region on account of the growth of domestic isolationist sentiment was never a credible one. The idea of avoiding entanglement in old Europe has always been accompanied by a sense of the Asia Pacific as the United States' natural frontier for expansion. In this sense, the intra-elite conflict in the USA has not been so much one between internationalists and isolationists, as one between in-ternationalists and 'Asialationists'.[119]

US expansion in the Pacific in the nineteenth and early twen-tieth centuries, which was as much a case of the flag following trade as trade following the flag, was pushed by an alliance between navalists seeking the extension of American strategic power, mercan-tilists within the bureaucracy, and corporate interests. During the Cold War, this alliance dissolved, as the United States put the pri-ority on Asian participation in the anti-Communist crusade and tolerated the mercantilist and protectionist trade and investment regimes put up by Asian governments which often disadvantaged

American businesses in the region *vis-à-vis* local industrial and trading elites.[120] With the Cold War over, the old alliance is being reconstructed, and it is likely that we shall see American military power being employed less and less for achieving the so-called universal good of regional stability and more and more to push specific American economic interests.

THE STRUGGLE FOR DEMOCRACY

Central to the future of peace and security is the spread of democracy. Democracies, it has been observed, seldom go to war with one another, whereas authoritarian governments have a propensity for war. The reason is simple: in democracies, though they may be no more than formal democracies, there are mechanisms which amount to checks and balances, such as the free press and public opinion, which assure that, even if a democracy has gone to war wrongfully, its policy can be reversed. But authoritarian regimes do not have such internal checks. Indeed, authoritarian regimes tend to channel outwards, sometimes into overt aggression, the internal tensions that have built up owing to the repression of political expression. It is a fair question to ask whether, had Indonesia been democratic in 1975, the invasion of East Timor would have taken place.

Indeed, the absence of democracy as an element of the vision that Asian elites are promoting is deafening. Instead, they have mounted an offensive to convince their populations of the validity of their own peculiar forms of governance, that they have their own brand of 'democracy' which does not have the Western emphasis on individual rights, electoral competition, the free press, free assembly and checks and balances. Asians, like good Confucians, says Lee Kwan-Yew, value order over change, hierarchy over equality, and cooperation and mutual respect over competition between the elite and the masses. Asians, we are told, fear that too much democracy may undermine the East Asian economic miracle.[121] But as some observers have pointed out, Lee's list of supposed Asian values come across less as values specific to Asians than as good British, upper-class Tory values.

The emergence of the thesis that there is a mode of governance peculiar to Asians in recent ideological debates is simply explained. It is a counteroffensive by alarmed elites against the great democratic wave that has been sweeping Asia since 1986, which has destroyed authoritarian dictatorships in the Philippines in 1986, Korea in 1987, and Thailand in May 1992. However imperfect these democracies are as forms of rule, however much they are characterized by political and economic domination by elites, the current systems of governance in the Philippines, Taiwan, Korea and Thailand are different from those in China and the so-called 'ASEAN Four' – Singapore, Malaysia, Indonesia and Brunei. And that difference is what Lee Kwan-Yew, Suharto, and other champions of Asian authoritarianism are trying to maintain.

Part of the strategy is to paint the democratic systems of South Korea, Taiwan, the Philippines and Thailand as alien Western implants that are out of step with the Asian psyche. In July 1992, for instance, in a much-publicized speech in Manila, Lee Kwan-Yew pinpointed Philippine democracy as the cause of the country's economic backwardness. His message then was equally, though implicitly, directed at Thailand, which had just a few months earlier unhorsed the Suchinda military dictatorship at the cost of many lives.

The authoritarian counteroffensive reached its high point during the UN Vienna Human Rights Conference in 1993, when the ASEAN authoritarian regimes and China were able to present what appeared then to be a formidable argument, to the effect that there was a correlation between their high-speed economic growth and their authoritarian political systems. 'Western democratic methods are not for us', they told the conference. 'Asians have their own unique methods of government that will bring about ordered change and avoid the crime, racial strife, drug epidemic, licentiousness, and moral breakdown of the West – all of which are propagated by liberal democracy'.

But the authoritarian counteroffensive has lost momentum in the last few years owing to a number of developments.

1. A succession of much-publicized events – including the conviction of a Singaporean reporter for releasing confidential government economic data to the press, a court case brought by the Singaporean government against the *International Herald Tribune* for an article critical of ASEAN judiciaries which did not even mention Singapore by name, the rush to execute a Filipino domestic, Flor Contemplacion, whose guilt was widely in doubt, and most recently, exposés of the Lee Kwan-Yew and the People Action Party elites' entrenched privileges,[122] including being on

the inside track of property deals – focused the international spotlight on Singapore's justice and political system in an unprecedented fashion. And what most of the world came away with was the image of a party dictatorship bent on staying in power through the efficient manipulation of the police, the judiciary, the press, and social engineering. Where previously the Singaporeans' recitation of their usual mantra of 'economic progress through political discipline' evoked tolerant nods, if not agreement, it now usually draws smirks and lies exposed for what it is: a thinly veiled justification for a continuing monopoly of power by Lee Kwan-Yew's People's Action Party.

2. In Indonesia, the expectation that with economic growth would come some liberalization was rudely punctured after 1994, when the Suharto government cracked down savagely on the labour movement, closed three of the country's leading newspapers for expressing increasingly independent views, and launched military-sponsored gang terrorism in East Timor. Hosting the APEC Summit in November 1994 was Suharto's supreme effort to whitewash his regime's repressive past and paint Indonesia as the newest 'Asian Tiger'. What mostly came across to the world, however, was the image of young East Timorese protesting at the Indonesian occupation of their country inside the American Embassy while hundreds of policemen eager to get their hands on them waited impatiently outside.

3. As for China, increased factional infighting in the Communist Party has undermined the post-Tienanmen Square justification that in this big and complex country authoritarian rule is the only means of ensuring a stable transition as the Deng generation dies off, and has underlined the fact that democratic competition, for all its surface 'disorder' and 'inefficiencies', is really a more effective solution to the problem of political succession.

4. Finally, over the last few years, the new democracies in South Korea, the Philippines, and, most recently, Thailand were able to pull off peaceful electoral transitions from one administration to another, indicating a more solid institutionalization of formal democracy in these countries.

In this context, it is now the authoritarian regimes that are perceived as out of step in their relationship to their peoples; and the democracies in Thailand, the Philippines, South Korea and Taiwan have re-emerged, despite all their flaws, as advanced political systems in the eyes of their neighbours still living under restrictive rule, rather than as alien Western implants, as Lee Kwan-Yew has tried to paint them. Lee himself is increasingly seen for what he is: a relic of East Asia's past. One might note that some of the region's younger leaders, like Deputy Prime Minister Anwar Ibrahim in Malaysia, are distancing themselves from the authoritarian position, with Ibrahim recently saying that human rights and democracy should not be subordinated to other objectives such as political stability and economic growth.

In the democratic countries themselves, however, the novelty of free elections, party competition and the separation of powers has worn off, and the citizenry is now wrestling with 'second-generation' issues having to do with the translation of formal democracy to 'substantive democracy'. These problems or dilemmas include the following:

- Rule by established elites can be just as effective, if not more so, through democratic competition as under dictatorial rule, since for the most part only the wealthy or people backed by wealth can afford to run for office, leading to effective control of the political system by economic elites that have the added advantage of legitimacy owing to their democratic election. In this connection, the eyes of many people in Asia's formal democracies are currently focused on the drama in Korea, wondering if indeed events there might lead to a breakthrough from monetary democracy to citizens' democracy.
- How does one translate formal political democracy into economic or social democracy, in which equality as citizens is translated into equality as economic actors? How can political democracy become an instrument for the redistribution of wealth rather than a mechanism to uphold the status quo, as has happened in Thailand and the Philippines?
- Can the institutions of formal representative democracy be modified to accommodate the 'NGO phenomenon', which represents an effort by citizens to go beyond mere electoral participation to more direct popular intervention in the political process? Not surprisingly, professional politicians see NGOs as a threat, while others see them as a step forward from representative to direct democratic rule.
- How can the interests of minorities, be they ethnic, racial or religious, be safeguarded under democracy, which by definition

is the rule of the majority? It is not at all clear, for instance, if democratic rule has been an advance over authoritarian rule for the Muslims in the Southern Philippines and Southern Thailand, where Christian and Buddhist majorities, respectively, have political sway.

These are, of course, the same problems that have confronted the older democracies in the West, but one thing is certain: the record of the Western democracies provides no guide to the newer or re-established democracies of Asia and the Third World. For the translation of formal to substantive democracy, the achievement of both political and economic equality, the transition to more direct forms of democracy, and the protection of the rights of the minority from the majority are the great unresolved issues of the democracies of the West.

Indeed, Asian democratic activists are very aware that there is currently in the United States and Europe a retreat from a positive approach to these challenges, as economic elites succeed in stripping the liberal democratic state of its already limited redistributive powers and inflamed racial and ethnic majorities increasingly restrict the rights of minorities. For instance, the Republicans' 'Contract with America' and California's Proposition is essentially a war against the poor, especially the non-white poor, but it is popular with the white American majority. Increasingly, the United States and Europe are turning out to be negative examples for Asia and the rest of the world, as democratic mechanisms become the vehicles for reactionary social and economic ends.

In short, Asian realities have not rendered irrelevant the progressives' message. Indeed, it remains as urgent as ever. But our analysis and strategy message must be restated, reformulated, and renewed for a post-Cold War Asia that looks with aversion at the failed experiment of centralized socialism, is becoming aware of the flaws of both market and state-led development strategies, and is unanimous in its demand for more democracy. Let us end by articulating the three elements of an alternative paradigm for change. We stake no claims to originality in this, for many NGOs and movements throughout the region are now expressing the same ideas, though not in exactly the same words.

SUSTAINABLE REGIONAL DEVELOPMENT

Against the model of high-speed growth, civil society organizations in the region have elaborated, with increasing specificity, the elements of an alternative development program.[123] In our view, sustainable development in an East Asian context will have to incorporate the following four concerns:

1. The fundamental mechanism of production, distribution and exchange will have to be something more sensible and rational than the ability of the invisible hand to coordinate the pursuit of their separate self-interests by millions of individuals into the common good. But neither the interventionist hand of the East Asian state nor the heavy hand of the socialist state is a good candidate for this role. Certainly, the state is essential to curb the market for the common good. But, as the East Asian experience shows, the common good is all too often defined as the good of state and economic elites. The thrust of sustainable development is to go beyond the invisible and interventionist hands, while not denying that market and state can play an important but subsidiary role in the allocation of resources. For development to be sustainable, the fundamental economic mechanism would have to be democratic and transparent decision-making on the key issues of production, exchange and distribution by local and national communities.

2. Production and exchange decisions can no longer be based solely or principally on the criteria of efficiency and profitability, but equally, if not more, on the values of equity, ecological stability, and community solidarity. In traditional economic terms many decisions will be viewed as inefficient and wasteful, but in broader societal and ecological terms, they will be functional and, in many cases, even optimal, for they respond to the reality of societies as complex creations bound by values that transcend the pursuit of material well-being rather than artificial boxes containing individual atoms concerned solely with accumulating wealth. Because, contrary to Margaret Thatcher's dictum that there 'there is no such thing as society', there *is* such a thing as society and it is something more than the sum of its individual parts. In short, instead of the dynamics of economy, as in the market paradigm, dissolving community and disrupting the link between community and environment, sustainable development is about

bringing economy and exchange back into the control of community.

3. Trade will have to be liberated from both the logic of the free market and the logic of neomercantilism of many East Asian states. In a sustainable development paradigm, trade relationships would develop in precisely opposite directions than they have developed in the region. Trade relationships must work to ensure that initial divisions of labour to facilitate trade do not congeal into permanent cleavages; that technological know-how developing from trade is spread around systematically to strengthen the capacity of both trading communities; that trade and investment contribute to developing an economy integrally rather than simply creating easily exhaustible natural-resource pools and cheap-labour enclaves which can easily be abandoned once wage rates go up; and that trade and development proceed along socially and ecologically sustainable paths rather than the strip-mine and community-dissolving patterns of current corporate-driven trade and investment practices.

4. The current regional economy must be transformed from an extension of the Japanese economy without becoming a free-trade area that simply serves to allow significant American repenetration of the region. The key is democratic planning at a regional level that incorporates more than just governments and industrial elites beholden to one economic superpower or the other but also NGOs, people's organizations and community groups guided by a strategy of sustainable regional development.

MULTILATERAL SECURITY

To move to the security agenda, against the managed anarchy at the level of state-to-state relations, Asian progressives need to make their own a crying need in the region – the need for a post-Cold War multilateral system of peace and security. But we must go beyond the limited formulations of figures like Australian Foreign Minister Gareth Evans to press for the creation of a regional system built on the principles of demilitarization and denuclearization – necessary conditions for lasting peace and security in the Asia Pacific. On this basis then can be built structures founded on an alternative notion of security, which would include environmental sustainability as well as wider access of the majority to basic development needs, such as food and water security, access to basic health care and education, and freedom from violence.

THE DEMOCRATIC CHALLENGE

Last on the political agenda, against 'Asian democracy' and other formulations seeking to give authoritarianism a facelift, we must build a regional democratic movement that assists those still living under authoritarian government to make the transition to democratic rule. But we must do it without becoming pawns of Washington's cynical politics; and we must distinguish our project from those of elite liberals who would stop at Lockean formal democracy by pushing democratic evolution in the region from formal democracy to substantive democracy.

Finally, while continuing to acknowledge the European Enlightenment's contributions to modern democracy, we must move to rediscover the mainsprings of democratic values in our cultures. Democracy is both Asian and universal.

NOTES

1. Wolfgang Munchau, 'German Workplace Consensus "Has Failed"', *Financial Times*, 25 April 1996, p. 3.
2. World Bank, *The East Asian Miracle* (Washington, DC: World Bank, 1993).
3. Alice H. Amsden, *Asia's Next Giant: South Korea and Late Industrialization* (New York: Oxford University Press, 1989) p. 139.
4. See, among others, Richard Doner, 'Domestic Coalitions and Japanese Auto Firms in Southeast Asia', Ph.D. dissertation, University of California at Berkeley, Berkeley, California, 1987, pp. 511–96.
5. Hal Hill, 'Ownership in Indonesia: Who Owns What and Does It Matter?', in Hal Hill and Terry Hull (eds), *Indonesia Assessment* 1990 (Canberra: Research School of Pacific Studies, Australian National University, 1990), pp. 54–5.
6. Testimony before US Senate Finance Committee, Washington, DC, 4 April 1995.
7. Nikhom Chandraveithun, *Thailand: The Social Costs of Becoming the Fifth Tiger* (Washington, DC: Woodrow Wilson Center, 1995), p. 2.
8. See Walden Bello and Stephanie Rosenfeld, *Dragons in Distress: Asia's Miracle Economies in Crisis* (London: Penguin, 1991), pp. 23–45.

9. See Song Byung-Nak, 'The Korean Economy', Unpublished manuscript, Seoul, 1989, p. 244; Cho Sun-Young, 'Farmers Fight for Survival', *Business Korea,* April 1991, p. 22.
10. Estimate by Sompop Manarungsun, cited in Pravit Rojanaphruk, 'Farmers Face Uncertain Future', *The Nation,* undated.
11. Amar Siamwalla, *Land Abundant Agricultural Growth and Some of Its Consequences: The Case of Thailand* (Bangkok: Thailand Development Research Institute, 1991), p. 39.
12. Quoted in Richard Kagan, 'The "Miracle" of Taiwan', Unpublished manuscript, Institute for Food and Development Policy, San Francisco, 1982, p. 37.
13. Sue Chang, 'World Shouldn't Have to Wait for an Open Market', *Business Korea,* December 1991, p. 21.
14. 'Farming Strategy to Uruguay Round Pact Discussed', *Yonhap Monthly Photo Journal,* March 1994, pp. 16–27; reproduced in *FBIS Daily Report: East Asia,* 2 June 1994, p. 50.
15. Neal Rudge, 'Edgar Lin', *Bang,* March 1988, p. 12.
16. See, among others, 'Polluters Considered "Criminals"', *Yonhap,* 25 March 1991; reproduced in *Foreign Broadcast Information Service (FBIS): East Asia,* March 26, 1991, p. 22.
17. Office of the National Economic and Social Development Board, *National Urban Development Policy Framework,* vol. 2 (Bangkok: NESDB, 1992), p. 18.
18. Interview with Dr. Oraphan Methaddilokul, Bangkok, April 14, 1994.
19. Interview with foreign expert, anonymity requested, Bangkok, April 25, 1994.
20. Huang Chi, 'The State and Foreign Capital: A Case Study of Taiwan', Ph.D. dissertation, Dept. of Political Science, Indiana University, February 1986, p. 189; Denis Simon, 'Taiwan, Technology Transfer, and Transnationals: The Political Management of Dependency', Ph.D. dissertation, University of California at Berkeley, 1980, p. 350.
21. Kim Kwang-Doo and Lee Sang-Ho, 'The Role of the Korean Government in Technology Import', in C.H. Lee and Ippei Yamazawa (eds), *The Economic Development of Japan and Korea* (New York: Praeger, 1980), p. 93.
22. Kent Calder, 'The North Pacific Triangle: Sources of Economic and Political Transformation', *Journal of Northeast Asian Studies,* vol. 7, no. 2 (Summer 1989), p. 5.
23. See, among other works, Hyun Young-Suk, 'A Technology Strategy for the Korean Industry', paper prepared for International Motor Vehicles Forum, Acapulco, Mexico, 1989.
24. Kang Duck-Joong, 'Structural Problems at Root of Illness, *Electronics Korea,* July 1990, p. 11.
25. Jacob Schlesinger, 'Hitachi Joins Goldstar in Plan for Chip Plant', *Asian Wall Street Journal Weekly,* 31 July 1989, p. 6.
26. Konomi Tomisawa, 'Development and Future Outlook for an International Division of Labor in the Automobile Industries of the Asian NICs', briefing paper for the First Policy Forum of the International Motor Vehicle Program, Cambridge, Massachusetts, 5 May 1987, p. 17.

27. Ibid.
28. Ibid.
29. Japan Ministry of Finance figures.
30. Rob Steven, *Japan's New Imperialism* (Armonk, NY: M.E. Sharpe, 1990), p. 116.
31. Diagram provided by Toyota Motor Company.
32. Okazaki, 'New Strategies Toward Super-Asian Bloc.'
33. Japan Ministry of Finance figures.
34. 'Deregulation the Key to Trade with Japan', *The Age*, 12 November 1994.
35. 'Japan's Survival Depends on Ties of Interdependence', *Asahi Evening News*, 4 December 1994, p. 3.
36. Japan Ministry of Finance figures.
37. Alan Rix, *Japan's Aid Program: A New Global Agenda* (Canberra: Australian International Assistance Bureau, April 1990), p. 40.
38. Quoted in ibid., p. 39.
39. Saburo Okita, 'Asian-Pacific Prospects and Problems for the Further Development of the Asia-Pacific Cooperative Framework', paper presented at the symposium, In Search of a New Order in Asia, Santa Barbara, California, 1–3 February 1990, p. 2.
40. Ibid.
41. Okazaki, 'New Strategies'.
42. Ibid.
43. Dick Nanto, Pacific Rim Economic Cooperation (Washington, DC: Congressional Research Service, April 3, 1989), p. 10.
44. East Asia Analytical Unit p. 98.
45. Okazaki, 'New Strategies'.
46. 'Japan's Survival Depends on Ties of Interdependence', *Asahi Evening News*, 4 December 1994, p. 3.
47. Urban Lehner, 'Taiwan Worries Its Reliance on Technology from Japan Could Hurt Its Competitiveness', *Asian Wall Street Journal Weekly*, 8 July 1991, p. 18.
48. 'New Strategies Toward Super-Asian Bloc', *This Is* (Tokyo), August, 1992, pp. 42–90; reproduced in *FBIS*, October 1992, p. 18.
49. Paula Stern, Testimony before the Subcommittee on Asia-Pacific Affairs and Subcommittee on International Economic Policy and Trade, Committee on International Relations, US House of Representatives, Washington, DC, July 18, 1995.
50. 'APEC to Fulfill US Goals', Kyodo News Agency, 2 November 1994; reproduced in *FBIS*, 3 November 1994, p. 1.
51. Ibid.
52. Testimony before the Subcommittees on Asia and Pacific Affairs and International Economic Policy and Trade, Committee on Foreign Affairs, US House of Representatives, July 18, 1995.
53. US House Committee on Appropriations, 'Department of Commerce, Justice and State, the Judiciary and Related Agencies', 104 Cong., 2nd Sess., p. 197. Y4. AP6/1: C73/2/497 Pt.S.
54. Cited in Kevin Watkins, 'Agricultural Trade and Food Security', Paper presented at the Southeast Asian NGO Conference on Food Security and Fair Trade, 13–16 February 1996, p. 17.

55. 'Japan Opposed to APEC Free Trade Area', *Kyodo News Agency*, 1 November 1994; reproduced in *FBIS*, 1 November 1994, p. 1.
56. 'No Action, No Agenda', *Economist*, 25 November 1995.
57. 'US Seeks to Blunt Division of APEC on Ethnic Lines', *Asian Wall Street Journal Weekly*, June 1994.
58. Tommy Koh, 'What Asia Wants from Bill Clinton', *Asian Wall Street Journal*, 9 November 1992, p. 14.
59. Quoted in Geoffrey Barket, 'Planners Agree on Key Policy Concepts', *Australian Financial Review*, 5 July 1995, pp. 23–4; reproduced in *FBIS*, 18 July 1995, p. 58.
60. Gareth Evans, 'Alliance and Cooperation', Speech delivered at the University of Texas, Austin, 9 October 1990.
61. 'APEC Military Taboo Broken', *The Nation* (Bangkok), 16 November 1995.
62. US Dept. of Defense, *United States Security Strategy for the East-Asia Pacific Region* (Washington, DC: Office of International Security Affairs, February 1995), p. 13.
63. Larry Niksch, *Regional Security Consultative Organizations in East Asia and Their Implications for the United States*, CRS Report for Congress (Washington, DC: Congressional Research Service, 14 January 1994), pp. 13–14.
64. Quoted in Parliamentary Research Service, *APEC and Australia: The Bogor Summit and Beyond*, Current Issues Brief No. 26, 15 November 1994, p. 2.
65. Geoffrey Barker, 'Australia Treads Cautiously in the Post-cold war Climate', *Australian Financial Review*, 6 February 1995, p. 18; reproduced in *FBIS*, 23 February 1995, p. 87.
66. US Department of Defense, p. 29.
67. 'ASEAN Views US Bases in Southeast Asia', *Suara Pembaruan* (Jakarta), 4 August 1995, p. 19; reproduced in *Foreign Broadcast Information Service East Asia Daily Report* (Hereafter to be referred to as *FBIS*), 7 August 1995, p. 1.
68. Arto Suryodipuro, 'Indonesia's Strategy and the South China Sea Dispute', *Kompas*, May 22, 1995, pp. 4, 5; reproduced in *FBIS*, 23 May 1995, p. 51.
69. Ibid.
70. Samuel Koh, *The Quest for a Just World Order* (Boulder: Westview Press, 1984), p. 36.
71. Inis Claude, Jr., *Power and International Relations* (New York: Random House, 1962), p. 52.
72. Henry Kissinger, *Diplomacy* (New York: Simon and Schuster, 1994), pp. 137–217.
73. Richard Grimmett, *Conventional Arms Transfer to Developing Nations, 1987–1994*, CRS Report for Congress (Washington, DC: Congressional Research Service, 4 August 1995), p. 10.
74. Tommy Koh, 'What Asia Wants from Bill Clinton', *Asian Wall Street Journal Weekly*, 9 November 1992, p. 14.
75. Quoted in Geoffrey Barker, 'Planners Agree on Key Policy Concepts', *Australian Financial Review*, July 5, 1995, pp. 23–4; reproduced in *FBIS*, 18 July 1995, p. 58.

76. Ibid., p. 54.
77. Desmond Ball, 'Arms and Affluence: Military Acquisitions in the Asia-Pacific Region', *International Security*, vol. 18, no. 3 (Winter 1993–4), p. 94.
78. Ibid.
79. Larry Niksch, *The South China Sea Dispute*, CRS Report for Congress (Washington, DC: Congressional Research Service, 29 August 1995), p. 6.
80. 'Supreme Commander Sees Need', *The Nation*, 7 February 1995, p. A4.
81. Compiled from, among other sources, Desmond Ball, p. 88.
82. Interview with Vice Admiral Winai Intharasombat, deputy chief of staff of the Royal Thai Navy, *Matichon*, 5 February 1995, p. 10; reproduced in *FBIS*, 8 February 1995, p. 53.
83. Micool Brooke, 'ASEAN Defense Chiefs Unsettled By Question of Potential Arms Race', *Bangkok Post*, 23 September 1995, p. 5.
84. Larry A. Niksch, 'Malaysia-US Relations', Foreign Affairs and National Defense Division, Congressional Research Service, 13 November 1966.
85. 'The Modality of the Security and Defense Capability of Japan: The Outlook for the 21st Century', Appendix A in Patrick Cronin and Michael Green, *Redefining the US-Japan Alliance: Tokyo's National Defense Program*, McNair Paper 31 (Washington, DC: Institute for National Strategic Studies, National Defense University, November 1994), p. 34.
86. In fact, according to one report, the United States raised questions about the report by asking: 'Does Japan plan to give priority to multilateral security?' See 'Toward Full-Fledged Reassessment of Security', *Asahi Shimbun*, 1 March 1995, p. 2; reproduced in *FBIS*, 2 March 1995, p. 3.
87. Quoted in ibid.
88. Shunji Taoka, 'US Armed Forces Need Japan', *AERA*, 10 July 1995, pp. 21–2; reproduced in *FBIS*, 25 July 1995, p. 3.
89. Barbara Wanner, 'Diet Approves US-Japan Host-Nation Support Pact', *JEI Report*, 17 November 1995, p. 6.
90. *Washington Post*, 27 March 1990.
91. Yoshiki Tadaka, 'The Japan-US Security Treaty Has Become a Dinosaur', *Voice*, 1 June 1995, pp. 85–7; reproduced in *FBIS*, 20 July 1995, p. 6.
92. Ibid.
93. Terumasa Nakanishi, 'A Decision for the Year 2010', *Voice*, 1 June 1995, pp. 91–4; reproduced in *FBIS*, 20 July 1995, p. 6.
94. Nicholas Kristoff, 'An Uneasy US Presence', *International Herald Tribune*, 4 December 1995, p. 4.
95. Wanner, p. 6.
96. Patrick Cronin and Michael Green, *Redefining the US-Japan Alliance*, McNair Paper 31 (Washington, DC: National Defense University, 1994, p. 11.
97. Ibid.
98. Admiral Charles Larson, Statement before the US Senate Armed Services Committee, Washington, DC, 13 March 1991.

99. Andrew Mack, 'A Nuclear North Korea', *World Policy Journal*, vol. XI, no. 2 (Summer 1994), p. 28.
100. Patrick Tyler, 'Pentagon Imagines New Enemies to Fight in Post-Cold War Era', *New York Times*, 17 February 1992, pp. A1, A5.
101. US Dept. of Defense, *United States Security Strategy for the East Asia Pacific Region*, p. 25.
102. James Morley, comments at the International Symposium on International Cooperation in the Asia-Pacific Region, Dokkyo University, Tokyo, 12–13 December 1995.
103. Robert Sutter, *China as a Security Concern in Asia: Perceptions, Assessment, and US Options* (Washington, DC: Congressional Research Service, 22 December 1994), p. 17.
104. Ibid., p. 19.
105. Ibid., p. 18.
106. Ibid.
107. Ibid, p. 19.
108. Ball, pp. 85–6.
109. Paul Dibb, 'The Future Military Capabilities of Asia's Great Powers', *Jane's Intelligence Review,* May 1995, p. 231.
110. Ibid.
111. Sutter, p. 18.
112. Grimmet, p. 66.
113. Ibid.
114. Ibid., p. 54.
115. Strobe Talbott, quoted in Geoffrey Barker, 'Australia Treads Cautiously'.
116. Note the following paragraph in an article that appeared in *Kompas,* well known as a government mouthpiece: 'The foreign policy of the Republic of Indonesia is partly based on our national assets – Indonesia's large size, strategic location, large population (about 190 million people whose skills are further being developed), and huge natural resources. In the history of mankind, big countries have virtually played a major role and exercised a great influence at least in their respective regions'. Arto Suryodipuro, 'Indonesia's Strategy and the South China Sea Dispute . .'.
117. See, among others, Kerry Dumbaugh, *China-US Relations*, CRS Issue Brief (Washington, DC: Congressional Research Service, 15 September 1995; 'Foreign Policy Changes Head for Clinton Veto', *Bangkok Post*, 30 March 1996.
118. Scott Kennedy and Michael O'Hanlon, 'Time to Shift Gears on China Policy', revised draft of article accepted for publication in *Journal of East Asian Affairs* (Winter-Spring 1996).
119. See, among others, Franz Schurmann, *The Logic of World Order* (New York: Pantheon Books, 1974).
120. For further discussion, see Walden Bello, *Dark Victory* (San Francisco: Food First, 1994), pp. 10–17.
121. For an analysis of the ideology of authoritarian domination in Singapore, see Walden Bello and Stephanie Rosenfeld, *Dragons in*

Distress: Asia's Miracle Economies in Crisis (San Francisco: Food First, 1990), pp. 317–30.

122. On the PAP and property deals, see 'Lee's Power and Privilege', *The Nation,* June 12–13, 1996.
123. See, for instance, the Kyoto Declaration prepared by the NGO Summit on APEC, Kyoto, November 1995.

Part IV

Representation and Accountability

10 Engineering Space in Global Governance: the Emergence of Civil Society in Evolving 'New' Multilateralism

W. Andy Knight

Several recent studies have demonstrated concern in one way or another with the issue of democratizing, or pluralizing, global governance.[1] The main issue being addressed is the extent to which existing, largely state-centric, multilateral institutions are willing to accommodate the interests and demands of individuals and groups that make up a recently empowered civil society which is apparently now being reconstituted along global lines.

Concerns with the issue of strengthening the role of civil society in global governance operations reflect, to a large degree, 'the vociferous demands of the range of social movements, and community and special interest groups which blossomed during the 1980s'.[2] They also indicate an increasing unease with the less than democratic aspects of multilateral institutions and point to the possibility of change, and perhaps transformation, in the way in which multilateral governance is conceived and practised. More importantly, for the purposes of this chapter, the above concerns force us to re-examine the nature of multilateralism and global governance at this particular historical juncture; a period of flux and transition.

I argue here that particularly over the past 50 years, the agitation and activities of certain non-state actors have, in effect, already etched out 'space' (which in the past has normally been reserved for state actors) for civil society within the global governance context. I also argue that out of the dialectical interaction of 'top-down' and 'bottom-up' forces, the outlines of a 'new' multilateralism is emerging which has the potential of allowing civil societal actors (by which I mean that broader community outside of political

255

authority) an expanded and increasingly important role in the workings of global governance.[3]

However, the creation of space in global governance for civil society is not unproblematic. There is no guarantee that multilateral governance will become more democratic or egalitarian as a result of the increasing activity of civil societal, or 'bottom-up', forces. Not all elements in civil society are benign or progressive. Some of them represent the criminal underbelly of society and others represent reactionary and exclusionary movements. Not all of them want to be placed under a governance structure of any type. Some of them prefer to be left alone in a space of anonymity. Not all of them are necessarily opposed to the existing structure of multilateralism and global governance. Some of them become co-opted by hegemonic institutions and ideologies. One thing is certain, however: for better or worse, as a result of the engineering of space in global governance for the various component parts of what we call 'civil society' we need to comprehend more clearly the nature of the current period of historical change and, in light of our understanding, to rethink precisely what is meant by multilateralism for today and for the twenty-first century.

This chapter explains the source of an evolving global governance structure that includes the simultaneous existence of 'top-down' and 'bottom-up' multilateralism (seen, most evidently at global conferences). The examples used throughout the chapter leave no doubt that the two forms of multilateralism not only co-exist but are also intersecting; but what is more interesting is the nature of that intersection. Is there an evident shift in the balance between the two forms of multilateralism? If so, in which direction is that shift headed? Since one of the primary normative concerns about the 'top-down' form of multilateralism is that it has tended towards an undemocratic structure and process of global governance, is the 'bottom-up' form of multilateralism more democratic? Furthermore, does the intersection of 'state-centric' and 'people-centred' multilateralism provide a corrective to the undemocratic nature of traditional multilateralism? In other words, is global governance any more democratic at the point of the top-down/bottom-up multilateral intersection? Can the 'top-down' multilateral process become more democratic as it tries to accommodate the demands of civil society? What sort of accommodations will be needed in order to bring this about?

After explaining the concepts of 'civil society' and 'space', this chapter is divided into three main sections (conceptual, descriptive and analytical). Section one is devoted to post-Cold War reconceptualizations of world order, multilateralism and global governance. The main purpose in this section is to demonstrate the linkage between these three concepts as well as to explore the connection between multilateralism and historical structures of world order and the nature of the social forces that will have an impact on the shape of future global governance.

Section two describes the expanded space in multilateralism being created by a broad range of civil societal groups (non-governmental organizations, new social movements, grassroots organizations and informal sector communities, as well as criminal entities such as the mafia, drug lords and terrorists) whose actions are facilitated, or circumscribed, by a configuration of social forces. Understanding the role that various forms of state-society complexes play in this process is an important part of this section of the chapter. After all, while in some cases civil societal actors may try to increase their autonomy from the state, states and civil societies are ultimately 'co-inhabitors of the public space'.[4] In addition, the intensity of transnational activity among societal actors may, at times, require state acceptance of it.

Correspondingly, state action in multilateral form may from time to time need to be legitimized by civil society. Section three of this chapter analyses the nature of the space that is created in global governance by and for civil society and what that means in terms of the 'top-down', 'bottom-up' intersection of forces in multilateral institutions. The space created is obviously a limited one in many respects, as is evident in the many recent calls for the democratization of existing multilateral bodies. However, the space that has already been created for civil societies in global governance arrangements indicates progress in the movement toward a 'new' multilateralism – one that takes into consideration the views and demands of the marginalized and repressed. This leads to a conclusion that grapples with an hypothesis which states that the struggle for change in the historical structure of world order is likely to take place primarily among the oppositional elements in civil society and, perhaps, outside the existing state-centric multilateral framework. If this hypothesis is to have any resonance, what will be required for the future is a strategy of mobilization that can unite the energies of the disparate groups that make up the social formation – civil society.

I

THE CONCEPT OF CIVIL SOCIETY: POST-COLD WAR RECONCEPTUALIZATIONS

The end of the Cold War seems to have coincided with a thawing of the minds of scholars whose ideas appeared frozen around such issues at the East/West superpower conflict and its concommitant arms race, geopolitical and military-strategic planning, the security dilemma and the maintenance of a precarious peace through balance-of-power and balance-of-terror mechanisms combined with notions of hegemonic stability and great power leadership.

The straightjacket imposed on our thinking by neo-realist, liberal institutionalist and Marxist theories, which led us to conceive of international relations and the governance of the globe in mostly statist terms, is being shed as a number of new paradigms emerge. The development of some of these paradigms has been aided, *inter alia*, by interdependence and globalization phenomena; an expanding conceptualization of security; an apparent erosion of the traditional concept of state; sovereignty due to the internationalization of the state, the tendency towards regional 'blocism'; and the revivification of civil society in relation to the state.

The paradigmatic shifts may also be related to what appears to be a movement towards a post-Cold War global agenda that privileges items such as demilitarization, democratization, sustainable development, environmental protection, cultural pluralism and other civilizational issues, human rights and justice, and multilateral approaches to global governance (as a means of dealing with the 'new world dis-order'). This refocusing of inquiry has given rise to what Richard Falk calls a potential 'counter-project' to that of the post-Cold War geopolitics.[5] At the base of this counter-project is a normative pre-occupation with strengthening the role of civil society at local, regional and global locales, which is generally viewed as an essential counterbalance to state-centric views of world order, multilateralism and global governance.

RETHINKING WORLD ORDER, MULTILATERALISM AND
GLOBAL GOVERNANCE

Robert Cox has pointed out the interrelatedness of the concepts
of multilateralism and world order.[6] Both of these concepts are in
many ways directly or indirectly linked to the notion of global governance.[7] Indeed, global governance can be taken as a starting point
for thinking about multilateralism.

The term global governance conjures up different meanings to
different people.[8] But, simply put, global governance can be viewed
as the attempt to orchestrate arrangements at the global, regional,
and local levels in order to resolve a multitude of transnational
dilemmas, ranging from socio-political and economic to military-
security concerns, that are proving to be beyond the scope of individual states to solve. As such, global governance incorporates
multilateral institutions, procedures, practices and activities which,
from the standpoint of a normative goal, strive to contribute to at
least a semblance of global order, sufficient to allow states and
other actors to engage in cooperative and mutually beneficial activity.[9] While global government may not be achievable under the
present conditions, the act of using multilateral entities in the quest
for the ideal of global governance is nevertheless considered worth-
while, particularly if at least some progress is being made in the
improvement of the living conditions of people across the globe
(by providing greater security for states as well as for individuals
and groups within civil society, by improving the social and economic
lot of people living in conditions of underdevelopment, by eliminating injustices, and by reducing the level of ecological degradation).

The linkage between global governance, multilateralism and world
order can be explained in the following manner. Given the unlike-
lihood that the conditions needed for achieving the normative goals
of global governance will be found in a totally anarchic international
system, some framework for global stability, ordering and steering
is generally deemed necessary. There can be several different hy-
pothetical forms of global governance (for example, world government or global empire, with a hierarchical form of coordination;
federalism, with a pluralistic form of coordination and interaction;
and multilateralism, with its apparently non-hierarchical arrangement and form of coordination).

Some people aspire towards the implementation of world
government, although the chances that this form of global governance

arrangement would be widely accepted under the present circumstances at this particular juncture are highly unlikely.[10] In his evaluation of the prospects of implementing world federalism, Inis Claude wrote of this potential form of global governance:

> It is an excessively mechanistic and rationalistic doctrine, relying upon the ingenious invention, rationally conceived, contrived, and accepted; in pseudo-Lockean fashion, it postulates a flash of creativity which carries mankind into the era or order. This is a dramatic and challenging conception, but its accuracy bears some examination.

He went on to argue that the foundations for this form of global governance simply do not exist at the moment.[11]

Much less ambitious, but more acceptable to the international community of states, are multilateral arrangements. These can come in the form of formal or informal international regimes (principles, norms, rules and decision-making procedures to which entities adhere) or they can be institutionalized in formalized organizations such as the United Nations system. While existing multilateral arrangements give the impression that they are non-hierarchical, the reality is that they can be used to mask hegemonic and counter-hegemonic struggles and dominant/subdominant relationships which exist within them. In any event, an historical account of the evolution of the UN system would reveal the extent to which this multilateral organization has been used to legitimate the post-1945 historical structure and thus to perpetuate the prevailing world order.[12] Nevertheless, for the moment, multilateral arrangements seem to be the preferred option for most states and for a large percentage of the global community. In other words, the multilateral concept provides a relatively well-accepted organizing principle for the attainment of global governance objectives.

MULTILATERALISM AND HISTORICAL STRUCTURES

In keeping with the realist tradition, multilateralism 'is conceivable at most as a series of transitory arrangements' designed to achieve the collective aims of a group of sovereign states that have discovered a momentary common interest. But multilateralism is best understood in a contextual sense – and that context being the historical structure of world order at any given juncture.[13] The historical structure of world order refers to a particular configuration of forces in the world system which imposes pressures and constraints on state, group and individual action, but does not necessarily dictate the form that action will take nor does it determine such actions in any direct mechanical way. While these pressures may be resisted or opposed, they cannot be ignored. Once a particular historical structure becomes institutionalized, it assumes certain hegemonic features which become characteristic of the world order at that moment in time.[14] Ideally, one way to resist successfully a prevailing historical structure of world order would be for states, groups or individuals to buttress their actions with an alternative emerging configuration of forces, or what Cox calls a counter-hegemonic or 'rival structure'.[15] The current actions of civil society in the multilateral realm indicates a potential for the development of such a 'rival structure'. However, it would take much coordination and mobilization for the forces of civil society to overcome the dominant forces in the prevailing historical structure of world order. Only when the rival structure prevails in its struggle over the once dominant historical structure can one then begin to speak of the emergence of a 'new global order'.

CONFIGURATION OF FORCES WITHIN THE HISTORICAL STRUCTURE OF WORLD ORDER

The forces that interact within any given historical structure can be lumped under three basic but inter-related heuristic categories:

1. *Material capabilities* – technological and organizational capabilities (in their dynamic form) and natural resources, stocks of equipment, and wealth (in their accumulated forms).
2. *Ideas* – consisting of intersubjective meanings (that is, shared notions of the nature of social relations that perpetrate routines, habits and expectations of behaviour) which are historically conditioned, and collective images of social order held by different groups of people which can exist in several forms that may be competing with each other.
3. *Institutions* – formal and/or informal organizational entities which reflect the power relations that prevailed at the time of their

origin but may, over time, take on a life of their own or become the site for hegemonic/counter-hegemonic struggles.[16]

Multilateral institutions can become the site at which the established order is institutionalized and entrenched. But they may also be 'the locus of interactions for the transformation of existing order'.[17] It is primarily because multilateral organs are viewed as potential engines of change that some civil societal actors are drawn towards them.

The reality, however, is that the current multilateral system has become entrenched within its differential levels of global social classes. At the apex of this system is a dominant class comprising what Gill calls 'globalizing elites'. These elites represent 'a directive, strategic element within globalizing capitalism'. They also represent that grouping of organic intellectual and political leaders which is found within the transnational fraction of the global capitalist classes. Some members of the globalizing elite are in key strategic locations in transnational companies, banks, universities, think tanks, media outlets, governments and international organizations such as the IMF, the IBRD, the OECD, and the G-7. As such, they occupy space in organizations at the apex of global knowledge, technology, production, credit and financial structures. Not only do these members of the 'global North' possess the bulk of the world's material capabilities, they are instrumental in the pervasion of their dominant neo-liberal ideology and control significant activities of the multilateral institutions of which they are members.[18]

Just beneath the globalizing elites is a cadre stratum – *l'encadrement capitaliste* or salaried functionaries. This group of individuals occupy an intermediate space between the globalizing elites and the marginalized class in developed capitalism. This stratum is comprised of technocrats (managers, administrators, bureaucratic personnel and technical specialists) who demonstrate a preference for rationalist planning and operate primarily at the state level but also, in certain cases, at the global level (as 'experts' on Commissions and Committees providing advice to multilateral bodies and other agencies of the state system, for instance).[19]

At the base of this multilateral system are the marginalized and exploited peoples of the 'Global South'; the product of a highly segmented labour force. Many social movements and grassroots organizations (for example environmentalists, rainbow coalitions, churches, farmers, women, youth, AIDS activists, indigenous people, the informal sector) fall into this category. Many of the 'new' social movements of this marginalized class reject existing legal and institutional arrangements at all levels, including multilateral arrangements.[20] They also seem, implicitly at least, to be jettisoning the traditional dualistic conception of private/public, domestic/foreign, and inside/outside spheres. While this marginalized class is engaged in a counter-hegemonic struggle with the dominant globalizing elites over the future of world order, its politics remain embryonic, and resistance groups, though increasingly autonomous in the management of their individual projects, are still knitted together within the framework of national politics.[21] Along the same line of argument, Drainville continues that the new internationalism of social movements does not take as its starting point 'universal categories' of people, but instead forms instant groups 'united by their immediate circumstances and by the exigencies of the moment'.[22] He points out that these 'gatherings' of people occur 'not as universal, transcendental, collective actors, but as site-specific coalitions'. Drainville's criticisms are worthy of serious consideration since too many scholars seem to imply a more positive, unifying dimension to these new social movements.

While it is possible to have coexisting historical structures, world order at any given juncture will be largely shaped by the dominant historical structure. The extent to which there is transformation from one historical structure to the next will be dependent on the extent to which the dominant historical structure is challenged by a rival structure and on when, as a result of that challenge, a new configuration of forces is aligned in a manner radically different from that of the outgoing historical structure. Thus, out of this dialectic, one would expect to see in the 'new' historical structure the emergence of a new form of consciousness (ideas) which results in, or is accompanied by, a shift in power relations (material capabilities) as well as a metamorphosis (not just tinkering) in the institutional arrangements of global governance. This kind of structural historical change fundamentally affects the parameters of world order and is, thus, to be differentiated from those epiphenominal changes that occur within a particular system of world order.[23]

Conceptually, therefore, world order is created through a dialectic process that pits hegemonic and counter-hegemonic actors against each other. Global governance arrangements can be conceived as the use of the existing historical structure of world order to address the problems faced by, and meet the demands of, states and civil society. Attempts to achieve the goals of such governance are made in a framework that combines dominant ideas, material capabilities, and multilateral institutions.

II

EXPANDED VIEW OF MULTILATERALISM: 'TOP-DOWN' AND 'BOTTOM-UP' FORCES

The prevailing historical structure over the past 50 years and more has been centred around the Westphalian state system. This fact is reflected in most studies of multilateralism since the turn of the century. These studies suggest that the dominant feature of multilateral evolution has been its 'top-down' characteristic. Thus, multilateralism is traditionally seen as a state-centric activity that addresses problems of security, defined in the traditional sense as military-strategic threats to the territorial and jurisdictional elements of the state ('high politics'). However, the concept and practice of multilateralism had to be re-examined once it was realized that military threats account for only one type of menace to the survival of humanity and that economic, social, technical and cultural interactions between people ('low politics') had become not only increasingly complex but also important to global governance and world order.

New material conditions of increased and complex interconnectedness called for an adjustment in the conceptualization of multilateralism, particularly if governments were to be successful in tackling 'the difficulties posed and the opportunities offered by the unprecedented international flow of commerce in goods, services, people, ideas, germs, and social evils.'[24] Revolutions in industrial technology, international communications and transportation along with the internationalization of labour, production, trade and finance provided the impetus for the development of functional and specialized institutions.[25] However, the emergence of issue-specific functional bodies also revealed another important dialectical development – the tendency in human history 'to establish territorial organizations' while at the same time attempting 'to transcend boundaries to the furthest extent permitted by technologies'.[26]

Not only did the scope of items requiring global administrative attention expand as a result of the above situation, but the possibility of augmenting the range of inter-state conflicts also increased as the areas of interaction broadened, and points of social contact multiplied.[27] The response to this development, toward the second half of the nineteenth century, was the creation of several public international bodies and hundreds of private international associations that covered a wide variety of fields and led to unprecedented levels of growth in socio-economic collaboration and cooperation at the international level.[28] As a consequence, the scope of the subject matter of multilateralism expanded to include areas formerly considered 'domestic'. This development was mirrored at the state level as governments in several countries expanded their administrative jurisdiction to cover almost every facet of social and economic life: areas which were normally considered to be outside the province of government. These developments resulted in a blurring of the domestic/international and public/private boundary lines.

Public functional bodies served

> as collection points and clearing houses for information, centers for discussion of common problems by governments, instruments for achieving the coordination by agreement of national policies and practices, and agencies for promoting the formulation and acceptance of uniform or minimum standards in the fields of their concern.[29]

In other words, these agencies performed norm-creation, service-oriented, facilitative, regulative and coordinative functions for the benefit of state governments, thereby contributing indirectly to 'top-down' multilateralism. At the same time, private international organizations, many of which mirrored developments among public international bodies, emerged as a number of national interest groups (dealing, *inter alia*, with humanitarian, religious, socio-economic, educational and scientific issues), initiated transnational meetings with counterparts from other civil societies.[30] These private associations are the forerunners of the non-governmental network we have today and provide clear examples of early 'bottom-up' approaches to multilateralism.[31] In one sense, they have tried to bridge the gap between sovereigns and civil society – a gap widened by 'top-down' multilateral conceptualization and discourse.

An expanded, or holistic, view of multilateralism which embraces analyses of both 'top-down' and 'bottom-up' varieties of multilateralism is something that was therefore needed for some time.[32] Why this did not occur probably had much to do with the pervasiveness of neo-realism and liberal institutionalism among those who documented the evolution of multilateralism. As Robert Cox notes, 'The Westphalian state system puts a theoretical barrier between state-centered multilateralism and the civil society that lies beyond it – a barrier that is breached frequently in practice but still presents a conceptual and often juridical obstacle'.[33] Despite the existence of this barrier, space has been engineered within ostensibly state-centric global governance arrangements to allow for the activities of civil society.

THE IMPACT OF SOCIAL FORCES

Despite the attempt by state governments to resist the encroachments of non-state actors within the UN system, it is becoming clear that the activities of global governance cannot be performed solely by states. At the very least, state-society relations have to be considered in any discussions of multilateralism, global governance and world order if for no other reason than that the state system is circumscribed and penetrated by other social forces.[34] In the same way that one can describe world structures as configurations of state power, one may also describe these structures in terms of the mode of arrangements of social forces. Cox proposes that the world 'can be represented as a pattern of interacting social forces in which states play an intermediate though autonomous role between the global structure of social forces and local configurations of social forces within particular countries'.[35] Randy Persaud's case study of Jamaica's insertion into the multilateral system bears this out.[36]

Because they operate above, across and beneath the state, these social forces play an important role in the determinations of various forms of state, of different forms of state/society complexes, and of regional/universal dynamics, as well as of the overall shape of historical structures. The complex interaction of these forces acts as a kind of propellant for the trajectory of contemporary and future global order and, in so doing, may help in the transmogrification of multilateral institutions and practices. The nature of the interplay between these forces may also provide obstacles and constraints to multilateral institutional change.

Primary among social forces is the global political economy, although other forces (subdominant or anti-systemic forces emerging from social class, gender, religion, ethnicity, indigenous peoples, migration and criminal elements) are becoming more visible and prominent.[37] Observers of the dominant globalizing economic forces describe these forces (globalization of finance, credit, production, labour, and so on) as extending and deepening the power of capital whilst simultaneously serving to disintegrate existing forms of state and social organization, marginalizing increasingly large numbers of the world's population, and endangering the delicate ecological balance.[38] It is not necessary to elaborate on the precise nature and activity of social forces, since such analysis is well covered in several of the MUNS studies. Suffice it to say that globalization forces exhibit dialectical tendencies (such as universalizing/particularizing, unifying/differentiating, integrating/fragmenting and progressive/reactionary tendencies) which produce the kind of contradictions that allows for the engineering of space for civil society ('bottom-up' forces) in 'top-down' multilateral governance structures.[39]

Certainly, recent analyses of the globalization phenomenon have forced a reconsideration of the nature of forms of state, state/society complexes and the intersection of 'top-down' and 'bottom-up' social forces. Such analyses reveal the complexity of the global system and make it much more difficult for international relations scholars to hold on to a state-centric conceptualization of the global system. Because of globalization and the internationalization of the state, the very abstract and traditional Westphalian concept of sovereignty is under attack. No longer can we consider states as being billiard ball-type autonomous entities which are impermeable to external forces and which can pursue their own self-defined national interests in an unimpeded fashion. Contrary to what classical International Relations theorists would have us believe, this situation may have never really existed – except perhaps in the minds of some practitioners and academics. Clearly, today we have become acutely aware of the extent to which national boundaries are being penetrated by external forces and of the degree to which state governments' domestic and foreign policy actions are constrained and shaped by economic pressures, computerization and telecommunications technologies, information flows, and population movements.[40]

STATE-SOCIETY RELATIONS AND COMPLEXES

Debate about the state's inability to grapple with societal problems as a result of globalization and other forces has led to a round of inquiry into state-society relations.[41] Some participants in this discussion focus specifically on domestic civil society and its interaction with the state. Others are more concerned with regional and transnational civil society and the assertion of its role in global governance activity.[42] Yet others are preoccupied with the oppositional tendencies of issue-specific, *ad hoc* grassroots movements whose purposes may lie 'in organizing gestures of regional solidarity that are inspired less by a particularly developed regional or internationalist consciousness than by the necessities to struggle against a regionally-constructed disciplining cadre'. The actions of the latter group are described by André Drainville as being 'constructed as a multiplicity of fleeting actions, gestures of solidarity, self-contained campaigns and punctual protests organized by social movements'.[43] Out of all these discussions and debates is emerging a better understanding of what civil society is and how it relates to the state, the state system, and global governing arrangements.[44]

The concept of civil society is a nebulous one because, in reality, civil society cannot be totally separated from the political and economic sphere. While liberal and neo-liberal scholars have tried to distinguish between the state and civil society, in practice this boundary is blurred. For example, Porter and Kilby argue that at least in one respect, the state is distinguishable from civil societal institutions and arrangements. As they put it: the state 'is distinguished from other institutions and arrangements, including civil society, mainly in that it seeks predominance over them and aims to institute binding rules regarding the other organizations' activities'.[45] Yet, one would not be too hard pressed to find examples of non-state actors who would endeavour to pursue similar goals.

Some Marxist scholars have used the term civil society in reference to classes that emerged as divisions of labour developed in pre-modern societies.[46] The current discourse on civil society, revived by Central and East European intellectuals, focuses 'on new, generally non-class-based forms of collective action oriented and linked to the legal, associational, and public institutions of society'. This social formation is generally differentiated not only from the state but also from the capitalist market economy.[47]

The term 'civil society' described 'the space of uncoerced human association and also the set of relational networks – formed for the sake of the family, faith, interest, and ideology – that fill this space'.[48] The dissidents in Central and Eastern Europe flourished within civil society. These relational networks are the stuff from which civility is thought to be produced and reproduced in the interest of 'the good life'. Civil society is the broader community outside of political authority – those agents that lie beyond the boundaries of family but stop short of the state. However, the most significant groups within civil society, in relation to the majority of International Relations scholarship, are non-governmental organizations, non-state actors, and social movements.

TOP-DOWN/BOTTOM-UP INTERSECTION

Alger reminds us that even at the founding conference of the United Nations, allowance was made for civil societal participation. Over 1000 representatives from non-state organizations were present in San Francisco and participated as consultants to some states and as unofficial observers.[49] While Killough makes the claim that these individuals 'had a measurable direct impact' on the text of the UN Charter as well as on opening up space for private organizations later on within the world body,[50] their contribution was somewhat marginal to the main thrust and spirit of the Charter.

The space that was created for private organizations was occupied by only a very small percentage of the vast number of non-governmental organizations that emerged out of the post-war period. The inclusion of 'We the People' in the preamble to the Charter can be viewed less as a significant contribution by non-governmental organizations and more of 'tokenism' on the part of the true members of the UN system, that is, state governments. Certainly, since the founding of this organization, UN members paid little homage to the sentiments of civil society, until recently.

The term non-governmental organization (NGO) is commonly upheld as a result of its specific inclusion in article 71 of the UN Charter. The application of this phrase must be separated from the designations intergovernmental organization (IGO), non-state actors, and social movements. Although not a collectively exhaustive usage of the term, Leon Gordenker and Thomas G. Weiss define a non-governmental organization as 'a private citizens' organization, separate from government but active on social issues, not profit making, and with transnational scope'.[51] In contrast, IGOs are sovereignty-bound, and non-state actors include an array of transnational entities from multinational corporations and financial institutions to mass media and criminal organizations.

The expansion of NGO activity in multilateral forums has been well documented. Gordenker and Weiss, citing figures from the Union of International Associations, illustrate the increasingly significant role NGOs are playing in multilateral activity: 'the NGO universe includes well over 15 000 recognizable NGOs that operate in three or more countries and draw their finances from sources in more than one country; this number is growing all the time'.[52] The UN's Economic and Social Council (ECOSOC) recognizes three categories of NGOs, designated as 'I', 'II', and 'the roster' – legitimated in ECOSOC Resolution 1296. Between 1948 and 1991, 'category I listings [grew] from 7 to 41, and in category II from 32 to 354 ... while an even faster expansion took place on the roster'.[53] One specific example of the recent sea-change in the relationship between the UN and NGOs is visible within the United Nations Development Program (UNDP). Antonio Donini observes that the UNDP 'did not have a framework for dealing with NGOs at the field level until the late 1980s;[54] and until recently, the field activities of UN bodies and NGOs were disconnected: 'the only significant exception ... was UNHCR which had traditionally devolved management and delivery of assistance to refugee camps to an array of specialized implementing partners (CARE, IRC, the many Caritas chapters, etc.)'.[55] However, since the late 1980s, NGOs have played a very significant role in UN activities – as will be documented shortly.

Already in several issue areas some NGOs are effectively positioned at the table with states. They have also been included as major partners in some multilateral agenda settings and at major multilateral conferences (as in the sustainable development conference in Rio de Janeiro, the Nairobi and Beijing conferences on women, the Vienna conference on human rights, and the population conference in Cairo). At the UN Conference on the Environment and Development in Rio de Janeiro alone, 1400 NGO representatives were registered – although only a minority were officially recognized as having consultative status.[56] After the Rio conference, the General Assembly and ECOSOC permitted NGOs which had been accredited at the conference rapidly to acquire roster status. In this instance, the 'consultative status machinery was bypassed, and this created an important precedent'.[57] More recently, NGOs have played a significant role in helping the UN and other 'top-down' multilateral bodies deal with humanitarian crises, for example in Somalia and Rwanda.[58] Also some governments have begun to include backbench members of parliament in their delegations at the UN General Assembly sessions, while others have even included NGO representatives in some of their delegations at major multilateral conferences. Pertaining to NGO personnel being included in national delegations to several UN bodies, Donini states that 'in many ways these links between non-governmental and governmental spheres of activity are a novel and welcome feature of the UN scene. This would have been unimaginable only five years ago'.[59] Peter Uvin observes five distinguishable roles played by NGOs at the international level: lobbying, consultation/information, surveillance/control, implementation/management, and decision making/policy making.[60]

The line separating the lobbying, consulting, and surveillance activities of NGOs is a difficult one to draw. As far as lobbying is concerned, Antonio Donini, a member of the Executive Office of the UN Secretary-General, remarks that 'it is the informal interactions rather than the formal variety that are the most interesting; the outside world has been changing much faster than the official rule book can record'.[61]

Closely related to lobbying is the consultative or informative role. The last activity has historically been the focal point of most NGO participation. Furthermore, this function has often been limited to UN-accredited NGOs. However, in the 1980s, 'IOs such as the UNHCR, UNDP and World Bank created institutional links for regular consultation with NGOs'.[62] In one specific example of the effects of this broadened function, Donini states that 'the preparatory work towards and the reporting on the implementation of the UN Convention on the Rights of the Child owe a lot to NGO action'.[63] Clearly, in relation to UN sponsored global conferences, the consultative role, along with the related lobbying, has been the most visible service of NGOs.

The performance of surveillance/control duties is another growing aspect of NGO influence. Whether the activity is human rights surveillance, election monitoring, or scrutinizing the efficacy of global declarations on a variety of issues, NGOs are shouldering a larger part of the international burden.

For many years the implementation/management role has been downplayed or non-existent; however, at the Rio Conference, each of the previous functions, as well as implementation, was undertaken by NGOs. Donini states that 'NGOs played a significant role in shaping the agenda . . . and in the international mobilization around the concept of sustainable development'.[64] He further points out that NGOs 'were rewarded for this role in Chapter 27 of Agenda 21, which gave full recognition to the role of "major groups" in implementing and monitoring the agenda'.[65] The extent to which non-governmental organizations at the international level have increased their power over implementation is seen in the activities of the UNDP which 'is now turning to civil society organizations, like NGOs and the private sector, for project execution'.[66] Donini states that this particular body was 'once the steadfast proponent of statism'.[67] Uvin goes as far as to say that implementation is now the 'favored' role for NGOs within the UN system:

> In the last decade or so, all UN resolutions urge governments to associate NGOs in the implementation of international programs. The World Bank, for example, publishes a list of 'World Bank-financed projects with potential for NGO involvement'. This involvement is usually that of implementation rather than design.[68]

The one activity in which NGOs have not made as significant inroads as in the previously highlighted roles is in decision making/policy making. As Uvin points out, 'Within the UN, at the level of regime creation, formal participation in decision making is impossible.'[69] However, there are some exceptions to this general rule. The International Labour Organisation (ILO), 'thanks to its constitutional links with trade unions and its tripartite system, provides elements of citizen representation and participation in decision-making'.[70] In addition, national constituents of the United Nations Educational, Scientific, and Cultural Organization (UNESCO), the United Nations Children's Fund (UNICEF), and the Food and Agriculture Organization's (FAO) Freedom from Hunger Campaign 'have built strong bridges with professional groups, NGOs and even individual citizens'.[71] In addition, it has been well documented that 'much goes on informally' between NGOs and national members in the General Assembly (in other words lobbying, discussion, attendance at hearings and the circulation of documents) – clearly much of this filters into the final legislation of UN bodies.[72] On the periphery of the UN system some quasi-decision-making roles are being undertaken by NGOs. At the Conference on Popular Participation in African Recovery and Development, which took place in Arusha in February 1990 and was organized jointly by the UN and the NGOs, 'an "African Charter in Popular Participation" was produced, which was later adopted by the UN General Assembly and OAU'.[73]

During the Cold War, when issues of 'high politics' dominated international discussion, NGOs were marginalized as a result of their almost singular concern with 'low politics'. However, with the demise of bipolar strategizing, and in a world increasingly affected by economic, social, technical and cultural interactions that are vital to the survival of our species, these civil societal organizations hold the keys to the kingdom, so to speak. In one specific instance, the United States has pledged to increase development aid channelled through NGOs from 25 per cent to 50 per cent by the turn of the century.[74] At the same time though, such a shift in responsibility from 'top-down' actors to members of civil society seemingly puts the latter on the cutting edge of leadership in many substantial ways. When the credit for these humanitarian operations is assigned, the power of nation-states is both implicitly and explicitly reduced.

The move away from 'top-down' multilateralism, though, has not been completely faultless. Although NGOs seem outwardly part of a 'bottom-up' process, Donini points out that these associations are an 'inescapably Western concept'.[75] Perhaps in an effort to escape the Western-dominated, 'top-down' multilateralism of old, contemporary society is moving in the direction of a different type of Western colonialism. Donini further argues that the rush towards 'sustainable human development', and the 'role of civil society therein, further encourages people to bypass the shrinking powers of host governments'.[76] As a result of the bypassing of state governments by NGOs, the failure of nation-states, with the attendant misery suffered by local segments of civil society, could be hastened.

Another major criticism of NGOs concerns the underlying values of some of these groups. In reference to NGO activity in the Rwanda crisis, Donini points out that:

In Goma, most NGOs seemed to have an inexhaustible supply of T-shirts with their colored logo on display; some were more keen on jockeying for TV-friendly locations than on professionalism; and many appeared vulnerable to media and public opinion shifts at home. On the basis of research in various conflicts and emergencies, one observer concluded that "we have yet to give the NGO community high marks for performance in even routine operational tasks" and that in the Gulf crisis "the prevailing picture of NGOs was one of energy and determination, mixed with confusion and disarray. Distinguishing the charlatan from the humanitarian proved difficult in the panic of the crisis".[77]

Donini argues convincingly that 'many NGOs with militant roots are being sucked into the business and are becoming service providers. Many others are simply born into the new world without the luxury of roots and values'.[78] Before indiscriminately championing the rise of NGOs in contemporary international politics, International Relations scholars ought more critically to analyse the behaviour of these groups in the roles that they currently undertake.

Beyond the expansion of NGO activities, the global community has witnessed the multiplication of new social movements since 1989. These movements operate at all levels: local, national, transnational, sub-regional, regional, transregional and international. Some of them represent a geographically distinct community, while others have a global agenda. Some have interests that are issue specific, while others have a wide spectrum of cross-cutting concerns. Their activities have been described in a variety of ways (from the 'new politics of protest', 'new populism', 'neo-romanticism', 'oppositional politics', 'disorderly politics', 'pressure group politics', 'anti-institutionalism', to 'revolutionary agitation'). The causes they undertake vary from concerns with animal rights, ethnicity, ecology, the manufacture and proliferation of nuclear weapons, war and peace, feminism, gay liberation, human potential, communalism, religion, indigenous peoples, urban renewal, inner-city crime, taxation, racial justice, youth, generation 'X', disabled groups, to the elderly.[79]

Some would argue that the increased activism of civil society, as witnessed within these recent social movements, is nothing more than a renewal of the seemingly immutable principle of political protest. However, as Joseph Camilleri and Jim Falk point out, these and other recent social movements may be the vanguard of a reconstituted civil society; a civil society that may no longer be quite satisfied to allow the old conceptualization of sovereignty to remain static. They argue that 'it is not that the older dimension of conflict has ceased to be relevant but rather that a new dimension has been added to it, which in a sense transforms it, makes for new actors, new patterns of interaction and above all new forms of political life'.[80] Once it was difficult for human beings to conceptualize a large gathering of humans; today it is increasingly difficult for human beings to conceive of themselves as members of a single artificial polity.

As previously evidenced, the process of globalization has allowed concerned citizens, some organizations, and select governments to concern themselves with the affairs of their brothers and sisters no matter where they might be specifically located in the world. The globe, as an increasingly more functional and practical component for analysis, is swiftly becoming the favoured forum for both problem identifying, and consequently problem solving, at the international level.

The most obvious example of a new social movement arose in response to the decision in June 1995 made by French President Jacques Chirac to renew nuclear testing. The ensuing protest included environmental activists, politicians, merchants, and consumers spanning the globe – and was made potent through a veritable panoply of multimedia communications devices. Although this particular movement was unable to prevent the French nuclear tests, Chirac, in the week before the tests, recorded the lowest popularity rating of any modern French president at a similarly early stage of his term, and pollsters blamed his adherence to nuclear weapons testing in the South Pacific.[81] In an attempt to demonstrate the sovereignty of France, Chirac instead provided a glaring example of how states are no longer absolutely sovereign as he apparently accelerated and shortened his initial testing plans.

Yet, even with these less favourable analyses of new social movements, it must be recognized that citizens everywhere appear to want a more direct voice in the political decision making that affects them. An ideal way to do this within the present multilateral structure would be for the UN system to undergo major structural reforms that would allow NGOs and other non-state actors more than simply the consultative status already allowed for in Article 71 of the UN Charter. But such changes are being resisted by most member states of the UN. And even if such reforms were undertaken, it is far from certain if all or most of these civil societal groups would desire inclusion in the UN system. Erskine Childers and Brian Urquhart point out that 'until quite recently the hauteur of secretariat and diplomatic officials about NGOs was matched by the disinterest and disdain of large portions of the NGO community for the UN as merely "another bureaucracy"'.[82] And surely many religious cults, neo-Nazi groups, or 'patriot' militias, to mention only a few associations, would be vehemently opposed to inclusion in the UN system.

The basic premise here is that the predominantly state-centric conceptualization of multilateralism held by traditional International Relations scholars is too narrow and unhistorical and, as a result, fails to capture many of the nuances of multilateral evolution.[83] Furthermore, while traditional realist and liberal institutionalist perspectives provide partial descriptions of aspects of multilateralism, they are less than fully adequate in accounting for the current changes in the practice and orientation of multilateralism or for predicting its future trajectory. What is required at this juncture is an historically sensitive perspective which will provide a more complete conceptualization of multilateralism and account better for its development and changing character.

The argument, simply put, is that multilateralism can be viewed as having two distinct characteristics: a) a 'top-down' trait that reflects a certain Euro-centric, state-centric bias which serves to suppress civil societies; and b) a 'bottom-up' attribute which has been present from the early beginnings of intersocial interaction and is becoming increasingly important today due to a reconstitution of civil societies. Although both versions have coexisted from the beginning of intersocietal interaction, the latter has been marginalized in the dominant discourse of International Relations scholarship whilst the former became entrenched owing, in large part, to that dominant discourse.

III

RECENT SYSTEMIC CHANGES AND THEIR IMPACT ON OPENING UP MULTILATERAL SPACE

A number of recent and profound systemic changes, often vaguely referred to by commentators as 'globalization', have sparked a call for the rethinking of multilateralism.[84] Most of these changes have struck at the very heart of one of the most fundamental elements upon which 'top-down' multilateralism has been based – the principle of state sovereignty. Unfortunately, the concept of globalization is being used by a variety of analysts in a diverse number of ways. For the sake of clarity, globalization is used here to refer to both an economic and political process.

In the economic sphere, Richard J. Barnett and John Cavanagh delineate four sectors of global economic integration: culture, consumption, production and finance.[85] In addition to the integration of global economies in these four significant areas, the recent development of regionalized trade and economic agreements and policies (the EU, NAFTA, and others), in contrast to the globalized or internalized practices of the period before 1970, as well as mass deregulation within the economic sector over the last two decades, has severely weakened the WTO-Bretton Woods mechanisms of post-1945. Today's international financial climate is formulated upon the principles of wide-open capital markets and the reduction of protectionism, regardless of whether the focal point for this liberalization of trade is at the national, regional or global level.

As for the political realm, technological advances in communications and transport have resulted in an increase in the level of complex interdependence.[86] Modern communications (in the form of television, radio, newspapers, telephones, fax machines, the internet and electronic mail, satellites, fiber-optics, and so on), appear to be uniting and fragmenting audiences, exacerbating social cleavages as well as bringing formerly disparate groups together, heightening existing antagonisms as well as providing a means through which such friction can be resolved, eroding national boundaries as well as propelling ultra-nationalist fervour, increasing political cynicism as well as raising the level of civil society's political consciousness. Individual citizens have been empowered as a result of the media's influence. At the same time, because of their adeptness with the utilization of communication systems, state leaders have also been empowered *vis-à-vis* civil society. Modern transportation has allowed people of formerly distant societies to interact more frequently. It acts as a conduit for bringing individuals from different countries with similar interests together.

The overall effect of the above 'double movement' has been a shrinkage in social, political, economic and cultural distances.[87] As a consequence of this phenomenon, formerly dense and opaque frontiers are being dissolved, thus breaking down the Westphalian notion of inside versus outside. National boundaries are no longer able to divide friend from foe. Indeed, the technological revolution has the potential of creating in the minds of people around the world a sense of global citizenship which could result eventually in the transfer of individuals' loyalties from 'sovereignty-bound' to 'sovereignty-free' multilateral bodies.

The changing relationship between the public and private spheres and the virtual collapse of the dividing line separating the domestic from the external environment suggests a fluid but closely integrated global system substantially at odds with the notion of a fragmented system of nationally delineated sovereign states.[88]

The globalization of trade, production and finance has resulted in a marked decline in governments' abilities to control these sectors and has challenged the traditional concept of state sovereignty. It has also expanded the number of players that can be involved in multilateral processes. From an international political economy perspective, Robert Cox sees the globalization movement and the seemingly paradoxical adherence to territorialism as two concepts of world order which stand in conflict but are also interrelated. He points out that the globalizaton of economic processes 'requires the backing of territorially-based state power to enforce its rules'.[89] But post-Fordism, the new pattern of social organization of production that is congruent with the globalization phenomenon, implicitly contradicts the lingering territorial principle that was identified with Fordism. The results of post-Fordist production have been, *inter alia*, the dismantling of the welfare state and the diminishing of the strength of organized labour. But it also has had the effect of increasingly fragmenting power in the world system, and providing fodder for 'the possibility of culturally diverse alternatives to global homogenization'.[90] If Cox is right, we can see how this dialectical 'double movement' of the globalization process can alter the relationship people have established with the political arena and how it can eventually cause a reaction leading to what Rosenau terms 'explosive sub-groupism'.[91]

GIVING CONTEMPORARY MEANING TO MULTILATERALISM

According to this perspective, multilateral norms, principles and institutions have a super-structural character and a facilitative function in terms of helping groups of states to achieve common ends. This position also holds that multilateral institutions cannot be independent of the states that bring them into being. They depend on states for their resources and remain instruments through which state governments can enact collectively derived policies.

A sceptical counter position to that of the neo-realists argues that multilateralism can provide legitimacy for measures which hegemonic powers wish to enact. In other words, it can provide a cloak under which the real ulterior motives of major powers are hidden, as well as a forum in which the acquiescence of the less powerful can be attained.

In contrast to the realist position are a number of paradigms which can be placed under the general category of liberal institutionalism. Each one envisions the emergence of multilateral 'institutions that would transform world order by progressively bringing the state system within some form of authoritative regulation'.[92] Included under this general category are functionalists, transactionalists, neo-functionalists, and the like.

Unfortunately, both neo-realist and liberal institutionalist theoretical perspectives on multilateralism have tended to obscure 'bottom-up' aspects of the phenomenon because these, primarily Western-dominated, positions have tended to focus on state-centred multilateral activity to the exclusion of the role that non-state actors from civil society have been playing in global governance.

The act of governance itself can be located at several different locales (neighbourhood collectives, town councils, multi-urban centres, the stock exchange, municipal, provincial or national government agencies, and regional and international organizations). The effectiveness of governing at any of these levels can be judged by how well-identified institutions are able to handle specific tasks of governance – in other words, their ability to manage, forestall or prevent sources of instability, conflict and risk; to mitigate effects of a crisis; to maintain global and regional space; to prevent abuse of power in international relations; to promote dynamic changes; to address sustainable economic development; to facilitate international flows of labour, trade, goods, services, technology and capital; to deal with global and regional disasters and humanitarian emergencies; to guard against the abuse of human rights; and to protect the interests of future generations (that is, protect the global commons).

In a sense, the UN system, although possibly a synthesis of the many perpetual peace plans, remains a state-centric, 'top-down' multilateral instrument. It can be considered part of an ongoing process designed to refine, adjust and fine-tune the multilateral instruments, structures and processes of global governance. However, the UN system is simply one of the recent, and most universal, expressions of the unfolding of multilateral evolution. It will not be the last. It represents the second generation of modern multilateral organizations. As such, we should expect that this organization, if it is to reflect continued changes in the institutions of multilateralism, must undergo change. Also, it must be borne in mind that the UN is not the only instrument of multilateralism. It is simply one of several such instruments. Others include: civil society, multilateralism itself, global governance, and NGOs. The negative phraseology of the term non-governmental organization may be 'inherently unsatisfactory' for some scholars,[93] but it does accurately reflect the fact that the grouping which falls under this category does not contain governmental organizations.

Although some civil societal actors are undoubtedly hostile to the UN, the growing prominence of NGOs, non-state actors, and new social movements on the multilateral stage today indicates that 'top-down' multilateralism is being challenged by, or at least being forced to intersect with 'bottom-up' multilateralism. What this indicates is that a highly decentralized, almost chaotic multicentric system (comprising subnational and supranational 'sovereignty-free' actors) is being forced to intersect with the relatively coherent and structured state-centric world of 'sovereignty-bound' actors.[94] The results have not been all that gratifying for civil societal actors. 'Top-down' multilateralism must either be reconfigured to accommodate these new social movements, NGOs and non-state actors by expanding its definition of what constitutes a legitimate political community, or it will be bypassed altogether. One author has advocated a possible way out for the UN system. He recommends that article 22 of the Charter be utilized to create a civil society-centric Parliamentary Assembly as a subsidiary organ of the General Assembly.[95] However, this particular proposal is highly problematic for a number of reasons:

1. Representatives would be elected by National Assemblies, rather than the general public within a nation-state.
2. It is difficult to see how the Parliamentary Assembly would be able to pay for the salaries and travel of what could be over 1000 representatives.
3. This proposal could increase the duplication and waste that already exists within multilateral bodies.
4. Very few UN member governments would actually support this proposal.

Other recent calls for 'new' multilateralism, however, recognize the emergence and importance of developing a cosmopolitan global culture and the operations of a global (transnational) community dealing with matters that refuse to be confined within state boundaries. Most of these calls are pushing for the creation of a body whose members are elected by world citizens rather than nominated by sovereign state governments.[96] Proponents of this measure argue that the creation of a global parliament would enhance the institutional linkages that already exist between states and civil society. The existence of such a body would also allow those that are most affected by decisions made at the international level to have a direct stake in their outcomes.[97] Calls for broadening the political participation, democratizing existing multilateral institutions, and empowering civil societies to take decisions that affect them at the international level are symptomatic of a desire to expand the concept of multilateralism to include the 'bottom-up' variety. If mainstream multilateralists continue to ignore such calls, it is possible that 'bottom-up' multilateralism will persist outside of the confines of 'top-down' multilateralism and could even pose a more direct challenge to it.

While one ought to be prudent in recognizing that 'top-down' multilateralism will endure as long as the state system exists, one also has to consider that the demands and needs of the new social and political movements may never be fully accommodated within that 'top-down' multilateral structure. Something will have to give! New social movements are forcing 'top-down' multilateral institutions like the UN system to acknowledge their existence and importance. Perhaps, out of the dialectical clash between 'top-down' and 'bottom-up' multilateral activity, a window of opportunity might be opened for emancipatory social and political movements to make substantial gains in what was once the preserve of states.

The Development of 'New' Multilateralism and its Impact on the UN

As a result of the agitation of non-state, or sovereignty-free, actors over the past few decades we have witnessed a movement toward a reconstitution of civil society. The significance of this activity has been the creation of a new domain of political action that challenges the restrictive ways in which dominant institutions, including sovereign states and the multilateral organizations they create, have sought to define both physical and social space. Some have labelled this phenomenon 'new multilateralism'.

The use of the qualifier 'new' before multilateralism does not signify novel or recent practices. It has simply been used by those in the MUNS project to mean 'contrasting with conventional usage'.[98] The theoretical basis for understanding 'new multilateralism' is 'new realism' – a paradigm which has much in common with classical realism in its focus on power relations, but which differs substantially from it by broadening the range of determining social forces beyond state power. The historical, contextual and critical approach used in 'new realism' sets it apart from neo-realism as well. Unlike neo-realism, 'new realism' is concerned with structural change in world order and with understanding this change in Braudelian *longue durée* historical terms.

Can a state-centric body like the UN system embrace the 'new' multilateralism? Will the UN system ever take greater account of the emergence of a global civil society that is demanding greater democratization of multilateral instruments, or will the world body continue to operate in a 'top-down' fashion, thus turning a blind eye to 'we the people'? If it is to be a relevant instrument of global governance for the twenty-first century and beyond, the UN cannot ignore the world-wide array of organized non-state activity nor can it disregard the growing call of civil society and other non-state actors to become involved in the management of their own affairs.[99]

Societal demands after World War II called for greater centralization of multilateral institutions to deal with threats to international security and any future world-wide economic depression. As a consequence, there was a clear focus on 'top-down' multilateralism at the expense of any attempts to institute a 'bottom-up' version. Today, however, societal demands are different. International Relations scholars should carefully consider the words of Robert Cox: 'Multilateralism can only be understood within the context in which it exists, and that context is the historical structure of world order'.[100] With the reconstitution of civil society, the development of transnational networks, and the outlines of what appears to be a global civil society, the call for, and the potential emergence of, a 'new' multilateralism should not be surprising.

If multilateralism is to be given contemporary meaning it must be conceived as the coordination of formal and informal relations, not only between states but also between non-state entities that operate on the global state using certain principles (such as law, diplomacy, indivisibility and reciprocity) in addressing common problems. The meaning of 'new' multilateralism ought to be broad enough 'to encompass all those entities that may be or may become relevant to negotiation concerning general issues or issues in specific sectors of policy, whether at the world level or at the level of a more limited grouping'.[101] The concept must also continue to presuppose a normative and purposive aspiration, 'a preference for dealing with problems arising among the entities by a process of negotiation or non-violent interaction among some or all of them'.[102] Through such governance, conflicting or diverse interests among the entities that operate on the global state can at least be accommodated.

CONCLUSION

As we head into the twenty-first century, we seem to be witnessing the intersection of 'top-down' and 'bottom-up' multilateralism; however, this does not necessarily mean that there is a linear direction to that shift. Clearly, the most powerful non-state actors in the contemporary global environment are transnational corporations and financial institutions. Are the universalizing cultural products of Disney not, in large part, similar in form and substance to the Roman Catholic Church of old? Therefore, is globalization merely weakening state power to the betterment of corporate power, thereby exchanging one mode of 'top-down' hegemony for another? Secondly, even if the shift is indeed away from 'top-down' multilateralism, does this inevitably mean that ostensibly 'bottom-up' actors will be more representative of majorities or minorities within civil society? Thirdly, should these more recently empowered civil societal actors anticipate some sort of 'closing down' response by 'top-down' power-brokers? These questions and others will occupy social scientists well into the next century.

Whether or not both versions of this phenomenon can be accommodated within the same conceptual model or merged into a single praxis is highly debatable at this point, owing to the lack of clarity that characterizes this particular transitional juncture. Very few International Relations scholars have focused on the 'bottom-up' version of multilateralism.[103] To do so would mean privileging the concerns and interests of the less powerful members of international society while at the same time recognizing the constraints imposed by the more powerful members. Developing such a research program would require a substantial movement away from traditional realist, neo-realist and liberal institutionalist scholarship.

No longer can we accept the notion that social and political activity must be viewed in the context of a world that is compartmentalized along state boundaries. Clearly, an alternative perspective has emerged which demonstrates that new social formations are effectively carving out, or have the potential to carve out, different domains of political space. As Joseph Camilleri and Jim Falk put it so well:

> ... we are living at a time when the hard certainties of an older political space are giving way to new but still only partially discernible constraints and possibilities. Shifting allegiances, concepts, identities and forms of authority are characteristic of our age. The complex forms of social, economic and political organization, the multiple tiers of jurisdiction, and the uncertainties over what is to follow reinforce the conclusion that we live in a time of transition.[104]

Their advice that, given the nature of the period in which we live, it is time to bring about a shift in our theoretical vantage point should be heeded. We need to try to understand the ways in which new forms of less restrictive political space are being fashioned so that civil society can be given a more central role in the shaping of future global governance arrangements. So as not to leave an inaccurate impression, it is crucial to point out that recognizing the emergence of 'new' forms of multilateralism does not as a consequence imply that the 'old' style of multilateralism is extinct – indeed it is not. The state-centric, 'top-down' approach to multilateral activity is still the dominant method of cooperating, reciprocating, and compromising over a number of issue areas in global politics. For this specific reason, I speak only of the intersection of 'top-down' and 'bottom-up' multilateralism. However, the recent systemic transformations that have split open the once-dominant economic and political orders will leave lasting marks. In both of these significant international areas, the concept of state sovereignty is being challenged. Demanding a seat at the global bargaining table, NGOs and some other concerned non-state actors are speeding into this increasingly gaping sovereignty vacuum. The 'top-down' multilateral order may still be attendant, but the emergence of new multilateral arrangements is unlikely to be hindered in a world that is witnessing the decline of state sovereignty. Given the inability of state leaders to agree on a formula for pluralizing the UN system, the reality is that future multilateral arrangements may, or may not, include the United Nations system.

NOTES

1. Among them are Yoshikazu Sakamoto, 'Democratization, Social Movements and World Order', in Björn Hettne (ed.), *International Political Economy: Understanding Global Disorder* (Halifax: Fernwood Publishing, 1995), pp. 129–43; a special issue of 'Nongovernmental Organization, the United Nations and Global Governance' in *Third World Quarterly: Journal of Emerging Areas*, vol. 16, no. 3 (1995), guest edited by Leon Gordenker and Thomas Weiss; Eric Fawcett & Hanna Newcomber (eds), *United Nations Reform: Looking Ahead after Fifty Years* (Toronto: Dundurn Press Ltd., 1995); The Commission on Global Governance, *Our Global Neighbourhood* (New York: Oxford University Press, 1995); Elizabeth Riddell-Dixon, 'Social Movements and the United Nations', *International Social Science Journal* (June 1995), pp. 289–303.
2. See Doug J. Porter and Patrick Kilby, 'Strengthening the Role of Civil Society in Development? A Precariously Balanced Answer', *Australian Journal of International Affairs*, vol. 50, no. 1 (1996), p. 31.
3. For an expansion of the concept of 'top-down' and 'bottom-up' multilateralism, see W. Andy Knight, 'Multilateralisme ascendant ou descedant: deux voies dans la quete d'une gouverne globale', *Etudes internationales*, numero special Multilateralisme et Securite Regionale, sous la direction de Michel Fortmann et Stephane Roussel, vol. xxvi, no. 4 (Decembre 1995), pp. 685–710.
4. M.J. Peterson, 'Transnational Activity, International Society and World Politics', *Millennium: Journal of International Studies*, vol. 21, no. 3 (1992), p. 376.
5. Richard A. Falk, 'Democratizing, Internationalizing and Globalizing', in Yoshikazu Sakamoto (ed.), *Global Transformation: Challenges to the State System* (Tokyo: United Nations University Press, 1994), p. 477.
6. Robert Cox, 'Multilateralism and World Order', *Review of International Studies*, vol. 18, no. 2 (April 1992).
7. See Mihaly Simai, *The Future of Global Governance: Managing Risk and Change in the International System* (Washington, DC: United States Institute of Peace Press, 1994).
8. See James N. Rosenau, 'Governance, Order, and Change in World Politics', in James N. Rosenau and Ernst-Otto Czempiel (eds), *Governance*

Without Government: Order and Change in World Politics (Cambridge, UK: Cambridge University Press, 1992), pp. 4–5 and The Commission on Global Governance, *Our Global Neighbourhood: The Report of the Commission on Global Governance*, p. 2.

9. For a good explanation of the traditional conceptualization of multilateralism, see James Caporaso, 'International Relations Theory and Multilateralism: The Search for Foundations', *International Organization*, vol. 46, no. 3 (Summer 1992).

10. For an excellent discussion of the question of the practical unattainability of this ideal see Inis Claude, Jr, *Swords into Plowshares: The Problems and Progress of International Organization*, (New York: Random House, 1984), pp. 414–20.

11. Ibid., p. 418.

12. See W. Andy Knight, 'Multilateral Evolution and Change in the United Nations System: The Quest for Global Governance', unpublished Ph.D. dissertation (Toronto: York University, 1995).

13. Robert W. Cox, 'Multilateralism and World Order', *Review of International Studies*, vol. 18, no.2 (April 1992), pp. 161 and 167.

14. Keith Krause and W. Andy Knight, *State Society, and the UN System: Changing Perspectives on Multilateralism* (Tokyo: United Nations University Press, 1995), pp. 8–11.

15. See Robert W. Cox, 'Social Forces, States and World Orders: Beyond International Relations Theory', in Robert O. Keohane (ed.), *Neorealism and its Critics* (New York: Columbia University Press, 1986).

16. Ibid.

17. Robert W. Cox, 'Multilateralism and World Order', p. 163.

18. Stephen Gill, 'Structural Change and Global Political Economy: Globalizing Elites and the Emerging World Order', in Yoshikasu Sakamoto, *Global Transformation*, pp. 182–4.

19. See Kees van der Pijl, 'The Cadre Class and Public Multilateralism', in Sakamoto, *Global Transformation*, pp. 200–27.

20. See Claus Offe, 'New Social Movements: Challenging the Boundaries of Institutional Politics', *Social Research*, vol. 52, no. 4 (Winter 1985), p. 827.

21. André C. Drainville, 'Resisting Integration in the Americas: Internationalism in One Country'? Paper presented at the International Studies Association Annual Conference, San Diego (April 1996), p. 14.

22. Ibid., p. 17.

23. On this issue see Robert W. Cox, 'On Thinking about Future World Order', in Robert W. Cox with Timothy Sinclair, *Approaches to World Order* (Cambridge: Cambridge University Press, 1996), p. 77.

24. Inis Claude, *Swords into Plowshares*, p. 34.

25. Industrial developments led to the need for improvements in technology and communications. The steamship replaced the sail boat. The railway replaced the stagecoach. The telegraph (which was introduced in 1837) increased the speed of message delivery. In 1850, the first submarine telegraph cable connected England and France. Each of these developments had a tremendous impact on the inter-

actions of states. For example, faster travel allowed for the quick convening of meetings between governmental representatives. The telegraph facilitated consultations between home governments and external representative of those governments.

26. Chadwick Alger, 'Citizens and the UN System in a Changing World', paper presented at an International Conference on 'Changing World Order and the United Nations System', held in Yokohama, Japan (March 24–27, 1992), p. 2. Also see Charles Pentland, 'Integration, Interdependence, and Institutions: Approaches to International Order', in David Haglund and Michael Hawes (eds), *World Politics: Power, Interdependence and Dependence* (Toronto: Harcourt Brace Jovanovich, 1960), p. 175.

27. The first evidence of the new functional issue-specific cooperation among states can be traced to the establishment of the Central Commission for the Navigation of the Rhine in 1815 and the European Commission for the Danube in 1856. This was followed by the Geodetic Union (1864), the International Telegraphic Union (1865) – later called the International Telecommunication Union; the International Meteorological Organization (1873); the General Postal Union (1874) – later renamed the Universal Postal Union; the International Bureau of Weights and Measures (1875); two International Health Offices set up in Vienna and Havana in 1881; the International Copyright Union (1886); the Central Office for International Railway Transport (1890); the International Union for the Publication of Customs Tariffs (1890); the United International Bureau for the Protection of Intellectual Property (1893); the Metrick Union established in France in 1901; the International Labour Office set up in Berne in 1901; the International Office of Public Health (1903) and the International Institute of Agriculture (1905) – viewed, respectively, as forerunners of the World Health Organization and the Food and Agriculture Organization.

28. See J.M. Keynes, *The Economic Consequences of the Peace* (London: Macmillan, 1919).

29. Inis Claude, *Swords into Plowshares*, pp. 34–6.

30. One of the first of these gatherings of non-governmental organizations was the 1840 World Convention called to address anti-slavery issues. In a few years, similar associations, like the International Institute for Agriculture, the Universal Peace Congress and the International Law Association were similarly convened.

31. L. Woolf, *International Government* (2nd edition, London: Allen & Unwin, 1916) and K. Skjelsbaek, 'The Growth of Non-Governmental Organization in the Twentieth Century', *International Organization*, vol. 25, no. 3, pp. 420–42.

32. W. Andy Knight, 'Multilatéralisme ascendant ou descendant: deux voies dans la quête d'une gouverne globale', *Etudes Internationale*, numero special, vol. xxvi, no. 4 (Decembre 1995), pp. 685–710.

33. Robert W. Cox, *Programme on Multilateralism and the United Nations System (MUNS)*, final report (Tokyo: The United Nations University Press, March 1996), p. 3.

34. Keith Krause and W. Andy Knight (eds), *State, Society and the United Nations System*, pp. 245–63.
35. Robert W. Cox, 'Social Forces, States, and World Orders: Beyond International Relations Theory' (1981), in Robert W. Cox with Timothy Sinclair, *Approaches to World Order*, p. 105.
36. Randolph B. Persaud, 'Social Forces and World Order Pressures in the Making of Jamaican Multilateral Policy', in Keith Krause and W. Andy Knight (eds), *State, Society and the United Nations System*, pp. 187–218.
37. For a depiction of the dominant forces see Susan Strange, 'Territory, State, Authority and Economy: A New Realist Ontology of Global Political Economy', in Robert W. Cox (ed.), *The New Realism: Perspectives on Multilateralism and World Order* (London: Macmillan for the United Nations University Press/Macmillan, 1997), and for an analysis of the anti-systemic forces see Rodolfo Stavenhagen, 'Peoples' Movements: the anti-systemic challenge', in ibid.
38. See Stephen Gill, 'Global Structural Change and Multilateralism', in Stephen Gill (ed.), *Globalisation, Democratisation, and Multilateralism* (London: Macmillan for the United Nations University Press 1997), p. 4.
39. In trying to understand the global impact of the Islamic revolution movement in Iran, Huizer adopts the view of 'globalization from below', that is, of 'linking people's movements rooted in their own local cultures'. Drawing on Esteva, Huizer explains that 'Grassroots movements can "regenerate people's space" by forming "hammocks"'. He places the struggle against apartheid in South Africa in this category. See Gerrit Huizer, 'Social Movements in the Underdevelopment of Development Dialectic: A View from Below', in Sing C. Chew & Robert A. Denemark (eds), *The Underdevelopment of Development*, (London: Sage Publications Ltd, 1996), p. 308.
40. For a discussion of this see W. Andy Knight, 'Foreign Policy: Coping with a Post-Cold War Environment', in Andrew Johnson and Andy Stritch (eds), *Global Imperatives, National Interest and Public Policy in Canada* (Toronto: Copp Clark, Ltd., 1996).
41. For a brief discussion of the debate see M.J. Peterson, 'Transnational Activity, International Society and World Politics', *Millennium: Journal of International Studies*, vol. 21, no. 3 (1992), pp. 374–6.
42. See for instance, Paul J. Nelson, *The World Bank and Non-Governmental Organizations: The Limits of a Political Development* (Basingstoke: Macmillan, 1995); Timothy Shaw & Fahimul Quadir, 'Towards Global Governance: (I)NGOs and the UN System in the Next Millennium', paper prepared for presentation to the Eighth Annual Meeting of the Academic Council on the United Nations System, New York (19–21 June 1995); Alejandro Col, 'The Promises of International Civil Society', paper presented at the International Studies Association Annual meeting, San Diego, California (16–20 April 1996).
43. André Drainville, 'Resisting Integration in the Americas: Internationalism in One Country?' Paper presented at the International

Studies Association Annual Conference, San Diego, California (16–20 April 1996), pp. 10–11.

44. Underlying all of these attempts at defining civil society are three persistent debates. The first is an old controversy within the field of democratic theory between defenders of elite versus participatory democratic models. The second is a primarily Anglo-American debate between 'right-oriented liberalism' and 'communitarianism'. The third debate is one that pits neo-conservative advocates of the free market against defenders of the welfare state. For a full discussion of these debates see the Introduction to Jean L. Cohen and Andrew Arato, *Civil Society and Political Theory* (Cambridge, Mass: The MIT Press, 1992).

45. Doug J. Porter and Patrick Kilby, 'Strengthening the Role of Civil Society in Development? A Precariously Balanced Answer', in *Australian Journal of International Affairs*, vol. 50, no. 1 (1996), p. 34.

46. See Lawrence Krader, *Dialectic of Civil Society* (Amsterdam: Van Goreum, 1976), pp. 7–8.

47. Jean L. Cohen and Andrew Arato, *Civil Society and Political Theory*, p. 2.

48. For a provocative discussion on this issue see Michael Walzer, 'The Idea of Civil Society', *Dissent* (Spring 1991), pp. 293–304.

49. Chadwick Alger, 'Citizens and the UN System in a Changing World', in Yoshikazu Sakamoto (ed.), *Global Transformation: Challenges to the State System* (Tokyo: United Nations University Press, 1994), pp. 304–5.

50. T. Patrick Killough, 'A Peace Made on Main Street: Private Americans Help Create the 1945 United Nations Charter', Address to the Southeastern World Affairs Institute, Black Mountain, N.C. (26 July 1991).

51. Leon Gordenker and Thomas G. Weiss, 'Pluralising Global Governance: Analytical Approaches and Dimensions', *Third World Quarterly*, vol. 16, no. 3 (1995), p. 360.

52. Ibid., p. 362.

53. Ibid., p. 363.

54. Antonio Donini, 'The Bureaucracy and the Free Spirits: Stagnation and Innovation in the Relationship between the UN and NGOs', *Third World Quarterly*, vol. 16, no. 3 (1995), p. 431.

55. Ibid.

56. Gordenker and Weiss, 'Pluralising Global Governance', p. 363.

57. Donini, 'Bureaucracy and the Free Spirits', p. 422.

58. See Andrew S. Natios, 'NGOs and the UN System in Complex Humanitarian Emergencies: Conflict or Cooperation?', *Third World Quarterly*, vol. 16, no. 3 (1995), pp. 405–19 and Donini, 'Bureaucracy and the Free Spirits', pp. 421–39.

59. Donini, 'Bureaucracy and the Free Spirits', p. 424.

60. Peter Uvin, 'Scaling up the Grass Roots and Scaling Down the Summit: The Relations between Third World Non-Governmental Organisations and the United Nations', *Third World Quarterly*, vol. 16, no. 3 (1995), p. 501.

61. Donini, 'Bureaucracy and the Free Spirits', p. 421.
62. Uvin, 'Scaling up the Grass Roots', p. 502.
63. Donini, 'Bureaucracy and the Free Spirits', p. 422.
64. Ibid.
65. Ibid.
66. Ibid., p. 437.
67. Ibid.
68. Uvin, 'Scaling up the Grass Roots', p. 504.
69. Ibid.
70. Donini, 'Bureaucracy and the Free Spirits', p. 422.
71. Ibid., p. 423.
72. Ibid.
73. Uvin, 'Scaling up the Grass Roots', p. 505.
74. Gordenker and Weiss, 'Pluralising Global Governance', p. 365.
75. Donini, 'Bureaucracy and the Free Spirits', p. 430.
76. Ibid., p. 437.
77. Ibid, p. 435.
78. Ibid., p. 437.
79. See Alain Touraine, 'An Introduction to the Study of Social Movements', *Social Research*, vol. 52, no. 4 (Winter 1985), pp. 774–82, Jürgen Habermas, 'New Social Movements', *Telos*, vol. 49 (Fall 1981), and M. Fuentes & A. Gunder Frank, 'Ten Theses on Social Movements', *World Development*, vol. 17, no. 2 (February 1989).
80. Joseph A. Camilleri and Jim Falk, *The End of Sovereignty? The Politics of a Shrinking and Fragmenting World* (Hants: Edward Elgar Publishing Ltd, 1992), p. 207.
81. *Journal du Dimanche*, 23 July 1995. See also *New York Times*, 11 August 1995: A3:2.
82. Erskine Childres and Brian Urquhart, *Renewing the United Nations System* (Uppsala: Dag Hammarskjöld Foundation, 1994), p. 172.
83. For a more detailed and comprehensive analysis of the phenomenon see W. Andy Knight, 'Multilateral Evolution and Change in the UN System: the Quest for Global Governance'.
84. For a more detailed discussion see W. Andy Knight, 'Towards a Subsidiary Model for Peacemaking and Preventive Diplomacy: Making Chapter VIII of the UN Charter Operational', *Working Paper Series,* Centre for Foreign Policy Studies, Dalhousie University (1995).
85. See Richard J. Barnett and John Cavanagh, *Global Dreams: Imperial Corporations and the New World Order*, (New York: Simon & Schuster, 1994).
86. To use a term coined by Robert Keohane and Joseph Nye, *Power and Interdependence: World Politics in Transition* (Boston: Little, Brown & Company, 1977), see especially chapter 2.
87. James N. Rosenau, 'Distant Proximities: The Dynamics and Dialectics of Globalization', in *International Political Economy: Understanding Global Disorder* ed., Björn Hettne (London: Zed, 1995), p. 65. Also see Mihaly Simai, *The Future of Global Governance* p. xvi.
88. Camilleri and Falk, *The End of Sovereignty?*, p. 88.
89. Robert Cox, 'Production and Security', in David Dewitt *et. al.* (eds), *Building a New Global Order*, pp. 141–158.

90. Ibid.
91. James Rosenau, 'Distant Proximities', pp. 60–1.
92. Ibid., p. 169.
93. See, for example, Rachel Brett, 'The Role and Limits of Human Rights NGOs at the United Nations', *Political Studies*, vol. XLIII (1995), p. 96.
94. James N. Rosenau, 'Patterned Chaos in Global Life: Structure and Process in the Two Worlds of World Politics', *International Political Science Review*, vol. 9, no. 4 (October 1988), pp. 334–5.
95. Dieter Heinrich, 'A United Nations Parliamentary Assembly', in Eric Fawcett & Hanna Newcombe (eds), *United Nations Reform* pp. 95–9.
96. Jonas Zoninsein, 'Implications of the Evolving Global Structure for the UN System: A View from the South', in Michael G. Schechter (ed.), *Innovation in Multilateralism* (London: Macmillan for the United Nations University Press, 1998).
97. The value preferences of this proposed global body would include greater social equity, greater diffusion of power, protection of the biosphere, peaceful resolution of conflicts, human security, and equality.
98. This was explained by Robert W. Cox at a MUNS symposium held at the European University Institute in Fiesole, Italy (Autumn 1992).
99. This was the subject of a conference sponsored by the Academic Council on the United Nations System and the Centre for International and Strategic Studies at York University, Toronto entitled, 'Nongovernmental Organizations, the United Nations, and Global Governance' (April 10–11, 1995).
100. Robert W. Cox, 'Multilateralism and World Order', p. 161.
101. Robert W. Cox, *Programme on Multilateralism and the United Nations System, 1990–1995*, 2nd Interim Report (Tokyo: United Nations University, September 1993), p. 2.
102. Robert Cox, *Perspectives on Multilateralism*, Programme on Multilateralism and the United Nations System (MUNS) (Tokyo: United Nations University, April 1991), p. 2.
103. One exception can be seen in the work of scholars involved in the *Programme on Multilateralism and the United Nations System, 1990–1995* or MUNS (headed by Robert W. Cox) sponsored by the United Nations University (UNU).
104. Camilleri and Falk, *The End of Sovereignty?*, p. 9.

11 Multilateralism from Below: a Prerequisite for Global Governance

Marie-Claude Smouts

NEW CHALLENGES FOR MULTILATERALISM

Multilateralism has long been analysed as a form of international relations falling exclusively under the institutional repertoire of states. It is ordinarily defined in terms similar to those used by Robert Keohane (1990): 'The practice of coordinating national policies in groups of three or more states'. This state-centred approach reflects a vision of the world that sees the state as the main (though not the only) actor in international relations and the principal mediator between citizens and world politics. The state has the power to decide whether to use force (power over war or peace) and is responsible for fostering the well-being and development of the population. Human rights are claims individuals can make on the state. World politics can only function properly when state policies are coordinated 'on the basis of generalized principles of conduct' (the very definition of multilateralism according to Ruggie 1992).

This approach remains partly valid but has become seriously deficient. It is unable to account for changes underway that increasingly blur the distinction between the public and the private sphere. Nor is it able to satisfy the need felt by many and in nearly every area to rethink the institutions that operate on the international scene. As this century draws to a close, the overwhelming majority of challenges facing the world can be met only by constantly renewed cooperation between public and private actors on an international scale.

As regards security issues, the main threats are no longer wars between states but societal fractures. The spread of civil violence, the proliferation of internal conflicts and the rise of particularisms and fundamentalisms all bear witness to this. Furthermore, and the remark is commonplace, the globalization of trade has weakened states. Faced with the constraints of competition, the weight of foreign direct investment (FDI) and the fickleness of an international financial market that is more and more disconnected from production and the actual economy, states have less and less control over their economic and monetary policy. The latitude they are left with is not nil but is considerably reduced. The growing gulf between globalized trade, mobile capital and territorially bound populations produces a sense of powerlessness among individuals. Citizens feel they no longer have a grip on their own destiny: their jobs, the future of their savings, the fate of their currency all depend on distant forces that are hard to perceive and that escape their control.

Added to this is a severe crisis of political representation. In many parts of the world, political identity is not necessarily forged through civil linkages and state allegiance. Nearly everywhere, even in long-established states, the rise of community-based demands, the decline of secular ideologies, the multiplication of sects and undercover groups acting on the fringe of national law attest to a breakup of the forms of political identification. Political entities form that meet no universal criteria, no common rationality. At the same time, the globalization of telecommunications has introduced a radical novelty: global time. The immediacy of cyberspace and multimedia is superimposed on the local time of the city, the region or the nation, sometimes dominating it. This sea-change in the time/space relations of human activity is still in its early phase. Its potentially disintegrating effects are awesome. Already the breach is widening between those who have the means to understand and play the globalization game and those who are disqualified from it. This cleavage no longer runs along a North-South axis; it cuts right through every society.

These four elements combined – spread of public violence, crisis of the welfare state, crisis of political representation, dissociation of territorial space and real time – make up a fast-changing world characterized both by interdependence and fragmentation. In this context, what is expected from the multilateral system today cannot be the same as 50 years ago. It is no longer a matter of ensuring better coordination among state policies. It is a question of dealing with change, interdependence, differentiation, so as to restore some sort of *meaning* to international politics by making it intelligible for all. This implies making people the focus of such activity. The success of such new concepts as 'human development', 'human security', and especially 'sustainable development' – at least as gauged by the lip service paid to them – indicates that a certain awareness is beginning to dawn among the international community.

THE CONCEPT OF GLOBAL GOVERNANCE

The ultimate goal of multilateralism is the dissolution of power into law, the substitution of a contract in place of domination. This can only happen through general political exchange among all the components of the economic and social policy-making sphere with the participation of as many of the actors involved as possible. A useful tool to analyse and describe this mechanism is found in a new concept: *'global governance'*.

The notion of governance first appeared in the field of public policy in the 1980s and referred mainly to urban policies. It came within the context of the major debate regarding the governability of Western societies that has been going on since the 1970s in Germany, the United States and Great Britain. Renate Mayntz (1993) brought to light how this concept was tied to failures of governments and their incapacity to steer increasingly complex and diversified societies. This perspective emphasizes the development of social subsystems and the proliferation of increasingly autonomous networks (consumer groups, public transport-user associations, and the like) capable of putting up resistance to government injunctions (Le Galés 1995). Traditional institutions are no longer adequate. New mechanisms of cooperation between state and society must be found to make action possible in the public sphere. Governance is first and foremost a form of social coordination (Kooiman 1993, p. 258).

> Governance can be seen as the pattern or structure that emerges in a social-political system as the "common" result or outcome of the interacting efforts of all involved actors. This pattern cannot be reduced to one actor or group of actors in particular: *"political governance in modern societies can no longer be conceived in terms of external government actors"* (Marin and Mayntz 1991). This emerging pattern forms the "rules of the game" within a particular system or, in other words, the medium through which actors can act and try to use these rules in accordance with their own objectives and interests.

The concept of governance has the merit of placing the emphasis on the multiplicity of actors in both the public and private sphere and on coordination. It views public action in terms of interaction and no longer in terms of power exercised from above over the people below. This notion has been transposed to International Relations in the famous work by J. Rosenau and E.-O. Czempiel, *Governance without Government* (1992). It found its way into diplomatic discourse in the report by the special Commission on Global Governance made following Willy Brandt's initiative after the fall of the Berlin Wall: *Our Global Neighbourhood* (see Knight 1995). According to this Commission (pp. 2–3):

> Governance is the sum of the many ways individuals and institutions, public and private, manage their common affairs. It is a continuing process through which conflicting or diverse interests can be accommodated and cooperative action may be taken. It includes formal institutions and regimes empowered to enforce compliance, as well as informal arrangements that people and institutions either have agreed to or perceive to be in their interest ... At the global level, governance has been viewed primarily as intergovernmental relationships, but it must now be understood as also involving non-governmental organizations, citizens' movements, multinational corporations and the global market. Interacting with these are global mass media of dramatically enlarged influence.

Defined in this manner, the concept of governance presents numerous advantages: it is flexible, adaptable, it takes nothing for granted; it encompasses a great diversity of actors and describes an ongoing process of interaction that is constantly changing in response to changing circumstances; it denotes a form of social coordination which can take into consideration various public and private interests in the management of matters of common concern and which takes responsibility for these matters collectively.

The difficulty resides in the fact that governance implies the participation of all the actors involved, consequently a high degree of democratization on the multilateral level. However, this is far from being achieved.

DEMOCRATIZING MULTILATERALISM

It is not easy to speak of democracy on an international scale.

1. Democracy is, in fact, a form of government that ensures communication between the governed and the governing bodies.
2. Voters choose representatives who make policy decisions on the citizens' behalf: this is representative democracy. In this form of government the definition of public good emanates from the people; the citizens express their preference. The expression of the people's consent ensures the legitimacy of decisions made in the name of common interest.
3. Democracy is a political system based on a set of institutions, rules and procedures that aim to ensure the respect of basic rights and freedoms known as civil liberties.
4. In a democracy, governing officials are accountable for their actions. The capacity of citizens to dismiss their leaders is one of the essential features of democracy, perhaps the most significant one (Manin 1994).

These four basic features of democracy imply both a rigorous definition of the actors (who has a voice and who is accountable?) and a territorial division of the voices into constituencies (what are the districts?). Neither of these elements exists on the international scene, which sharply curbs the possibility of creating democracy on an international scale, unless its processes are envisaged in quite a different manner (Held 1995a, 1995b).

The question of democratizing multilateralism can be broken down into at least three sub-dimensions.

1. Democratization of Inter-State Relations

How can it be arranged so that all states, great or small, are represented, can make their voices heard and participate in multilateral decision-making? More importantly, how can it be ensured that a coalition of major powers, or even one single super-power, cannot impose its will, its objectives and its system of standards and values on small and medium powers?

This question is a perpetual one. It was already at the centre of debates in San Francisco in 1945. It periodically reappears with regard to the International Monetary Fund (IMF) and the World

Bank. At the risk of being somewhat provocative, I maintain that, in any case, this is not the most pressing issue and that little can be done to improve the existing arrangements for equitable representation. On the legal and institutional level, considerable progress has certainly been made since the European Concert. Organizations with a universal vocation have proliferated in all sectors. All states can make themselves heard, either individually or as a group. Not only does the principle of 'one state, one vote' prevail most of the time in plenary assemblies but, for the past 20 years, multilateral decisions are increasingly adopted by consensus. Even in the IMF or the World Bank, where the voting system in principle resembles suffrage by might (or wealth), in practice a consensus is observed. Moreover, an unprecedented event was witnessed in Madrid in October 1994: a 'rejection front' organized by India and Brazil and backed by Saudi Arabia opposed a G-7 proposal on Special Drawing Rights (SDR). (Some weeks later, in Washington, a new wind of rebellion rose up with regard to the doubling of the General Agreements to Borrow, GAB).

The situation is admittedly far from perfect, and institutional improvements would still be welcome but, if they are to come about, giving priority to greater democratization in this area would be at the expense of huge and exhausting efforts for what would ultimately result in only minimal gains. The task of democratization between states is not of a legal and institutional order. The real issue is not the control of decision-making mechanisms within international organizations but the control of the process of production and allocation of resources on the global scale. What is happening in international organizations is merely the more or less subdued reflection of competition that occurs outside these organizations and over which they have little control. Nothing is more detrimental than feigned ignorance. Each time the discrepancy has been too great between the control exercised by a majority in an organization and its actual power on the international scene, the organization has suffered and in the final analysis the majority has gained nothing: from this standpoint the 1970s and the failure of the New International Economic Order drove home a hard lesson indeed.

The reason is simple: the most basic notions of the sociology of organizations taught us long ago that an organization can function only if it guarantees its members a minimum level of satisfaction (Simon 1972), particularly its 'strategic' members, those whose participation is critical to the organization's activity (Miles 1980). The history of the UN, UNCTAD, UNESCO, UNIDO and many others has verified this axiom time and again. Having failed to achieve a minimal degree of satisfaction for the industrialized countries, these multilateral organs have been left paralysed by tensions that have squandered their resources and effectiveness.

States – and international bureaucracies – are now intensely aware of this. The quagmire in which UN reform has floundered is significant in this respect. Ideally, the Security Council must be reformed. Politically, no state or coalition has made a staunch commitment to attempting to push through a reform by submitting the same proposal year after year, which would end up creating irresistible pressure. The status quo is most certainly detrimental to the Security Council's representativity and international legitimacy. Yet things go on as though reform of any kind would generate still more dissatisfaction.

2. The Right of Populations to Break Free of their Governments and Promote their own Views and Demands[1]

By definition, global governance implies that individuals take charge of matters that concern them by sharing the management and responsibility of them with public authorities. This implies improving opportunities for citizens to participate in setting the multilateral agenda and to discuss the bases for international public action. Yet citizens still have little access to these opportunities.

In authoritarian countries, by definition, political debate on public decisions is out of the question. In many democratic countries, foreign policy is considered to be too technical and complex to be handled directly by citizens. Popular participation is generally expressed only through lobbying by organized professions or by street demonstrations of angry citizens such as the rice growers' demonstrations in Japan or breeders' protests in Europe (against the Uruguay Round), 'hunger riots' in Egypt and Morocco (against measures imposed by the IMF), and so on.

The management of international affairs is largely technocratic and unchecked by the population. Governments and experts pose as the natural mouthpiece for social movements on the foreign scene. It is they who define the content of the international public order. In many cases this situation leads to flagrant injustices and social disasters. Examples are found, for instance, in the implementation of structural adjustment programs prescribed by the International Monetary Fund and the World Bank. Most of the time, governments make the poorest bear the weight of adjustment pressures (Adda and Smouts 1989): cutbacks in public services and social benefits rather than land reform or reductions in military spending and curbing of clientelist payoffs.

3. The Voice of the Global Civil Society

This third dimension of democratizing multilateralism is the most complex one (Falk 1995). It ties into the other two while being expected to provide its own answers to the new demands of complex interdependence by enabling the world system to function in a more balanced manner.

The current situation is in fact paradoxical. Decisions made by power centres (states or corporations) have repercussions beyond these centres. They affect populations in neighbouring states, in the region, and more and more on the global scale (the environment, relocations, financial speculation, and so on). But the forms of individual participation and control remain territorially grounded (Held 1991, 1994, 1995, Robertson 1992). International public law and *lex mercatoria* occasionally provide for the reparation of damages to populations once they have occurred but practically no provisions are made for preventing such damage. The recipients – and the victims – of decisions made outside of their territory have no means of participating in the decision-making process. Particularly in the economic realm, as it has been underscored, globalization has occurred from above (Falk 1995). Corporations devise global strategies for a global market and build a global system of production and trade that is often unfettered by territorial boundaries and, consequently, political control. Individuals and political communities wind up enmeshed in a multitude of transterritorial networks that link them together without their being able to see the logic of them. How, then, can one tell friend from foe? What are grounds for solidarity and what are grounds for struggle? In a world that is both interdependent and increasingly hostile to political control, at what level should the social compromise be made that is vital to the functioning of any society? The city, the region, the world? By sector (textiles, timber, steel, or similar)?

The emergence of a global civil society might contribute a partial response to the extent that it would mean the emergence of new forms of representation and legitimacy to enable compromise and coordination of interests of both conflicting and complementary actors, with a view to satisfying human needs (Smouts 1995). It remains to be seen what mechanisms must be brought into play and how to reconcile the diversity of social practices with the universality of the human condition.

CIVIL SOCIETY: DARK SPOTS AND RAYS OF HOPE

Countless suggestions have been made to accelerate the emergence of a global civil society defined as 'a network of institutions through which groups could represent themselves at the international level' (definition derived from Gramsci's notion that civil society stands 'between the economic structure and the state', borrowed from Martin Shaw 1994). Propositions to advance toward a 'cosmopolitan democracy' (Archibugi and Held 1995) range from the multiplication of regional parliaments to holding referenda on a global scale, and include creating new General Assemblies and, of course, reforming the Security Council; they range also from establishing a Social Council as a principal organ of the UN that should have a standing Advisory Board composed of individuals and groups involved in social and human rights policies (Ford Foundation 1995) to calling an annual Forum of Civil Society (Commission on Global Governance 1995). All of these proposals include something worth while and may some day become a reality. However, they all have the disadvantage of implying reforms decided on high to develop democratization from below. But the entire multilateral system has developed extremely effective avoidance strategies with regard to this sort of reform (Smouts 1998). More importantly, these suggestions attempt to raise certain mechanisms of democratic representation to the international level which are known to function poorly and are no longer sufficient on the domestic level.

Rather than reason in institutional terms, rather than look to models that are partially obsolete, it would make more sense to start with existing social achievements and examine what pitfalls must be avoided and what dynamics should be encouraged. The idea of direct representation of the civil society on an international level has made considerable progress since 1945. The first task is to analyse its accomplishments. The growing role of social movements and associations on the international scene is certainly the prelude to a vast transformation in international regulatory mechanisms (Camilleri and Falk 1992, Chapter 8). Already in the fields of environmental protection, human rights, minority rights, indigenous people's rights and public health, social movements and non-governmental organizations have demonstrated their influence. This influence is perceptible mainly in the setting of multilateral agendas: it is often these movements and organizations that identify issues and force them to be considered on the international level. It is often they who impose the language and form of qualification that set the tone for multilateral negotiations. By their very presence alongside states and the pressure they exert on public opinion, they have managed to weigh in the decision-making process in numerous instances. However, to maximize this potential, one must steer clear of a certain romanticism that sees in associations (Hirst 1994) and social movements (Walker 1988) the cure for all the failings of the state and the interstate system.

Social Movements and Grassroots Communities

Social movements are collective endeavours to question the established order, opposing citizens and those in power without going through the usual channels of representative democracy and the mediation of elites. They aim to change the social or political structure by non-institutionalized means. (There is a tendency in the International Relations literature to group under the same term all spontaneous social groupings, thus amalgamating social movements, citizens' movements and grassroots communities. There is no room in the present chapter to take issue with this sociological heresy). Because they are the spontaneous expression of the people, because their imaginative and innovative capacity is boundless, these forms of social mobilization bear signs of hope. Encouraging citizens to take their own affairs in hand and ensuring that they are better taken into account in national and international public policies is an integral part of a process leaning toward global governance.

Several problems arise, however, which must not be underestimated:

• How can the focus be shifted from the local to the global level? Social movements gel for the purpose of defending a topical issue, for the immediate protection of an activity, an asset, a way of life and conditions conducive to pursuing it. Rallying a local population around a particular interest does not automatically transpose to rallying international support to defend a general cause.

- An interest has been taken in social movements because they resist institutionalization and consequently offer an alternative to a hierarchical structure of social relationships that flows from the top down. But experience shows that citizens' movements attain credibility in the public sphere only once they represent an 'organized collective interest'. As R.B.J. Walker (1994) puts it, rightly: 'To make contact, social movements and world politics require some kind of mediating agent'. The actual alternative becomes the following: either these movements remain uninstitutionalized but run the risk of never achieving participation in public action and losing the limelight, or they become institutionalized and then fall into all the typical traps of structuring and being co-opted by the elites for classical political purposes.

- The overvaluing of social movements or grassroots communities in discussions on the democratization of International Relations (references in Alger 1994) too easily dodges the question of conflict and the possibility of betrayal. No more than the coexistence and the free competition of economic actors spontaneously spawn harmony and the common good, does the coexistence of and competition among social movements, citizens' movements or grassroots communities naturally spawn harmony and common good. Even on the smallest, most local scale, sources of conflict are numerous. Anyone who has the slightest experience with micro-development projects in small communities, in Africa for instance, can cite many examples: breeders versus sedentary farmers, populations whose village has dug a well versus neighbouring populations that come to draw from it, and so on. On the national scale, the whole task of pluralist democracy is precisely to arbitrate these oppositions and define the terms of a social compromise. At the international level, divergent perceptions and interests are multiplied infinitely. Brazilian peasants in the Amazon forest or the Masai in East Africa have little in common with Western environmentalists clad in their certainties. How these various 'representatives of the civil society' perceive the earth, nature or the environment have strictly nothing in common. And the gap can reach a point where the living conditions of vulnerable social groups are destroyed with no regard to compensation, under the influence of foreign non-governmental organizations who are the self-proclaimed guardians responsible for the preservation of mankind on this planet (Constantin 1994).

Apart from inevitable conflicts between social movements, the eventuality of betrayal within these movements must not be neglected. Certain actors have a talent for investing the mass media and the various corridors of influence that include international bureaucracies, the major NGOs and international conferences, all to their own advantage. In a world made up of networks and inter-organizational relations (Jönsson 1993), they easily shift grounds, from grassroots community to transnational micro-societies operating according to their own codes in the name of the higher interests of mankind, at times far removed from the local populations they are said to represent.

Associative Movements

The same questions arise with regard to associative movements and international non-governmental organizations (INGOs). Associations represent structured collective interests that interface individual interests emanating from the civil society and state action that is supposed to incarnate general action. When they manage to form a network, NGOs play a major role on the international scene. They help define issues, set agendas, keep an eye on the implementation of decisions. Their role is one of watchkeeping and expertise as well as presenting demands and mobilizing forces.

NGOs have up to now been the essential impetus for democratizing multilateralism (Weiss and Gordenker 1996). They take on a role of vertical mediation between the grassroots level and the upper echelons: it is they who bring the demands of social movements and grassroots communities before those who are in political power and who voice these demands on the international scene. They also play a role of horizontal mediation by ensuring the liaison between the various grassroots communities or citizens' groups, helping them to transform local and specific demands into causes of general interest: from the defence of the African peasant woman, for instance, to the definition of intergovernmental conventions on women's rights in general; from denouncing the situation of children making rugs in Pakistan to denouncing all modern forms of slavery. In return, local protest movements can resort to proceedings and conventions drawn up by international bodies at the impetus of NGOs to defend their claims against their national political authorities.

Associative movements draw their legitimacy from their ability to make demands in terms of collective needs. It also derives from their innovative capacity to suggest ways to meet these needs. Their informative, educational and socializing role make them structuring actors of the civil society.

Representativity is a problem for associations, however. First of all, most influential NGOs on the international scene are from the northern hemisphere. The costs of maintaining a continual presence in multilateral circuits and the expense of the indispensable media campaigns to convey a message are far too high for southern NGOs. The demands of the most indigent southern populations only make it to the international scene if they are taken up by heralds from the North who interpret them according to their own culture and in their language. (And it is a known fact that certain NGOs are direct offshoots of state agencies). Furthermore, the extension of associative power in turn produces a new form of elitism. In some countries, particularly the poorest African states, NGOs organize and finance entire areas of social policy: health care, training, local savings schemes, rural community action, and so on (Coussy 1994, pp. 241–6). These NGOs proclaim themselves representatives and instruments of the civil society and drain what remains of the state's legitimacy by adopting a purposely anti-state stance that disseminates foreign schemes for the emergence of a civil society. Just as there is a patrimonial power and a clientelist power, there is now an associative power that can be seen as a contemporary version of the power of the Notables.

A strange collusion is thus taking shape between the partisans of ultra-liberalism and those who claim to be its detractors. Both agree to denigrate the state and force it to restrict its scope of intervention. The international organizations have programmed the economic disengagement of the state. NGOs are holding out the social safety nets.

The disintegration of state infrastructures goes hand in hand with the dispersion – and internationalization – of economic decision-making *loci*. With the exception of a few large industrialized countries, most countries in the world are witnessing the dismantling of the powers and attributions once reserved for the nation-state. Major macroeconomic balances are discussed down to the smallest detail at the IMF and the World Bank. Loans are negotiated in clubs

(Paris, London). Investments are a factor of the financial market. The broad principles by which basic needs are satisfied are determined by the World Bank and implemented by other UN agencies. Matters of food security are discussed by donors of food aid (Coussy 1994).

Faced with this transfer of power over economic policy to international experts and decision makers who pride themselves on their autonomy with respect to local groups, citizens' movements and associations supply no real alternative to the state. The state remains the obligatory intermediary and maintains the power to block things (Hirst and Thompson 1996). Yet at the same time, experience shows that no development project imported from the outside can be accomplished successfully without the support of local groups and entrepreneurs determined to implement it. Consequently, international organizations, including the World Bank and the IMF, wind up having to elicit much greater participation from the state than they care to, in assessing the powers of social groups, predicting risks of social unrest, designing arbitration schemes and making domestic policy wagers. Thus a sort of conflictual tripartite collaboration is established between the state, international organizations and representatives of the civil society.[2]

RETURN TO *JUS GENTIUM*

On the domestic level and even more so on the international level, the potential vectors of democratization remain extremely nebulous. Myriad social movements and associations operate according to rules of their own, trying to strike an uneasy balance between opposition and partnership with national and international public authorities in a context where the combined effects of globalization and the crisis of the state multiply points of social conflict and amplify differentiation among actors. Faced with such fragmentation, building an international order that will foster more respectful practices of a population's needs implies that assessment criteria and decision-making guidelines must be defined.

It is foolish to think that democratization will naturally spawn from competition among more or less organized social actors each defending a specific interest on the international scene. The uncontrolled eruption of contrasting subjectivities in multilateral activity can only engender new cleavages and new types of domination.

The construction of a universal social linkage requires a set of general rules enabling one to distinguish what is authorized and what is prohibited. The law should be the means by which the principal interdictions and shared positive values are expressed. It should enable individuals and groups to understand one another and act within a pre-existing framework. The current trend is not moving in this direction.

Far from contributing to the establishment of a common legal framework, the proliferation of 'regimes' has produced a mass of legal texts that obey a functional rationality alone. The aim of this frenetic legal production is not to build a law 'common to the people' linking populations organized into societies within the great society of man (*totius humani generis societas*) but to devise forms of case-by-case regulation to deal with a particular field. Transnational actors in the private sector – banks, insurance companies, multinational corporations, and so on – seek to define rules of good conduct amongst themselves, with the aid of public administrations and the major corporations that are their customers or their suppliers, the sole aim of these 'laws' being to ensure that business can be conducted properly in a context of global competition. As to regional organizations, they multiply legal procedures to the same ends. The European Community's legal frenzy has been superimposed on that of states. The result is that it has been years since anyone has known for certain what European law is in effect. On the other side of the Atlantic, NAFTA has already become a legal hydra (over 2000 pages), the provisions of which are still unclear to the businesses most directly affected.

Democratization of multilateralism would imply that citizens are at least minimally aware of the legal regulations that apply to their activity. This knowledge has been confiscated by experts. Furthermore, the primacy of functional and financial rationality over the quest for the global good has considerably diminished one of the law's basic functions: its capacity to classify, to categorize, to say what is permitted and what is not, thereby guiding people's actions. In their frantic pursuit of a minimum consensus, international organizations contribute to the weakening of the power of law. The legal texts they produce, sort of 'non-legally binding, authoritative statements of principles for a global consensus' (Rio Environmental Conference statement on forests), promote an 'aesthetics of the wishy-washy' that reveals the current uncertainty about the content of law and the foundations of its mandatory nature (Chemillier-Gendreau 1995).

The adoption of the notion of *jus cogens* (Vienna Convention 1969), a peremptory norm that is 'accepted and recognized by the international community of states as a whole as a norm from which no derogation is permitted' established the existence of a universal legal community founded on specific values. It affirmed the primacy of peremptory norms on the contractual conception of law. State resistance and the legal emancipation of transnational actors have prevented these peremptory norms from being formulated clearly. Each has defined them in its own manner to serve its own interests and position in the international system. Still today, no enumerative text exists.

The concern with political regulation takes precedence over the clarification of values and consolidation of principles. The human rights field is no exception. The International Conference on Human Rights (Vienna 1993) was able to incorporate the principle of the universality of human rights in its final statement only by simultaneously reaffirming the 'universal and inalienable' nature of the right to development. Since then several Asian countries (Singapore, Malaysia, China) have brandished an 'Asian' vision of human rights, utilizing the legitimate concern for the respect of differences for political ends.

Moral and legal relativism is in fashion. It comes as a counter-attack on the propagation of 'universal' models imposed by the West since the dawn of capitalism and colonization. It is true that since time immemorial mankind has asked the same questions about life, death, sexual mores, labour and its relationship to nature, and that since time immemorial civilizations have come up with different answers. But differences in social practices do not preclude the possibility of a 'minimal specification of human interests acceptable to all'. Imposing a minimal standard of conduct on all international actors is not justified as a consequence of what states, peoples and societies owe to one another to put a semblance of order in their relations. It is a consequence of what each owes, as a human being, to other human beings who are fundamentally of his or her own kind (Puchala 1995).

PUTTING THE CONCEPT INTO ACTION

The proliferation of special conferences that devote part of their agenda to civil society and its major groups marks a basic transformation in multilateral activity. Henceforth the driving forces of civil society are involved in developing law; they have become incontrovertible partners in the elaboration, implementation and enforcement of recommendations that result from these big jamborees. Since the second Rio Conference it would appear that the proceedings are cumulative. Not only do special conferences treat specific subjects (population, women's rights, social development, habitat, and so on) but they also present an opportunity to tie the subjects together, to hone down ideas, to hammer out messages. The preparatory studies are high in quality. The final reports are often substantial. Combined, they offer a new repertoire of meanings established on a global level through close cooperation between the public and private spheres. Ethical considerations occupy a significant place. It is still too early to gauge the effects, but a dynamic is under way; it remains to be seen whether it will be able to triumph over the context of frenetic competition that governs international relations.

Yet the control over decisions that structure the world's economic and financial system in practice escapes all democratic control. The civil society is a victim of these decisions. Some take advantage of them, others make do with them, many try to circumvent the negative effects on employment and work conditions by switching over to informal and barter economies. New forms of organization and solidarity are being created on the group and local level that clamour for considerable independence from public authorities. These self-defence mechanisms will not suffice to solve the problems as this century draws to a close, but they may prefigure society in the future: atomized and unmanageable from a centralized standpoint for having failed to organize in time the participation of citizens involved in the global governance of affairs that concern them.

Most effective protest activity still occurs at the local level where civil society reaches the point of face-to-face confrontation with multinational firms, the main financial institutions, the nation-states. NGOs and major groups have all the more chances to obtain results on a multilateral level if individually they have managed to besiege individual key actors in a given field. Effective action is one that hits the most sensitive weak points: commercial risk, shareholders' confidence, prestige. The means are not immense and some are not used sufficiently. As regards publicity, for instance, campaigns to inform parliamentarians, professors and opinion makers about international conventions that exist but are disregarded in their own country are not sufficiently deployed. In the legal field, associations too rarely bring cases in which international treaties have been breached before their own domestic courts. In the economic field, shareholders hardly take advantage of their right to demand that large corporations guarantee compliance with social or ecological standards in the course of their activity.

The definition of what is or deserves to become acceptable to all was first the affair of philosophers, theologians, and magistrates pondering the duty of princes (Vitoria, Grotius, Pufendorf, and the like). Since the seventeenth century international public law has become the work of diplomats in the service of the state, international private law being the work of merchants in the service of commerce. In the next century could law possibly emanate from the carefully reasoned decisions of free men and women in the service of humanity?

NOTES

1. See Falk 1994.
2. The 1994 World Bank's progress report on cooperation with NGOs shows 115 or half of the 229 projects approved by the Bank in the fiscal year 1994 had provisions for NGO involvement. Indigenous NGOs represented 70 per cent of NGOs involved in Bank-financed projects, 40 per cent were grassroots organizations. Of all NGO-associated projects 33 per cent have been in Africa; 22 per cent in Latin America; 19 per cent in East Asia; 9 per cent in Europe and Central Asia; 13 per cent in South Asia; and 4 per cent in the Middle East and North Africa.

REFERENCES

Adda, Jacques and Marie-Claude Smouts 1989, *La France face au Sud. Le miroir brisé*, Paris, Karthala.

Alger, Chadwick 1994, 'Citizens and the UN System in a Changing World', in Sakamoto 1994, pp. 301–29.

Archibugi, Daniele 1995, 'From the United Nations to Cosmopolitan Democracy', in Daniele Archibugi and David Held (eds), *Cosmopolitan Democracy: an Agenda for a New World Order*, Cambridge: Polity Press, pp. 121–62.

Camilleri, Joseph A. and Jim Falk 1992, *The End of Sovereignty. The Politics of a Shrinking and Fragmenting World*, Hants, Edward Elgar.

Chemillier-Gendreau, Monique 1995, *Humanité et souverainetés. Essai sur la fonction du droit international*, Paris, La Découverte.

Commission on Global Governance 1995, *Our Global Neighbourhood*, Oxford: Oxford University Press.

Constantin, FranHois 1994 (ed.), 'L'homme et la nature en Afrique', *Politique africaine*, 53, Mars 1994.

Coussy, Jean 1994, 'Les ruses de l'Etat minimum', in Jean François Bayart (ed.), *La réinvention du capitalisme*, Paris, Karthala, pp. 227–48.

Falk, Richard 1994, 'Democratizing, Internationalizing and Globalizing', pp. 475–502 in Sakamoto.

—— 1995, 'The World Order between Inter-State Law and the Law of Humanity: the Role of Civil Society Institutions', in Archibugi and Held, pp. 163–79.

Ford Foundation 1995, 'The United Nations in its Second Half-Century', the report of the Independent Working Group on the Future of the United Nations. New York: Ford Foundation.

Gill, Stephen 1994, 'Structural Changes in Multilateralism: the G-7 Nexus and the Global Crisis', in Schechter 1998.

Held, David 1991, 'Democracy: the Nation-state and the Global System', in David Held (ed.), *Political Theory Today*, Cambridge, Polity Press.

—— 1994, 'Globalization and the Liberal State', with Anthony McGrew in Sakamoto 1994, p. 57–84.

—— 1995a, 'Democracy and the New International Order' in Archibugi and Held, *Cosmopolitan Democracy*.

—— 1995b, *Democracy and the Global Order. From the Modern State to Cosmopolitan Governance*, Cambridge, Polity Press.

Hirst, Paul 1994, *Associative Democracy*, Cambridge, Polity Press.

Hirst, Paul and Grahame Thompson 1996, *Globalization in Question*, Cambridge, Polity Press.

Jönsson, Christer 1993, 'International Organization and Co-operation: An Interorganizational Perspective', *International Science Journal*, pp. 463–77.

Keohane, Robert O. 1970, 'Multilateralism: An Agenda for Research', *International Journal*, 45 (Autumn), p. 731.

Knight, W. Andy 1995, 'Beyond the UN System? Critical Perspectives on Global Governance and Multilateral Evolution', *Global Governance*, 1, May–August.

Kooiman, Jan (ed.) 1993, *Modern Governance*, London, Sage.

Le Galés, Patrick 1995, '*Du gouvernement des villes à la gouvernance urbaine*', *Revue française de science politique*, février, p. 59.

Manin, Bernard 1995, *Principes du gouvernement représentatif*, Paris, Calman-Lévy.

Marin, B. and Mayntz, R. (eds) 1991, *Policy Networks*, Frankfurt/Boulder, Campus/Westview.

Mayntz, Renate 1993, 'Governing Failures and the Problem of Governability: some Comments on a Theoretical Paradigm', in Kooinman 1993, pp. 9–20.

Miles, R. 1980, *Macro-Organizational Behavior*, Glenview, Scott Foresman and Co.

Puchala, Donald J. 1995, *The Ethics of Globalism*, John W. Holmes Memorial Lecture, The Academic Council on the United Nations System, Brown University.

Robertson, Roland 1992, *Social Theory and Global Culture*, London, Sage.

Rosenau, James N. and Ernest-Otto Czempiel 1992, *Governance Without Government: Order and Change in World Politics*, Cambridge, Cambridge University Press.

Ruggie, John Gerard 1992, 'Multilateralism: the Anatomy of an Institution', *International Organization*, 46 (Summer), p. 568–74.

Sakamoto, Yoshikazu 1994, *Global Transformation. Challenges to the State System*, Tokyo, United Nations University Press.

Schechter, M.G. 1998, *Innovation in Multilateralism*, London, Macmillan for the United Nations University Press.

Shaw, Martin 1994, 'Civil Society and Global Politics: Beyond a Social Movement Approach', *Millennium* (Winter), vol. 23, pp. 647–67.

Simon, H.A. 1972, 'Theories of Wounded Rationality', in Radner R. McGuire, *Decision and Organization*, Amsterdam, North Holland Pub Comp., pp. 161–72.

Smouts, Marie-Claude 1998, 'United Reform: A Strategy of Avoidance', in Schechter, 1998.

—— 1995, *Les organisations internationales*, Paris, Armand Colin.

Walker, R.B.J. 1988, *One World, Many Worlds: Struggles for a Just World Peace*, Rienner: Boulder, CO.

—— 1994, 'Social Movements/World Politics', *Millennium*, Winter 1994, vol. 23, pp. 669–99.

Weiss, Thomas and Gordenker, Leon 1996, *NGOs, the UN, and Global Governance*, London, Lynne Rienner.

Books and Articles Published (or to be Published) through MUNS

Robert W. Cox, 'Multilateralism and World Order', *Review of International Studies* 1992 (1) 161–180. Based on a 'concept paper' written at the launching of the MUNS programme.

Yoshikazu Sakamoto (ed.), *Global Transformation: Challenges to the State System* (Tokyo: United Nations University Press, 1994). Based on the symposium held in Yokohama in 1992.

Keith Krause and W. Andy Knight (eds), *State, Society and the UN System: Changing Perspectives on Multilateralism* (Tokyo: United Nations University Press, 1995). Based on the symposium held in Toronto in 1992.

Robert W. Cox (ed.) *The New Realism: Perspectives on Multilateralism and World Order* (London: Macmillan for the United Nations University Press, 1997). Based on the symposium held in Fiesole, Italy, in 1993.

Stephen Gill (ed.), *Globalization, Democratization, and Multilateralism* (London: Macmillan for the United Nations University Press, 1997). Based on the symposium held in Oslo in 1993.

Michael G. Schechter (ed.), *Innovation in Multilateralism* (London: Macmillan for the United Nations University Press, 1998). Based on the symposium held in Lausanne in 1994.

Michael G. Schechter (ed.), *Future Multilateralism: the Political and Social Framework* (London: Macmillan for the United Nations University Press, 1998). Based on the symposium held in San José, Costa Rica, in December 1995.

James P. Sewell (ed.), *Multilateralism in Multinational Perspective: Viewpoints from Different Languages and Literatures* (London: Macmillan for the United Nations University Press, forthcoming).

Robert W. Cox, *Multilateralism and the United Nations System: Final Report* (United Nations University Press, March 1996).

Sequel to the MUNS programme

Michael G. Schechter, Martin Hewson and W. Andy Knight, *Global Governance for the Twenty-First Century: The Realistic Potential* (London: Macmillan, forthcoming).

Tables of Contents of Titles in MUNS Subseries

Stephen Gill (ed.), *Globalization, Democratization and Multilateralism* **(London: Macmillan for the United Nations University Press, 1997).**

Michael G. Schechter (ed.), *Innovation in Multilateralism* **(London: Macmillan for the United Nations University Press, 1998).**

Michael G. Schechter (ed.), *Future Multilateralism: the Political and Social Framework* (London: Macmillan for the United Nations University Press, 1998).

James P. Sewell (ed.), *Multilateralism in Multinational Perspective: Viewpoints from Different Languages and Literatures* (London: Macmillan for the United Nations University Press, forthcoming).

2   A Survey of Russian Scholarly Work on Multilateralism
    Yevgenia Issraelyan
3   Chinese Literature on Multilateralism and the United Nations System
    Zhang Xinhua
4   Francophone Literature on the Study of International Organizations
    Jean-Philippe Thérien
5   Multilateralism: The Case of Egypt
    Hassan Nafaa
6   Survey of Scholarly Work on Multilateralism: the Netherlands
    Monique Castermans-Holleman, with Peter R. Baehr, Dick A. Leurdijk and Nico J. Schrijver
7   Scholarly Work on Multilateralism in Hungary
    Károly Nyíri
8   Latin American Views of International Law Principles and the United Nations System
    Alberto Cisneros-Lavaller
9   A Study of Multilateralism in Iran: the United Nations and the Iran-Iraq Conflict
    Djamchid Momtaz
10 African Perspectives on Multilateralism: the View from Anglo-Africa
    A.J. Samatar
11 Pragmatism, Displacement and the Study of Multilateralism
    James P. Sewell

Michael G. Schechter, Martin Hewson and W. Andy Knight, *Global Governance for the Twenty-First Century: the Realistic Potential* **(London: Macmillan, forthcoming).**

1   Introduction: the MUNS Programme, Key Issues and Lacunae
2   What Has Changed?
3   The State System on the Eve of the 21st Century
4   Civil Society and Multilateralism: Global Governance on the Eve of the 21st Century
5   Key Policy Issues
6   Conclusions: Policy, Process, Normative and Theoretical Implications

Index of Names

Index of Subjects

2